A HUNDRED HOUSES

The story of
Irene Rowley

by
Anne Rayment

D1332882

Christian Focus Publications

© 1991 Anne Rayment & Irene Rowley
ISBN 1 871 676 770

Published by
Christian Focus Publications Ltd
Geanies House, Fearn IV20 1TW
Ross-shire, Scotland, UK.

Printed and bound in Great Britain
by Cox & Wyman Ltd, Reading

Cover design
by
Seoris McGillivray

CONTENTS

FOREWORD

It is said that moving house can be one of the most traumatic things that a person can go through, along with divorce or the death of a loved one. So the title of this book tells you immediately that you are not in for a cosy read.

People who have a romantic vision of missionaries and their work will have their thoughts severely challenged after reading this honest, down to earth book.

It tells of Irene Bateman's strict and dour upbringing in the North of England, her conversion after hearing the words of a hymn which seemed to sum up her family, and her on/off friendship with Joe Rowley who she eventually married, after which they travelled to Brazil to begin their missionary work. We learn of the restrictions put on married couples at missionary school and the tensions which resulted, and later on in Brazil, the slow and laborious work hampered by occult forces, lack of resources, and of good food.

It contrasts the clean and spacious houses of Lymm in Cheshire - where I spent part of my childhood, and where I first met Irene and Joe in the early seventies - with the heat and dust of Brazil, where people at first seemed to be dishonest and lazy. The book is frank enough to record Irene's changing attitude towards the Brazilians as she begins to understand some of the problems of the people of that country. We learn how the Rowleys' faith is tested as one baby dies and another is found to have development problems.

The book relies heavily on the letters that Irene wrote to her family and friends and includes some interesting insights on what it means to be a 'MK' (Missionary Kid) by their daughter.

In a day and age when some Christian books give the impression that Christianity is about floating from one pink cloud to the next, the book is refreshingly frank. It will challenge you and leave you thinking.

David Waite
June 1991
Witney,
Oxfordshire.

'I don't count sheep at night, if I'm unable to sleep because of the heat, or the noise coming from the street below.

In my mind's eye, I take a front door key in my hand and walk down an English street. The street may be lined with rows of terraced houses, like the ones in Salford that I remember from my district nursing days. On the other hand, it may be an avenue of semis, with driveways and neat front gardens.

In my mind's eye, I will build up a picture of the type of house I want to enter. I consider the outside of it in detail, from the length of the drive to the height of the trees that surround it. Then I walk up to the front door, which I open with my key.

Everything inside the house then belongs to me, from the carpet on the stairs to the pictures on the walls. There may be a piano in the lounge for me to play, and there may be a large fireplace with a nearby footstool, placed there for me to sit on.

When the dream reaches this latter stage I usually fall asleep. I seldom get to visit any of the other rooms of my imaginary house, but it doesn't matter, because I know I'm home...'

Irene Rowley
Portel,
Brazil.

Part 1
MISSIONARY
IN THE
MAKING

Everyone who has left houses or brothers or sisters or father or mother or children or fields for my sake will receive a hundred times as much and will inherit eternal life. (Matthew19:29).

1
January 1966
ADVENTURE

So this was Brazil! Who would have predicted humidity like the clinging, heavy fog of steam from a Turkish bath? Who would have imagined the sun would beat down like a blowtorch, scorching fragile English skin? How extraordinary that stars could shine so dazzlingly bright in a velvet night sky filled with the noise of laughter, the honk of car horns and the barking of dogs! How delightful to eat exotic, tropical fruit for breakfast and be driven in a taxi down teeming, colourful streets at speeds that take your breath away! A whole new world of sights, sounds and smells, bombarding the senses!

Already retreating into the memory was the romance of Paris, and a hotel on the banks of the Seine with their own marble bath and decadent feather bed. Then there was the glimpse of mysterious Madrid, the Straits of Gibraltar, and the vast, sandy wastes of Africa as the plane carried them over the ocean and ever further west towards their new country.

They were dizzy with tiredness by the time they arrived at their final destination and were warmly greeted in Belem by their hosts.

With gratitude, Irene and Joe passed their baby daughter to less weary hands, and gave smiles of relief and thankfulness to the English friend who offered them a cup of tea. An English voice at last, after the meaningless babble of foreigners on the plane! How pleasant it was to have something in that alien place reminding them of their distant, cherished home.

All the places and people that Irene and Joe held dear were now as inaccessible to them as the moon that gleamed so hugely above the mission headquarters where they were to spend the next nine months.

Irene's parents and Joe's family were a world away in Manchester where both fledgling missionaries had grown up. Irene knew that her Mum would be praying for her and thinking of her, as would her sisters and brother. Her family were proud of her, and she was determined not to let them down. After all, she had been preparing for this work nearly all her life, right from the days when aeroplanes had been no more to her than remote specks of silver, soaring high above the Bateman family's modest home in Moston.

Irene had felt called to this work since her childhood Sunday School days at the Albert Memorial Church when all she had ever seen of dark-skinned people were the pictures of negroes she collected for her album.

She had always wanted to tell unevangelised people that Jesus was their Saviour and had always imagined she would have a great love for them, originally envisaging herself in the Sudan. She had encountered her first non-whites while nursing at Manchester Royal Infirmary and had been so agreeable to a few of the male patients that she had artlessly elicited more than one proposal of marriage.

The proposals had taken her completely by surprise and had disturbed her, such had been her innocence. Her stable, lower middle-class home life had left her unprepared for a great number of surprises.

One big surprise in the future would be the sharp contrast between her own golden dream of a missionary life and the harsh reality.

Another big surprise would be her instant dislike of the very people she had been called to 'reach'. Class prejudice, that had made her turn up her nose at 'dirty' children in Sunday School, would follow her to Brazil.

Then there were the hardships and privations of the missionary life: friction between co-workers, the miseries of tropical disease, emotional stress caused by family problems, and hostility from the Brazilians. One of those who had referred her to the Unevangelised Fields Mission had expressed doubts as to Irene's suitability for the work. He had considered her to be not quite the 'type'. Was he right?

2
1938-1954
THE PERFECT FAMILY

The home was a three-bedroomed semi in Moston, the father a clerk in a cotton warehouse, the mother well practised in making a little money go a long way. Irene was born the third of three girls, soon to be followed by a brother.

Her mother, Edith, took a tailoring course so that she could make clothes for the family, and found time to be a good neighbour in between feeding the chickens and keeping the house spick and span. Alfred Bateman struggled to pay the mortgage and took pride in his duties as church-warden at the (low-church Anglican) Albert Memorial.

Alfred thought the world of Edith and tried hard to please her, as did all the children. Edith's warm and generous nature prompted their love and respect: a love and respect so deeply ingrained in the minds of the children that all their moral dilemmas were instantly resolved upon consideration of her preferences. She was their conscience. Alfred went to church because it was what Edith wanted, though her family's devotion was inspired rather than enforced. Edith could not have been domineering even if she had wanted to, because of Alfred.

Alfred did not have to shout or bully in order to govern the collective mood of the household: he only had to come home from work looking tense and an ominous silence would fall on the family at the tea-table. Edith and the children loved him, but they feared him. They knew how to keep quiet so that Dad would not lose his temper. He was by nature melancholy and deeply emotional, finding it impossible to rejoice in affection. If he was given a Christmas present he would burst into tears, embarrassing everybody. He appeared dour at weddings when the rest of the family wanted to be happy. They could not smile if Dad did not smile.

To the close fellowship of the Albert Memorial Church, the Batemans were a faultless family: clean-living and hard-working, with a keen and active interest in the religious life of their community. The Batemans themselves were proud of the image they projected and would never have let each other down by admitting publicly to their shortcomings. Each of them attended all the appropriate church meetings, but never prayed together in the home. Irene would play sad hymns at the piano when she was alone, just to make herself cry and thus relieve her inner tension.

They had high standards and stuck to them. When, at Alfred's instigation they fostered an adolescent boy, they cared for him as a Bateman. When he rebelled and left home to marry at an 'unsuitably' early age, Edith endured a sense of personal disgrace and failure. She was hurt by the boy's betrayal, and for a long time could not bring herself to speak to him.

Margaret, Dorothy, Irene and Neville played house often, huddling under a blanket thrown over a clothes horse. They played house in the bushes in Boggart Hole Clough (a local park) and giggled together under the dining table in wartime when there was an air-raid and Dad was out driving the ambulance for the Air Raid Precautions (A.R.P.). Irene's recurring nightmare in wartime was that of German paratroopers landing in the Batemans' back garden and invading their home. Her fear of Germans left a legacy of prejudice that lingered into adulthood, but which was eventually overcome with the help of prayer.

They were happy children who enjoyed each other's company and supported each other in adversity. When boys bullied Neville in Boggart Hole Clough Irene (a tomboy) would fearlessly chase them away. All the children shared a single bedroom, Irene and Neville even sharing a bed until she was twelve and he eleven - long after they had begun to feel awkward about it.

Irene attended primary school at Moston Lane where she gave an average academic performance. She was a chatterbox, her effusiveness once earning her the punishment of being made to stand in the classroom waste-paper basket, ridiculed before all her friends. Wounded pride had a salutary effect on the lanky, blonde ten-year-old, and the penalty did not have to be paid a second time. At the age of eleven she conspired with a similarly-minded pal to fail the eleven-plus exam, as neither wished to change schools. The plot worked, though Irene later thought better of it and decided to pass at the next opportunity. Thus she eventually graduated to St. Mary's Road Central and acquired a new blazer with a home-embroidered badge.

The Batemans travelled to church by bus if they could afford the fare, and on foot if they could not, attending three times each Sunday. The children sat patiently through sermons even as infants, continually tracing their thumbnails over the embossed covers of hymn-books to pass the time. If Dad was in a good mood he would sing the hymns more lustily than anyone, and if he was in a bad mood would not sing at all. Mum had a beautiful voice and loved to sing at all times.

All three girls attended the Campaigners youth movement through the Church and it was a great source of pleasure to them. Campaigners taught them how to memorise Bible verses and play the fife. They learned how to evangelise and march in step. It was at a Campaigners meeting that Irene, aged fourteen, first testified to her faith.

Her spiritual turning-point had occurred some time previously, at Manchester's Houldsworth Hall. David Shepherd (now Bishop of Liverpool) was the speaker there at a youth rally which Irene attended. She listened eagerly enough to the sermon, but it wasn't until the closing hymn that the gospel message finally sank home. Something about the words of that final hymn struck a chord in her soul:

> Out of unrest and arrogant pride,
> Jesus, I come! Jesus, I come!
> Into thy blessed will to abide,
> Jesus, I come to thee!
> Out of myself to dwell in thy love,
> Out of despair into raptures above,
> Upward for aye on wings like a dove,
> Jesus, I come to thee!

'Arrogant pride'! The words resounded in her head and she pondered them gravely. A child of the Bateman family - she knew something about pride. Jesus Christ was one of the very few unimpressed by the Bateman facade: Irene had to give account of herself to him. He could see beyond the mask to the sins deep within her, and there was no concealing them from him. There was nothing for it but to confess those sins and seek forgiveness for them, through the Son of a holy God, crucified in her place to take the punishment that ought to have been her own. With tears, she submitted her will to that of her Saviour. It was a decision that changed and coloured her future.

Edith, Margaret, Dorothy and Neville were delighted with Irene's conversion and encouraged her in the disciplines of the Christian life. Edith confided to Irene her own youthful desire to be a missionary nurse (an ambition thwarted by family commitments) and Irene promptly vowed that she would achieve that which her mother had not.

The new convert began to support the Sudan United Mission and to attend missionary meetings with renewed zeal. She joined the St. John Ambulance Brigade nursing cadets and would gaze wistfully at nurses through the railings outside Booth Hall Hospital.

At Whitsuntide in Manchester, contingencies of the various Christian denominations regularly marched through the city: Protestants on Whit Monday and Roman Catholics on the Friday. In 1954 Irene (aged 16) was on duty with the St. John's in Picadilly, while the Catholics 'walked' with their banners and vestmented priests. It was her first official turn of duty, and she was very nervous. A male cadet of her own age agreed to shepherd her, and they chatted as they strolled along the road watching for 'fainters'. Irene told Bryan about her new found faith in Christ, but he was not a believer and showed little interest in her testimony. A newspaper photographer took their picture, and Bryan asked for Irene's address, so that he could mail her a copy of the photograph when it appeared in the paper. Even the naive Irene wondered if Bryan might not have an ulterior motive for acquiring details of her place of residence and she returned home that evening in a romantic daze, her mind filled with pleasant musings on the theme of love.

Bryan was the first lad to have shown any interest in her. There were lads at church - but they were brothers rather than beaux. She had learned something of the 'facts of life' through her older sisters, and had a healthy interest in boys. At the age of thirteen she and a girlfriend had formed the habit (for a while) of following a boy home from school - surreptitiously, of course. They had sighed dreamily as he entered his house, and then caught the bus home. Apart from that fleeting passion, however, there had been nothing - till now.

Summer came and went, but there was, to

Irene's dismay, no word from Bryan. Another series of Houldsworth Hall rallies commenced, and Irene attended with Marjorie, a close friend. At the end of one gospel meeting, the girls were shuffling down the aisle with the crowds on their way to the exit, when they heard a shout - someone was calling them! Irene was overjoyed to recognise Bryan, paying little attention at first to the lad at his side. Bryan introduced himself to Marjorie, then returned his attention to Irene.

'I'm a Christian now,' he declared.

Irene was thrilled at this news. It was so unexpected, after his lack of interest in the faith at their last meeting.

'Oh,' Bryan continued immediately, indicating the lad at his side, 'and this is my friend, Joe Rowley.'

Joe was nice. He had a handsome face and laughing eyes. Irene and Marjorie were nearly overcome with shyness, but both tingled with excitement as the lads escorted them to their bus stop. All four arranged to meet the following week at the mission hall in Ancoats attended by the lads.

Thus began a 'foursome', the young people attending each other's churches in turn, no pairs being formed. However, it was not long before Bryan wrote Irene a letter, asking her to choose between himself and Joe.

Irene was upset by the letter because she liked both boys, and did not want to offend Bryan by admitting that she actually preferred Joe. After consultation with Dorothy, therefore, she wrote back to Bryan informing him that she had no particular preference for either lad.

For some reason, Irene's response caused Bryan to back off. He soon started to court another girl. The field was now clear for Joe Rowley, who was head over heels in love with Irene.

3
1954-1965
LEARNING FOR LIFE

A very pleasant member of the form; steady, intelligent; forceful but respectful; helpful and energetic; reliable child; could be less talkative.

That was what her teachers thought of her, and it was true. Joe Rowley, however, was to bring out a quality that had remained dormant within her Bateman character: a sense of humour. It was Joe who provided the antidote to her inherited melancholia and taught her how to shrug off tension with a laugh. Irene's new-found ability was to prove an indispensable asset in the near future.

Joe's father was an engineer in a Manchester factory, bereaved of his wife when Joe reached fifteen. The Rowleys were not believers, but were good, upright people. After the death of his mother Joe had learned to be self-reliant and could wash clothes and keep house for himself - attributes which were later to be of value.

He was converted at the age of fourteen through the witness of a neighbour and soon showed himself to be a Christian of great zeal: dynamic and active in evangelism. He was baptized at the age of seventeen and preached at street corners even as a teenager.

Soon after his baptism Joe went to London to pursue a year-long course in preaching run by the Protestant Truth Society. In return for his tuition Joe had to work for the organisation for three years, a period of estrangement from Irene which caused her to have doubts about their future as a couple.

Irene's own life did not undergo such a dramatic post-conversion change as did Joe's - after all, she could scarcely have been more committed to church life than she was already. Her only post-conversion divergence from accustomed practice was to be baptized as a believer whilst on holiday at the age of nineteen.

The change for Irene was rather more inward: hymns became imbued for her with new meaning, and she gained a greater awareness of the 'why' of religious custom to add to her existing familiarity with the 'how'.

She was more shy in her Christian witness than Joe. If non-church friends asked her to dances or the cinema (pastimes of which Alfred and Edith, for religious reasons, did not approve) she would hide behind convention and not explain precisely why the Batemans refrained from those activities. 'Our family don't do that' became her pass-phrase out of embarrassment, when a less dismissive explanation might have afforded her the opportunity to share something of her faith.

It was not that she was unsure of her faith, nor did she ever regret the promises she had made to Christ at her conversion. Far from backsliding as a young Christian, she became ever more emotionally and actively committed to the doctrines she held dear.

Irene did not rebel against the restrictions imposed by her family and never longed for the dances and cinema trips forbidden to her. This was not because she was weak-willed and easily manipulated - for she was far from that. She was always leader of her particular gang at school and was boldly outspoken. Within the confines of her own home she had a reputation as the only one who ever dared argue with Dad.

She was an emotional girl who did not inherit her father's undemonstrative nature. Certain hymns affected her deeply, and she would give free rein to her feelings when thus moved. On one occasion in school assembly the singing of *When I survey the wondrous cross* so touched her that she burst into tears and ran from the hall, mystifying her teachers.

Because she was accepted by Manchester Royal Infirmary for future nursing training when she was sixteen, she left school at seventeen in order to earn money for the family before beginning as a nurse the following year. She found an office job for that intervening year and enjoyed her time there. She was not tempted, however, to give up her aim of becoming a nurse and obeying her deepening call to mission.

Irene fretted at having to live away from home when she commenced her nursing training and suffered greatly from homesickness. Joe was by now in London and a poor correspondent, so offering her little comfort. However, there were Christians among the teaching staff in the nurses' home who saw to it that Irene was never short of friendship. The Nurses' Christian Fellowship was of great practical and spiritual assistance to her in those early days, and Irene had the pleasure of seeing two or three of her fellow students come to faith.

Her studies demanded much of her time, but she was still able to go for spiritual encouragement to the annual Christian Convention at Keswick. It was there that she committed herself publicly to full-time Christian service.

The occasion was a tent meeting attended by herself and Joe, who was sitting three rows in front of her while they listened to the speaker. When the invitation came for all Christians committed to full-time service to rise to their feet, Irene obeyed the summons, but could observe that Joe did not. At that point Irene decided that if Joe would not serve the Lord full-time, she would put an end to their relationship.

She caught him up in the crowd as it spilled out of the tent after the meeting. Grabbing him by the arm she declared: 'I've got something to tell you!' To her surprise, Joe rejoined:'Don't say it - I've got something to tell you!' Irene ignored Joe's command and told him anyway, whereupon Joe held up a sheaf of leaflets. Irene could tell by their covers that he, too, had been called to full-time service. He just hadn't stood up.

Irene resumed her nursing studies back in Manchester with renewed vigour. She enjoyed the work and made many friends among the patients with whom she would correspond long after they had left her care. Her diary reveals some of the few difficulties she experienced:

'Nov. 9th, 1957. Scared of going to theatre. Sat in the toilet and read Daily Light before I went on. Sister accused me of nearly killing a patient. I was dead upset. She came and apologised afterwards.'

The same diary reveals some of the ups and downs in her relationship with Joe, who would come from London to visit her.

Aug. 4th. My birthday. Didn't get either a card or present from Joe. I query my feelings.

Aug. 14th. Walked around Cheadle with Joe who wasn't very friendly.

Aug. 20th. Joe and I went for a walk - quite friendly.

Aug. 21st. Joe didn't say much to me.

Aug. 26th. Didn't hear from Joe.

Aug. 27th. Still not heard from Joe.

Oct. 8th. Joe kissed me through the window of the train to London. Didn't seem sad to see him go; went and bought myself a hat.

Dec. 20th. Joe (home for Christmas) has had his hair cut - lovely to see him.

Dec. 23rd. Joe came and we went to Margaret's; had a lovely time.

Dec. 24th. Joe gave me a handbag; had a lovely time.

Dec. 27th. Went with Joe to Jean and Derek's; had a lovely time.

The couple broke off their relationship for a year, but got back together again and began to consider marriage and a future in the mission field. Irene proposed to Joe just before she took her finals, and he accepted.

Her minister at the Albert (the Rev. Blowers) expressed doubts as to the wisdom of Irene and Joe's decision to wed before going abroad as a missionary couple, fearing they would drift away from the plan to serve abroad, settling down, instead, in England. It had happened to other would-be missionary couples. Irene's ex-Sunday school teacher shared the minister's reservations, but both were happy to be proved wrong.

Irene looks back fondly on her nursing days, and recalls with particular affection the Christians she encountered on the wards.

She remembers a girl in her early twenties suffering from aplastic anaemia, a fatal blood disease. The girl was a Christian, and Irene recalls her peaceful submission to death, as well as the joyous assurance of eternal life that helped to comfort her grieving parents. Another girl with the same ailment was the first corpse Irene had to 'lay out', and was not a Christian. As she had approached her end, the girl had been angry and her mental anguish had added to her suffering. The bereaved parents had only hopelessness at her death. Attitudes to death differed widely between believers and non-believers, and comparisons were unavoidable.

Irene was to find, invariably, that Christian patients always experienced peace with God in the final stages of terminal illness. Non-Christians never displayed the same feeling. Irene herself would sense the believing patient's own special nearness to God when they were close to death. The radiance of the love of God always showed in their faces.

She also witnessed the death of babies and children, and would often cry all night (as did the other nurses) when an infant passed away. Nurses who were not believers would ask Irene how she could still maintain belief in a caring God when she could see such awful suffering, but it was an experience that never shook Irene's faith. She believed that all little ones who died went to heaven, and never lost her trust in the lovingkindness of the Lord, in spite of what she observed on the wards. Her experience of death confirmed her faith rather than disturbed it.

4
1962-1965
PREPARING FOR SERVICE

(1) Marriage

Irene, in bridal white, walked sedately up the aisle to meet her future husband on July 7th, 1962. Tall, willowy and swan-like in her flowing gown, no-one would have guessed her inner confusion and ambivalence of feeling.

She *liked* Joe very much. She was very fond of him and he was attractive. He was her friend. She did not feel terribly romantic about him, but that wasn't really the problem. The problem was that she doubted their compatibility.

They were *both* dominant. They were *both* assertive. They were *both* outspoken. They were *both* leaders. In a conflict of wills, who would be the winner? Irene believed that a wife should submit to the will of her husband, but was less sure that she could comply without resentment. Only time would tell.

During their eighteen-month engagement they had applied to various Bible colleges in order to receive training before going abroad. All but one of the Bible colleges had refused them entrance, and the one that had not had simply neglected to respond to their application.

Bible colleges in those days did not admit married couples wishing to live and study together. Some colleges did not admit couples at all, and even the most broad-minded establishments insisted that married couples live apart, address each other as 'brother' and 'sister' and refrain from holding hands in public. The reason given was that married life might distract individuals from their devotion to study - but so far no college had ventured to test the theory.

Irene and Joe had almost resigned themselves to the demise of their missionary ambitions, when, during the second week of their honeymoon, they took a day trip to the Keswick Convention. They were strolling down a street in the town, past stalls set up by various religious organisations, when they happened to pass that of the only Bible college which had not responded to their application. The college in question was the Birmingham Bible Institute, and its stall was manned that day by the bursar.

The bursar asked Joe and Irene if they were interested in missionary work. Something about the forcefulness of their affirmation made him regard the couple inquisitively.

'Are you the Rowleys?' he enquired.

'Yes.'

'Oh. Why didn't you reply to our letter offering you an interview?'

'What letter?'

The letter had been lost in the post. Irene and Joe had two months in which to order their affairs and move to Birmingham. The BBI had decided to 'experiment' with a married couple living together.

(2) Birmingham Bible Institute

They were given an attic room in a Victorian hostel, above the communal dining-room. They had to share a bathroom with other students. It was not ideal. The personality struggles Irene had anticipated prior to their union were now to be given a public airing.

Irene and Joe were a curiosity to the college because they were 'guinea-pigs'. Everyone was keeping an eye on them. This meant that every argument became common knowledge within minutes. Irene would dread going down to the dining room for a meal after she and Joe had had words, because she knew that her facial expression would be instantly interpreted. Female students were particularly fascinated by the Rowleys' private lives and would ask searching questions.

The exposure added greatly to the strain of adjusting to life as a couple.

The course was two years long, during which time Joe learned a variety of skills: car maintenance, printing, building, dentistry and electrical installation - even elocution. One of the most significant and useful skills the Rowleys learned was not, however, on the syllabus. The subject bore the broad heading *Endurance* and covered the related sub-topics of *Patience* and *The Art of Living Harmoniously with Other People*. This was the truest spiritual training: living cheek by jowl with other Christians, suffering the petty rules and regulations of Bible college, and putting up with the damp and cold of the hostel. Once mastered, the craft was never lost.

Joanne was born in 1964. The Rowleys had by then been moved to another attic room and shared a kitchen with an elderly couple also living in the house. The baby made predictable and normal demands on Irene, but the new mother was not short of help from the students whose interest in the couple was now rather more welcome than before. Everyone rallied round to assist the new mother, including other married women who had recently been admitted (with their husbands) to the college - the BBI had evidently judged the 'experiment' a success.

(3) The Call To Brazil

On their very first night at BBI, all new students had had to declare their 'calling' at a meeting. Irene had stood up and declared her 'calling' to the Sudan, whereupon Joe stood up and declared his to Brazil. Of course everyone at the meeting thought that was hilarious, and it only added to the students' curiosity about the married couple.

Joe felt called to northern Brazil simply because scarcely anyone else did - in fact only three missionary societies were currently operating around the Amazon river. One of them was Unevangelised Fields Mission (UFM).

Irene submitted her will to Joe's and went with him for an interview at the UFM Headquarters in London, abandoning her desire to be a missionary nurse upon the discovery that she would not be allowed (under Brazilian law) to practice nursing in that country. UFM accepted the Rowleys, and they returned home to raise financial support for themselves from churches and friends, as they had done in order to go to BBI.

(4) June 1965 UFM

Joanne was nine months old when Irene and Joe arrived in London for the candidates' course. This short course, however, was packed with training as well as strict rules. Almost as soon as they got there, Irene was told to grow her hair.

They were informed that, in Brazil, only loose women wore their hair short. Irene's hair was short, so she grew it. She was also informed that, in Brazil, only loose women wore red. Irene accordingly disposed of every stitch of red clothing. Oddly enough, however, she was to find no evidence to support either of those ideas in the country itself. Her information must have been outdated, for quite decent women paraded short hair and red dresses in Brazil, entirely without shame.

Further studies in the subject of *Endurance* resumed in London, brotherly love being tested to its outer limits within the walls of the mission hostel. The hostel was run under a strict regime, great patience having to be exercised on an almost daily basis by all residents.

Life was hard there, but soon the course was over and Joe and Irene returned home to Manchester to gather sponsors. They had to raise all their travelling expenses and twenty-five £1 monthly promises. Diverted funds from missionaries expelled from the Belgian Congo boosted the Rowleys' finances.

It was a bad time for missionaries, worldwide. A number of them had been murdered by Simba tribesmen in the Congo uprising, and missionaries were unwelcome in many other African countries moving towards independence. There had been no missionary persecution in South America, but the mere contemplation of hostility still made Irene nervous now that she and Joe had responsibility for a baby. She forced herself to swallow her fear, and trust in God.

The fund-raising period lasted six months, during which time Irene returned to nursing (in Salford). In December she and Joe got the all-clear to go to Brazil and set about obtaining visas, medicals and vaccinations. They gave their furniture away and packed three oil drums with belongings ready to be shipped out to their new home. They had been told they were going to the UFM Language School in Belem for nine months, followed by three years or so in the mission 'field'. Joe and Irene didn't know which area of the 'field' they would be given, or what to expect when they got there. It was all a bit of an adventure.

Part 2
MISSION
FIELDS

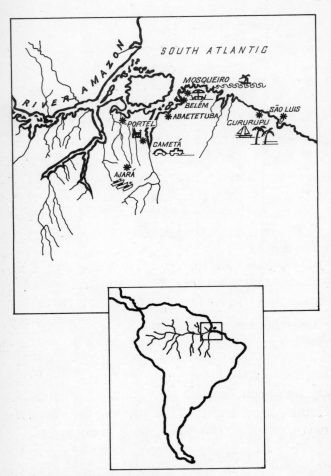

SOUTH AMERICA

5
1966
LANGUAGE SCHOOL, BELEM

The adventure begins

Belem,
Para, Brazil.
January 17, 1966

Dear prayer partners,
First of all, we must ask you to praise God with us, because we are here at last. Secondly, we want to thank each one for your faithfulness in prayer for us. We are writing straight away to you from Brazil.

Our last two weeks at home were such a rush, and there are so many of you we would have liked to have seen, but we just couldn't manage it. Thank you each one for the gifts and the hospitality you gave us. It is 'marvellous in our eyes'!

We were excited at the thought of flying to Brazil, after our comparatively ordinary life in England. We flew from London to Paris on the 5th and then had to stay overnight there because of fog in Madrid. It was fascinating to see the river Seine and other landmarks that we'd only ever heard about.

Then we flew to Madrid and then on to Dakar in West Africa. We were thrilled to see the Swiss Alps and later on we flew for hours over the Sahara desert. We felt so small and inadequate looking at these wonders of God that we had to glorify him again and again for his own greatness who made them all.

As we stepped off the plane in Recife, (a city on the eastern seaboard of Brazil,) we were amazed by the humidity of the atmosphere. It was like walking into a laundry full of steam! We stayed overnight in a modern hotel before flying on the next day to Belem.

It became hotter as we neared the equator and we flew over jungle, of which we only had glimpses because of the layer of cloud above it. Finally we landed in Belem, very hot, very tired, but really thrilled with the Lord's goodness.

We are staying at present in the mission headquarters, and it is really lovely. We expected things to be very strange, but apart from one or two things we feel quite at home. The rainy season has just started so we feel even more at home! It rains usually each day, in the afternoon: a really heavy downpour which cools us off nicely.

The houses have shutters instead of windows,

which we found strange at first because they're open all the time unless it rains. Also, we sleep under mosquito nets, but even Joanne doesn't object to that.

The people are very handsome on the whole; this of course is our first impression only, and we are in a big city here. They seem to be either very rich or very poor. They stare at us a lot when we're out, especially at Joanne. They would like their own children to be fair-haired and blue-eyed.

It is conference time at the base and we are having a time of blessing with Pastor Graby from North America. The theme of the conference is 'I will build my church.'

We want to remind you to pray especially for our study of the language, which begins on the 21st, also for our health and that of Joanne. She is settling down well, but cannot understand the heat. She plays with just pants and shoes on - how different from England!

Every good wish to you all and our dear love,
Joe, Irene and Joanne Rowley.

This was the first prayer-letter written by Irene from Brazil to their supporters in England. The writing of prayer-letters was a duty performed each quarter-year. The letter would be sent to England where it would be copied and circulated to all concerned by one of the Rowleys' supporters. Most missionaries keep in touch with their prayer-partners in this way.

Irene's letters to her mother were written far more frequently than once a quarter. They give deeper insights into the mind of the missionary as well as more vivid descriptions of their environment. Here are some extracts from Irene's letters to her mother penned at the same period:

'It seems so strange to hear everyone speaking a strange language. The people have bronze skins and black, oily hair, some straight, some curly. They seem a really nice people, but there is a mixture of course. There are lots of beggars and yet the majority seem decently dressed. We are in a better class area, though. Some of the houses in our area are really beautiful, absolutely palatial, with drive-in garages underneath them. Then right next door you have a scruffy hovel with only half its roof.'

'Brazilians are really happy-go-lucky and just don't mind how long they keep you waiting for things, just standing about. Poor people have got electricity and water and not much else. Whole families live in one big room and at night they hang up their hammocks on hooks in the walls. Everyone sleeps in hammocks here except the Europeans unless it's necessary. We went to visit a woman in a very poor house - there were three families living in the same house. They hardly had any windows at all. The walls were sort of mud, and no carpets anywhere. Just a couple of cane chairs, a Singer sewing machine, and a wireless.'

'We went to Mosqeiro beach. It was the first time Joe and I had been outside Belem. We soon got away from civilisation and wow! wasn't everything different! Just outside Belem we passed along what was left of a railway line that the British had started to build or had used. The Brazilians wouldn't use it after the British left. There were coaches and engines lying rusting all over the place, but the Brazilians are like that - they're very lazy and won't clear away anything.'

'Today I have hardly done anything, it is so warm. It is now 3.30 p.m., the hottest part of the day. We have all been lying down since about 12.30. I have to keep stopping writing, it is so hot. Joe has gone out with a couple of missionaries to do a meeting. He seems to have settled down reasonably well - I think the fact that he sweats a lot may have something to do with it. We are well, much better than I thought we would be. I think we're going to enjoy the language school very much. Everyone is so nice to us.'

'We started language school on Monday and the week has just flown by. We get up about 6.30 and have breakfast at 7a.m., then at 7.30 there are English prayers in the big house. There are two large houses and we have a chalet. We all have our meals in the big house. At 8.15 we do language study, until 11.15. There are six of us and we have three teachers. Dinner at 11.30, siesta from 12 till 2. We have to go to one mid-week prayer meeting in Portuguese and the Sunday services.'

'Some things are very cheap and some very dear. Omo is 3d for a giant packet - the Omo is in a plastic bag inside the box because of the humidity. I could do with plastic bags for other things as well. Joe's blazer is getting a sort of fur on it. Nothing ever feels really dry. Joanne has got a sweat rash on her shoulders and neck. We've acquired an ancient pushchair for her - typical Brazilian - falling to bits and tinny.'

'It's carnival time here in Belem. It began yesterday and goes on till Wednesday. It's absolutely vile! The processions are meaningless and end in a drunken orgy. It goes on right through the night - you can hear the drums beating, etc. I'm glad we're in the back and away from the front road.'

Irene was beginning to find out more and more

about Brazilian life, and didn't like everything she saw. She was also homesick. Flo Lawson, one of our colleagues, recalls: 'Language school was a traumatic experience for Irene. It was not that she had any problems learning Portuguese, but she really missed her family, and in particular her mother. I was so happy when I could 'borrow' Joanne and take her for a walk. This helped Irene get some rest to study.'

Irene and Joe were to value the support of their friends more than ever when they received shattering news from home.

*   *   *

> Belem,
> Para, Brazil.
> May 1966

Dear friends,
Thank you for your continued prayer and support which we really appreciate. We have now been here for four months and so much has happened. The Lord has been very near to us as we have been getting used to the climate and the country. We are all well in health, despite the heat.

Our first language exams were held in April, the results of which were quite satisfactory. Keep praying, though, as Satan uses language problems to discourage us.

I play the organ at the women's meeting at the

small mission hall on the outskirts of Belem. There are only a few women but they are all saved and testify each week of the Lord's goodness to them. After the meeting they all go visiting the homes of other women taking with them the gospel. In one house we saw a group of women sitting talking in a group around a little old lady who was dying in her hammock. It is the custom for all the relatives to come and wait when death is imminent.

We read a few verses of scripture and prayed with them. I had tears in my eyes as I saw the poverty and darkness of the people. The other women looked pathetic, suffering hardships which we'd never dream of, yet still without hope. I asked the Lord to use me to win them for himself as soon as I can speak the language.

Joe's father died suddenly in February...'

They received the news by cable. Irene describes Joe's reaction in a letter home to her mother:

'I still can't believe it, and Joe is walking around in a dream. We've hardly slept all week thinking about everything and wondering what would be said because we weren't at the funeral. Joe was relieved to read your letter today telling just how his Dad died because it seems he didn't suffer. He is very upset though and gets really depressed.'

Time healed the wound, however, and life eventually reverted to normal. Irene's letters home related more experiences of Brazilian life.

'Another fiesta in a house - everyone singing and dancing - it felt really evil. There was no escaping the noise at all. I felt sorry for any neighbour who wanted to go to bed early or who was a Christian and didn't want to join in. But that's how they live and why their lives are so immoral. They have no privacy at all.'

'I can hear next door's TV playing the theme tune of 'Bewitched'. It seems just like home - they get quite a lot of American programmes here. Went to Belem airport to see a demonstration involving a British plane. Got talking to several English mechanics. It was nice to hear English voices, even though they were Londoners. Anyway they were interested to hear about the mission. They couldn't believe it was winter here because it was so hot. It made me feel really homesick and when they left I nearly cried. The plane had the Union Jack on the tail. Needless to say we talked of nothing else all day.'

'Saw a beggar - he looked horrible with just a body and head and two bits for arms and only stumps for legs. I felt sick and Joe did too. Another fellow had crippled legs but at least he sat with his back against a wall: the first man was right in the middle of the pavement! Then just as we were waiting for a bus we heard a shout and a lad running with a wallet he'd just pinched. A couple of people tried to chase him but the rest just laughed. I was amazed, but it did seem funny though I felt sorry for the owner of the wallet.'

'On one bus trip saw a woman with a baby that looked dead. The baby was beautifully dressed and she was taking it to the hospital. The guard was sitting behind me and said 'Is it dead?' It wasn't, but it looked it, poor thing. It wasn't thin either. It had a really pretty face and she said it had had a transfusion, but that can mean anything in this country.'

'Visited a church up river; friendly people all in their Sunday best. The only work they do is pick cocoa beans and fruit called acai, and occasionally coconuts and bananas, but they're lazy and only pick what's there; that's why they're so poor. The children sang some choruses and the adults one or two solos. I've never heard such terrible singing; they have hard, coarse voices and they picked the worst songs, bless them!'

'Corpus Christi - the first R. C. procession we'd

seen, and it was an eye opener. Crowds of children all neat in school uniform, then priests all dressed up, and boys in white surplices. Then came the Archbishop with his gold staff, and the 'host' in a great big gold thing on a pole. There was lots of incense and bells and boys. Everyone bowed down to the host - even the folks on the pavements and at windows and balconies. We just stood there like great big foreigners, looking.'

* * *

Belem,
Para, Brazil.
August 1966.

Dear praying friends,
Our last term of Language School. It is hard to imagine ourselves out in the work at last. We have been allocated for a temporary period to a town called Cameta, which is further up the Amazon from Belem. We will live in the house of the Ackland family who are now home on furlough. Early October is the date set for our move, and we would value your prayers as we go to this town of some 10,000 people.

After our second set of language exams we had a holiday with Winnie and Maurice Sloan, who were in Bible college with us in England. They have a mission station on the coast at Parnaiba...

Please pray for Joe as he stands in the market

as a witness and sells Bibles to Brazilians who have a hunger for the things of God. Praise God for conversions in our little suburb church run by the language students. God reigns. Our love to you all,

Joe, Irene and Joanne Rowley.

Dear Mum,
Joanne is getting tall but bonny as well. She says lots of things in Portuguese now. I'd give anything for a tin of Heinz baked beans with pork sausages in them. The ones we have here are very spiced. I go shopping quite a lot. It's like going down town at home, in a way. In some ways it's more modern because of the American influence...

We are going go Cameta, everybody says it's a nice place. I hope so. The river is called the Tocantins, it's off the Amazon. We can speak quite a bit of Portuguese now. We can understand nearly everything that is said.

I have had a perm this week.

I seem to be losing weight, so I am taking vitamins...

Dear Mum,
Sorry not to have written sooner but have not felt too well. I had a stye on one eye, and then two more, and the whole of my face swelled up. Winnie is on a fattening campaign for me.

We think Flo is expecting. She keeps being sick, poor thing. I do feel sorry for her. I've taught the Sunday School the past two weeks and last week I had to give a talk in Portuguese in front of the students in school. I think I managed O.K.

Yesterday we went to a fabulous Brazilian wedding. I've never seen such gorgeous food and loads of it too. The cake was in two parts and the other food was super, all sorts of savouries and sweets.

Please send vitamins for me and books - I'm dying for a change of something to read. Did I mention Germolene too? It would be good to have some.

Love, Irene.

p.s. Just had a letter from the other couple in Cameta to say the house has just been broken into and the stove, gas bottles and a bike and sewing machine have been stolen! Hope they get some of the things back before we arrive!

6
1966
CAMETA

Corner of a foreign field

Caixa Postal 123
Belem,
Para, Brazil
December 1966

Dear praying friends,
Greetings for Christmas and the New Year from
Cameta.   May the Lord give each one of you his
richest blessing.

We came to Cameta in October and have had
two very busy months.   Our senior missionary
(Ron Combs) was ill when we arrived and within
three days of our arrival he was in hospital in
Belem having treatment.   Two days later his wife
and children went also to have check-ups - and
here we stayed alone - the only English speaking
people among thousands of Brazilians...

Irene and Joe had been thrown in at the deep
end. For these newly-qualified missionaries there

would be no gradual acclimatisation to the altered living conditions, and no-one to show them the ropes. They just had to get on with the job as best they could. Their prayer-letter continues:

Language School Portuguese fades into the background in the face of a host of people conversing rapidly. The people of Cameta aren't trained to pick out our words...

Cameta has had missionaries for about six years but it is known to be a very hard town. There is little fruit (i.e. converts) and we are praying for the Lord's will to be done to keep us here, concentrating on the town itself. A few miles away is a prospering work for which we praise him, but we feel there is an urgent need to work here right in this city.

The city used to be the capital of the state of Para but it is too far away from civilisation to accomplish much. Belem, being on the river mouth, is a far better location. The city has one piece of tarmac road which is full of ruts. It has only two cars - the R.C. bishop's car which is about four years old, and our jeep which is twenty-two years old! We are praying about a new jeep - will you join us?

The people here are very poor, and food is a constant problem. I feel so sorry when we have so much in comparison. Our neighbour's house is more or less typical of those of the poor: it's made of a type of bamboo lashed together with strong grass. The wooden floor is raised off the ground to keep things dry when the rainy season comes.

The front room has one chair - on which Irene usually sits when visiting - and a selection of hammocks. Clothes either hang on nails in the wall or over the rafters. The roof is made of palm leaves. A single plank connects the front room with the back room. To one side is a windowless bedroom. The kitchen (the most important room) has to be seen to be believed. It has no back wall. The stove is a table of wood on which a fire constantly burns. We keep expecting the roof to catch light, but it doesn't. The sink is open to the air. It's a sort of table with wooden slots through which the used water drains. Our neighbour's house has pigeons in the rafters and a duck with eggs underneath the fireplace. A dog, a cat, chickens and turkeys wander in and out as they please. When animals wander onto the family's land they just shoo them off and shrug their shoulders at the damage. Some houses are better than this, and some are worse.

Please pray for these people as their standards of everything are so low. Pray for Joanne's health (and manners) as she associates with this family who use one bowl and spoon between them all - and Joanne too when I'm not about! Pray for our testimony as close neighbours: they are very quick to get offended if you make one false move. We are constantly fighting a warfare which has so many facets that at times we are confused. But with the knowledge that you are upholding us before the Lord, we can carry on...

Cameta was to prove a very severe testing ground, as Irene's letters reveal. The difficulties faced in Belem were as nothing compared with the difficulties to be faced in the field. Here is an extract from Irene's first letter home to Mum:

'Ron and Lois Combs' house is absolutely gorgeous and brand new - all wood. I was surprised that it was so modern, but I was surprised in a different way when we saw our own house: dear me, I just cried.

The front half is cement, the back is wood, but it is not in good condition. We've worked for two days cleaning it and raised so much dust I've got a very sore throat and keep sneezing. The house is quite big, and now we've got our own things in it we feel a bit better.

Today I had a maid - dear me it's no fun when you can't speak the language properly. I visited her family yesterday - she's a nice girl, Cara, but I've never seen such a poor home. They were all eating their dinner off the floor: one enamel plate in the middle of them. A filthy little baby was sharing it too. Cara's clean, though. She's about sixteen. She doesn't know much about cooking, but if she washes and irons and cleans and washes up it'll be a good help. It's so hot here. It feels more so than Belem - I think it's because of the dryness.

Joe found a sick boy. The poor child was yellow. I gave him half a tube of antiseptic cream but you have to be so careful or else the whole town will be at the door...'

In spite of the prohibitions of the law, Irene became an unofficial nurse to the people of Cameta simply because she could not allow them to suffer when she had some means of relief at her disposal. She kept her own supply of medicines (some of which were donated) and became something of a missionary nurse after all. She found that the local people knew nothing of the basic rules of hygiene, as illustrated by these extracts from letters to Mum:

'The people eat a fruit called acai for nearly every meal and a local fish. Their diet never changes, it is so sad. We've had acai off the neighbours yesterday and it's the done thing to send something back in return. I sent three tomatoes, which they can't afford to buy. You've got to be so careful, though - when the acai came I put it in the fridge, and then when the maid wasn't looking I put two chlorine tablets in it to disinfect it because they'd mashed it up with river water! I wouldn't like to offend anyone.'

'We were up late last night with a woman Joe brought back from church (he has been preaching and I take Sunday School). The woman had a septic finger. People's poverty and backwardness depress me. I suppose it's because I can see ways to improve things that they probably *don't* see - or they're not bothered. Joanne has gone through the fence to next door *again*. I've given up trying to stop her. If she catches anything I'll just have to treat it when it comes.'

'Joe met the woman with the septic finger again. She said it's got worse - probably because she took off what I put on and put on a leaf instead. Ah well...'

'Have just been to the woman's house. Gave her an injection of penicillin and in walked another woman with a baby for me to inject as well. Not very sterile, but...! I talked to several women on my way home but they're all cadgers. I pity them, but I can't give them all stuff. Just gave the neighbour three eggs because she said they've got nothing for tea. Still, she does give me odd bits now and then. We're down to our last cabbage and that's three weeks old. Am feeling very homesick but it's no use. Keep praying. I've never felt so cut off. I can only speak English with Joe. I'm sure I'll cry with relief when I meet another English-speaker. It really is so foreign at times.'

'Yesterday I gave an injection and cut three people's hair! Joe baked cashew nuts in the garden all afternoon so we've enough to last three weeks. The fresh food is getting scarce till someone comes from Belem, but we've still got meat in the freezer from three weeks back - thank goodness. I don't know what we'd do without the freezer. Just had a lovely cup of tea. We're going through loads of it but it helps me feel normal. We're all right really.'

'The responsibility is terrific here and Ron sent a letter with lots of things to do. He doesn't expect to return for another two weeks yet. I don't know what to do about Christmas programmes (for church) or anything.'

'This morning a man (supposed to be a Christian) came with two children (girls) and left a present of acai for Joanne. It's the custom to give presents in return so I gave him three tin cans full of cashews.

They were pleased because they will use the cans to drink from. But as they were going the littlest girl came and asked if she could have a pan, as her mother had asked for one! I was taken aback and refused. Then afterwards Cara said the girl was lying: her mother hadn't asked anything of the sort. But I was really upset, because this chap had taken three batteries without offering to pay for them, and asked for a Bible which he says he'll pay for. It's awful not being able to trust people. I've bitten my nails awful this week. These people are so different from us - you've no idea! I'm getting a reputation for being strict.'

'Joe has been ill. He had a rigor and high temperature, and vomited once, then a touch of diarrhoea. He is still hardly eating and I want him to have a check-up in Belem. He's actually looking a bit thinner.

It is very different from home here. People are in some ways civilised and in others not. I have to be so careful all the time. I can't make real friends or they'll take advantage. I've been very worried about Joanne in our neighbour's house as they are so dirty in their habits. I keep telling her not to eat things and not to drink the water but she doesn't understand. I hope she'll get the message soon. But the neighbours are sly and give her things when I'm not looking.

We are practising for a Christmas programme. It is short this year as Ron and Lois are only just back. I've been visiting a lot: it's the only way I can get Joanne away from the neighbours. I'm looking forward to conference in Belem and a change from here. It's a real strain living so close to the people - that's putting it mildly!

Our maid has been bothering me a bit. This week I'm giving her a list of things to do in strict order. She messes about so much. Lois says she is taking advantage of me because she was someone else's maid before and thinks she knows it all. Anyway, we're looking around for another house now because since this one was robbed the atmosphere around here has been painful. People think it was our neighbour who is so friendly - she knows folk are thinking this.

We are all trying to be friendly and yet everyday things are coming to a head. I think perhaps Cara knows something and this is what is making her act funny. She told me that she thinks by February we'll have the sewing machine back - but she says all sorts of funny things. I told her not to come in on Sundays so today feels strange to have no-one else wandering about. I said to Lois, "I must be very British. I like to have my home to myself" - but here it is impossible. Please keep praying for us. Times are very discouraging, especially for poor old me who falls for everything, then is disappointed. They are scroungers, these people. That woman who had the septic finger is now suspected of having taken part in the robbery - what a let down! It's all very upsetting - you've no idea what it's like not to be able to trust anyone. I'm even a bit doubtful about Cara, but time will tell. We're just waiting for someone to make a false step.'

'Had a Brazilian boy and his sister to stay for a week. I didn't really enjoy it. The boy was four and his sister eleven. He caught his foot in the back wheel of his mother's bike and nearly ripped it off. They're a Christian family and live miles from anywhere in the jungle so I said he could stay while he had treatment. He was OK as far as homesickness was concerned, but was just so un-civilised I nearly came to blows. He ate with his fingers (which they all do) but the floor was such a mess after he'd finished! I made his sister clean up after him. One other thing: he refused to say please and thank you for anything! In the end I didn't actually give anything to him but always worked through his sister.'

Christmas came and went, and the Rowleys gladly departed Cameta to attend the annual conference at Belem in the Language School. They both had medicals which revealed roundworm in Irene and a liver disorder in Joe. All three Rowleys were discovered to have nits, though Joanne was otherwise completely healthy. Irene cheered herself up with shopping and had a perm before the family returned to Cameta, where they found a new house big enough in which to hold meetings, though it would be some time before they would be able to move in. They aimed to gather a nucleus of believers which they would then encourage to start a church of their own. Irene decided to form a women's sewing group in the new building, as a means of spreading the gospel. The warfare continued.

7
1967 - 1968
CAMETA

Forever England
Caixa Postal 123
March 1967

Dear praying friends,
Greetings to everyone from Cameta. What a time of blessing and fellowship we had in Belem! What a wealth of old truths and new things were put before us! Also what a good time of chatting with old friends, getting up to date on news, and making new friends! We returned to Cameta more confident and very refreshed, to begin our work here in earnest. The people of Cameta gave us a real welcome back and we felt they were sympathetic towards us.

Irene commenced a girls' class in our home, beginning with a devotional followed by handiwork. This appears to have gone very well, as the Brazilians are very neat and clever with their fingers. There are about 15 girls coming regularly so far, aged 10-18.

Joe's boys, with whom he plays volleyball and

football on a Saturday afternoon, have begun to come to the Saturday morning Bible class for adults, which is also fairly well attended by the neighbours who show a keen interest in the Bible.

Two weeks ago Joe, along with Ron Combs, visited a man who was a backslider from the faith. He was very repentant and showed a real desire to be back with the Lord. He's been to each meeting since, Sunday and weekday. Please pray for him. His name is Raimundo and he has ten children. His wife is a Christian.

Sometimes we think these people are as civilised as we are, then one comes upon something to show their great ignorance.

We were in the house of Christians where there was a baby of three months. The baby had hiccoughs, and a lovely old Christian lady leaned across and asked an older child to bring her a piece of paper, which she did. The old lady then ripped off a tiny square of the paper and stuck it on the baby's forehead. At first we just looked, then asked her why she did it. She answered in all sincerity that it would stop the hiccoughs. She took the paper off there and then, and of course it hadn't worked! I suppose she thought it was our fault!

Dear Mum,
We received a telegram today saying Flo had had

a baby girl. Was thrilled for her!

Last Sunday morning Joe killed our dog - it had gone mad! I think it was rabies.

When we move into the new house we will have as a near neighbour the bank manager, who is a Baptist. They've got four children who seem quite nice kids so perhaps Joanne will get on OK with them. His wife is a nurse and very nice and I look forward to getting to know her, also the other better class folk who live nearby.

May: This afternoon none of the girls turned up for my class because there was a do on at the school up the road for Mother's Day which is tomorrow. Our neighbour is having a mass in her house every night this month - Mary's month!

Had a letter today telling us they're thinking of dividing the mission into zones because of doctrinal differences between the Americans and the British. The British are more easy-going about certain things than the Americans. Have also heard that the Indian Protection Society are asking our Mission to move all Americans off their stations. We're not sure if this means all Americans or all foreigners (it means the same out here) as there are also a lot of Europeans. Please pray - we may be home before we think!

A fellow was converted last night at the Bible study. He's a nice fellow and has talked a lot about wanting to become a Christian.

Do you know what I'd like? A food parcel - with tins and packets of things English. Nothing here tastes the same and tinned fruit is expensive. I wander around the house sometimes just longing for something English to eat like chocolate or liquorice allsorts! You can buy chocolate in Belem but it tastes musty.

We called at the new house and were told it would be finished by the fifteenth so we'll see! We are all quite well again, although we all get very tired at times and the noise from the fiestas is terrible.

Wednesday night there was Joe's meeting in the church, an R.C. mass in our neighbour's house, plus two fiestas! The clash was terrific!

*   *   *

Caixa Postal 123
June 1967

Dear prayer partners,
Hello and greetings in the Lord from Cameta. We're in the process of moving into a brand new house in the town centre, right behind the home of the priests and very near to the biggest R.C. church in Cameta. We decided to move when it was felt we could stay and do town-based work.

The house is rented and not too big, but a change from leaking wooden walls and tiles that hide insects of all types. We're so close to the neighbours on one side that if we had windows on that side we'd have all their smells and conversation.

Our house is clean, white-painted, and although simply built, looks neat. Our neighbours' house is a rambling mud-brick type with half the mud washed away to leave holes which you could look through if you were so inclined. A picture of our witness here for Christ, is it not? We have hearts cleansed and free from sin by our dear Lord, uncluttered by worldly things. Their hearts are crumbling ruins because of their sin, and so dark inside that even when you try to get through to their conscience it is full of sinful vices and will not admit the light. Please pray that our personal lives may be continually clean before God so that our witness may be unblemished before him.

The Lord is encouraging us. A few weeks ago, at our Wednesday evening Bible study, Joe was preaching and the words seemed to get all tangled up and the right ones wouldn't come, he was so tired. Then at the close of the meeting a fellow came to know the Lord. Oh, how we praised him when we got home that night! Help us to believe God will always work even in our every weakness.

Join us in praying for a united conference in September when we hope to invite all the Christians from the outlying places for fellowship, finishing with a baptism of new believers. We hope to make it a real 'Keswick' for believers and a time of salvation for unbelievers. Thank you for your letters and continued prayer. Yours in his work here,

Joe, Irene and Joanne Rowley.

Dear Mum,
I've never been so tired for a long time as I am today. We moved into our new house last Monday and it took till Wednesday to get it more or less straight. Then on Wednesday afternoon three American airmen arrived - phew! Joe had invited them to stay with us because there was nowhere else for them to go - so I'm running a guest house! You would never know me if you saw me, Mum! Without Cara I'd go mad! They've given me loads of things which are very acceptable, like Tide and toilet rolls, steel wool, white soap, scrubbing brush, and fly spray! I've even got the loan of a bicycle!

* * *

Caixa Postal 123
Belem,
Para, Brazil.
August 1967

Dear praying friends,
Greetings again in the Lord from Cameta. What a busy few months we have had! About six weeks

ago three people were converted at our evening meeting - we were so thrilled. One is an epileptic and we would value prayers for her, that her decision may be real for the Lord and not just an opportunity to get the missionaries to buy her medicine.

There is also another convert, Vincent. We are not too certain how real his decision was. Pray for our dealings with him.

Joe discontinued with the football after the scamps ran off with the ball. We haven't seen it since. One or two still come to the meetings and we'd value prayer for their conversion. Where we now live it is difficult to play football.

Irene continues with the girls' class. Last Saturday there were eighteen - please pray for these girls...

Dear Mum,

I now have ordered clothes through an American magazine in case we have to split with the Americans mission-wise...

One of our airmen is awful: he was spoiled by his mother when he was a little boy and is a terrible eater. He picks at his food and wastes things. He went to a public school and insists on a napkin! Ah well, these things are sent to try us. Cara is ill and I've got a new girl - she's very slow. I'm still keeping a good weight and Joanne is massive. Joe is the same - on the thin side. The Americans have bought us an electric heater for the shower, so we can have warm water! Joanne keeps having an eye infection. I treat it and it goes away, then recurs.

Must go and cook the dinner. This girl can't cook! I have a bit of a cold but have to carry on - it's twice as hard with this girl.

Dear Mum,
Thank you, thank you for the gorgeous parcel we received on Saturday - I nearly cried! The Bird's Custard Powder is on show and at last I've used a little. Oh! It's gorgeous after the Brazilian stuff! Also the milk is so different from the powder we use here! Everything was crisp! The biscuits went in five minutes! The Smarties next, but I'm trying to make the rest last a bit. It makes me feel just that bit nearer to you when I see different things that are English.

You don't sound too well, Mum. Please go carefully. It worries me when we are so far away.

I'll be glad when the Americans go. It's hard work finding food that they like when there's no choice anyway. Still, I must go, this girl in Cara's place is a dope. Hope Cara comes back in August. She at least can cook anything I tell her to.

There's a commission coming from England to discuss this split or whatever it is, so Joe has to go into Belem, to meet with all the other Europeans. Don't know for certain if the Acklands will come back then - we'll have to see what happens.

*   *   *

Caixa Postal 123
Belem,
Para, Brazil.
November 1967

Dear praying friends,
Hello again in the Lord from Cameta.

Our work in the little church continues and the numbers seem to have increased somewhat. About fifty attend the morning Sunday School. Our three converts are doing well, but Vincent hasn't been near us for several weeks. When he sees us arriving for a visit he nips off into the forest!

You will be wanting to know how our 'Keswick' went! Well, a week before we were due to go to Belem for a conference we received a telegram saying that our speaker had to take his wife home to the U.S. because she was seriously ill. It was about three weeks before the meetings were planned to begin. We were so disappointed, but of course prayed earnestly for our friend in his trouble. We could not ask anyone else at such short notice so felt we had to cancel it. We plan to have it nearer January, when our fellow missionaries will be planning to come to Belem anyway. Several of the interior Christians were glad in a way to cancel because we had an early rain and they wanted to get their crops well planted before the big rains come, so it seemed to be of the Lord, and we know he is the best organiser in the world.

We have begun some new ventures. The first was to start a Sunday School in our home. The first Sunday saw us with 22, the second with 33, then last week there were 43. We must tell you that although these folk are very poor they are very respectful of anything religious and wouldn't dream of coming without shoes to the Sunday meeting even if they spend the rest of the week playing in and out of the house in bare feet!

On Tuesday nights from 6 till 8 Joe has organised a Y.P. night. The young people play table tennis and other smaller games for the first hour, then have a 'break' during which they get the gospel. It is well accepted especially by the parents as it keeps their children out of mischief.

Thursday saw the start of Irene's dream of a women's meeting. There were only six the first two weeks but she is finding it a good opportunity to speak about Christian matters that affect women only...

Dear Mum,

I'm so tired, please forgive my handwriting. I think I'm heading for bronchitis. I've started taking tablets so that I can make it to meetings - penicillin every four hours. Joe too has a runny nose and is coughing. Thanks for the tape. It made me homesick.

Met my first witch doctor! A baby was ill and I went to ask about him. There was this old woman sitting there in the house stroking a bunch of leaves all over his head and body. I thought at first she was playing with him, but no. Maria paid her some money and off she went. She kept glancing at me out of the corner of her eye all the time and had a most evil look on her face. I guess she knew I was a Christian. I don't wonder the baby is ill, though. She doesn't wash him enough. His nose was all running and I felt like saying, 'Clean his nose out, then he won't get stuffed up!'

Joanne has been playing with an American boy and has picked up a drawl - I heard her telling someone her name in English and she said 'Jowan' just like an American would - it's a scream! She would like us to have a baby, so she says. I told her we'd have to ask Jesus. She really needs someone, still I guess the Lord has it all planned - it's only me that's bothered. I've been so worried about not having another baby yet. Winnie had a baby girl.

The Acklands are not coming back now till next December - did I tell you?

Joe's got a bad septic finger, the second in recent weeks. I don't know what's up with him. Joanne had worms so I gave her some worm medicine, but it blocked her up and she was rolling around her bed in agony. In the end I gave her an enema.

You have no idea how we appreciate parcels and post. I thought I might have been getting less homesick, but it isn't so. Even Joe nearly cried last week when he heard Land of Hope and Glory played on the radio.

We heard on Sunday that there had been a wedding service in the jungle between two men. It was made worse for us because rumour had it the wedding had been conducted by our church! I saw this awful, screaming and shouting wedding procession coming down our street with the 'couple' in the middle, one dressed as a woman with a veil, etc. I was so upset - in the end the authorities arrested the men. Apparently the rumour began because one of them had previously been with the Seventh Day Adventists, and of course these ignorant people call anyone who isn't a Catholic a 'believer'.

During conference we sorted out all the problems with the Americans and now everyone is happy again...

Dear Mum,

Surprise, surprise! The Acklands are coming back to Cameta and we are on the move! Guess where? Down south, to a place called Cururupu - it's a boarding school! Joe is to help with maintenance and we'll have several children living with us in term time - I'll tell you more about it later. It's by the sea and is supposed to be the most beautiful station in the field - I'm thrilled! I might relax a bit more when I'm not stuck in the centre of a town with just Brazilian neighbours. We will have our own house in the grounds of the school in a mission compound - must rush and pack!

8
1968-1969
CURURUPU

Paradise Lost

The location was lush, verdant, and almost like
Eden: the sort of typical jungle mission station
that seemed at once familiar. A wide clearing had
been hacked out of dense forest to make room for
the Bethany Institute, and several small buildings
dotted the slope that eased down to the muddy,
slow-moving river. Within the compound was a
school for the children of local converts, and
dwellings for the pupils and their Christian leaders. It appeared orderly and disciplined: each
person's daily duties regulated by the homely
clang of the school bell.

Irene and Joe were to be houseparents to ten
eight-year-old boys in a small mud-and-wattle
house with no bathroom or running water. The
boys were unhealthy, noisy and mischievous, but
Irene did not mind, so relieved was she not to have
to reside in a town with Brazilians. She was among
her own kind, now. She was living with English-

speaking Christians, so life was bound to be easier.

The boys in their care were cheerful and lively, always joking amongst themselves or charming Irene and Joe with their artless wit and naivete. In times of difficulty for their houseparents, the humour of these boys was to lighten the load considerably.

There was a village nearby which she could visit, dispensing medicine to local people who were as ignorant of nutrition and hygiene as those of Cameta, nine hundred and fifty miles to the north. In this remote place disease ran as rampant and uncontrolled as the abundant vegetation, and there was much need for her knowledge, though she doubted the Brazilians' willingness to act upon sound advice. She doubted they even bothered to take the medicines she gave them. Still, there was always the enclosure to return to, where people at least understood how to live.

There was plenty for Joe to do: as well as supervising the unruly pupils and maintaining the grounds and equipment he had the opportunity to preach at the local church. Joanne had the company of other children and was growing tall and beautiful. Well-provided American missionaries donated clothes for her wardrobe and contributed to the development of her accent.

Some of the flaws of Bethany were obvious: lack of fresh fruit and vegetables meant a diet of rice occasionally garnished with meat, subsequent malnutrition accounting for ill-health in pupils and staff. Water had to be boiled before drinking because of the risk of disease, and Joe was to be severely afflicted with malaria. Irene fretted at her inability to conceive and suffered the continual ache and downward drag of homesickness.

These burdens were unavoidable: were the less obvious burdens also unavoidable? Were the secret flaws of Bethany as inevitable as disease in an unclean place?

Irene and Joe had experienced something of strife among missionaries at the Language School: personality conflicts, that interfered with the work of spreading the gospel, threatened to destroy the credibility of Christians, and discouraged those already engaged in intense spiritual warfare. They had seen it at missionary training college. It was not new to them, and yet here, in the closed universe of the mission, strife was fiercer and tension more oppressive than ever before. Strife was like the jungle that always threatened to overwhelm their fragile colony of civilisation, obscuring the work of God and plunging the land once more into deep darkness.

Strife rarely took the form of open conflict. Instead, it ate away at the foundations of friendship, undermining trust and gnawing at understanding. At its surface it had a crust of pettiness and irritability, criticism and intolerance, whilst beneath seethed frustration, hatred, and profound hurt. Irene and Joe sought love and rationality, comfort and calm, whilst endeavouring (not always successfully) not to fall victim to the infection themselves.

Bethany was a haven without peace: a claustrophobic prison of unrest that made Irene long to live once more among Brazilians. She would rather have been agony aunt to the unsaved than succour the converted. Surely, she reasoned, this was not what was meant by 'missionary work'. She did not feel emotionally equipped to deal with this. She wondered how much of the physical ill-health within the compound was due to diet, and how much to stress.

*　　*　　*

Prayer-letters gave no hint as to the precise nature of the situation at Bethany. Personality struggles were shameful and private, and Irene did not want to cast slurs on character. In June 1968 she would only say: 'Discouragement is not a thing we want to go into at length, but if you know it comes, then you can pray for us more readily.' October's prayer-letter would only admit: 'You have no idea how much you help us by your letters and assurances of love and prayer.'

Of course, Mum could be privy to all the details

and was the only one to whom Irene would name names, in the assurance that the confidence would not be broken.

Irene became pregnant in October 1968 and planned to travel to Belem in March in order to receive treatment for a Rhesus condition. She would take Joanne with her and remain there until the baby was born. Joe would have to endure the tribulations of Cururupu alone, until term ended and he could join his wife and children. At least, that was the plan.

Cururupu,
May 1969.

Dear praying friends,
Greetings to you all in the precious name of Jesus.

You must all have been praying extra hard these days, because we have felt the closeness of the Lord in an even greater way than ever before...

Irene went into Belem as requested and there the blood picture had become a lot worse. Consequently, when Irene began to go into labour on the 22nd April, and our baby only lived two hours, we were more or less prepared. We were disappointed, but at the same time knew the Lord's will was being done.

Thank you for your prayers, dear friends, and may the Lord uphold you and lead you in his ways, too. The words of a sacred song came to our minds at the time and we have been singing it to ourselves ever since:

He giveth more grace, when the burdens grow greater,
He sendeth more strength when the trials increase.
To added affliction he addeth more mercy,
To multiplied trials he multiplies peace.

We have something always to praise the Lord for, and we want to praise him for our experiences these past two weeks. We have learned of the love of the Lord in many ways, not the least in the care of our American fellow missionaries for Irene. They undertook everything that Joe was not able to do through his absence, and our sense of fellowship and oneness was doubly sweet...

While Joe shed tears of despair as he awaited the plane that could take him to his wife's bedside, this is how Irene broke the news to her mother:

Dear Mum,
Well, loves, how are you? I hope this letter won't be too much of a shock. I started in labour on Tuesday morning at 6 a.m. here and they got me straight into hospital. I had the baby about 8 a.m. and it lived for only a short time. I knew as soon as I started the pains that I couldn't expect it to live. I was only in the seventh month. I called it Janet for the sake of the documents and also after

a kind friend who helped me. Janet said it was a good sized baby, about five pounds, and had a pretty face, but she said it was very swollen.

I feel very tired, that's all. I've explained about the baby to Joanne and she seems OK about it. Joanne knows the baby died because it was too small to live. She still wants a brother or sister though so we'll see what happens when we come home on furlough. I'll go and see a specialist and find out what he says about trying again. If it's impossible for me to have another baby that will live, we might think of adoption. Ah well, the Lord knows. Joanne is actually proud of the fact that she had a baby sister who died - here in Brazil they talk a lot about these things.

I came out of hospital today, they looked after me really well. I'm not sad. Don't feel too sorry for us - just pray about us doing the Lord's will. I do hope you're not too depressed about our news, I'm very well really and as I get stronger I feel better about it all...

Dear Mum,
Got your letter yesterday. I'm sorry you were shocked but do hope that by now you will have recovered and realised that all things do work together for good to those that love God. I was talking to a friend who said she didn't understand how one can be happy when things go wrong, but

I think that as long as you know you are where God wants you to be, then you are happy. Keep looking up. God is the only comforter, you know. I believe he asks us to go through the experiences we do in order to come out better for him. I certainly know that without him, the past few months would have been terrible. He can give us peace in all our situations. I'm saying all this to myself as well as to you. I'm not very spiritual, but all I have is due to him...

Irene eventually became pregnant again, and came back to England at the end of September 1969, bringing Joanne with her. Joe had to remain in Cururupu. He was continually weak and ill and she worried about him, but at last he, too, was able to return home.

Their time at the Bethany Institute was over. Only in later years were Irene and Joe able to value the spiritual lessons they had learnt there. Bethany's days were numbered, and after another two years it closed down.

Despite the flaws of the mission station, the voice of the gospel was not drowned by the clamour of dispute at Bethany. Despite the faults of the messengers, the message of Christ won the hearts of many people. Despite the weakness of God's agents, God did not lose strength. All of those whom God called, he justified.

9
1971-1975
PORTEL

Opening Doors

Nigel was born on March 12th, 1970 after a labour induced in anticipation of Rhesus condition. To everyone's surprise, however, the tiny, premature baby boy was not afflicted with the illness that had caused Irene's previous miscarriage. He was jaundiced and underweight, but needed no transfusion.

Irene was delighted to be safely delivered of her son in her home country. Willingly she resigned herself to a few weeks of sleepless nights and two-hourly feeds whilst Nigel matured. Lack of rest was a necessary and unavoidable sacrifice, though Nigel was to demand more sacrifices and sleepless nights than anyone predicted.

Irene and Joe were overjoyed to be once more in England, savouring the beauties of the Cheshire countryside with the heightened appreciation of exiles. They had a proper, solid English house in which to live, and could relish the sort of meat-and-two-veg diet denied them in Brazil. Bird's Custard Powder could once more be taken for granted.

Joe's health was slowly restored and he was able to perform the required task of touring churches giving reports of their work. He preferred actually doing the work to talking about it but was aware of the need to refer back to those who had upheld the family in prayer and sacrificial giving.

One church that gave the missionaries a particularly warm welcome was Lymm Baptist in Cheshire. The Albert Memorial had closed, and Lymm was soon to fulfil the role of 'home church' to the Rowleys. Friends made at Lymm were to provide Irene and Joe with much-needed practical help and Christian love in the future. The home church became their domestic HQ: a spiritual base camp and source of supply.

Probably even more than their missionary society, Lymm Baptist would become a mooring post in England's harbour of comfort and familiarity. Irene and Joe knew that wherever they had been and for however long, Lymm would open its arms to them and welcome them home.

*   *   *

Nigel's broken nights continued for a far longer period than that expected of most premature infants. As a consequence Irene became exhausted, irritable and almost suicidally depressed - and this during a year set aside for recuperation.

At eight months the baby was still not sitting unsupported and was unable to grasp small objects with his hand. Irene also discovered another problem one day as she was pushing him out in his pram. A particularly noisy lorry passed them in the street making the sort of thunder and rattle that would cause most babies to flinch. To Irene's dismay, however, her son displayed no reaction.

He was given a hearing aid and speech therapy and began to show some improvement. The hearing aid, in fact, opened up a whole new world of experience for Nigel, revolutionising his perception. By the time the Rowleys returned to Brazil in September 1971 Nigel could walk and was a better sleeper, and could soon dispense with his hearing aid altogether. The missionaries were tired, however: it had not been an entirely restful period.

*   *   *

Portel was a river town in an oppressively hot climate. Local industry was dominated by an American-owned sawmill. The Rowleys' missionary society had asked them to settle in Portel and help build up an existing small congregation.

At first they were given a small rented house on

a town square, then after a time moved into the mission house which until then had been occupied by a church deacon. Their new house was a large, single-storey wooden edifice on stilts, with verandahs front and rear and a loud generator too close for comfort. Water was drawn from a well. The house had been built nineteen years previously by Cecil McMullen, the first missionary to Portel, and was situated in a large garden, facing on to an unmade road. It was surrounded by a fence. Not far from the house was the church, located in uneasy proximity to a frequently uproarious Catholic place of worship.

Joanne was sent to boarding school at AVA (the Amazon Valley Academy) as a suitable education was not to be procured for her in Portel. She lived with houseparents during term-time and came home to her parents for holidays.

Irene found it very hard to be separated from her daughter and missed her terribly, worrying about Joanne's initial homesickness and hoping that she would eventually be content in the distant school. The certainty of Irene's own calling preserved her from any sense of guilt about sending Joanne away, but did nothing to diminish her maternal instincts. However, she realised she had to trust entirely in God for the care of her child or lose all peace of mind and become ineffective in his service. Once she learned to trust she was able to sublimate her natural frustrations as a mother by immersing herself totally in the work to which she had been called.

Soon after the Rowleys began work in Portel, the congregation of the Christian Evangelical Church increased in number. Irene taught local women to read and held children's and Sunday School meetings. Joe involved himself in youth work and preached upriver to isolated Christian communities as well as ministering in Portel. With another missionary he instigated a ministry course for local men in order to pass on skills in preaching and church leadership. He lost weight and began to go bald as a result of his hectic lifestyle and continued ill-health.

Locals began to be drawn to the missionary couple, as Brazilians often flock and attach themselves to an admired leader. Attendance at young people's meetings soon exceeded fifty, and many adults dedicated (or re-dedicated) themselves to the work of the fellowship. Sunday School numbers rapidly increased to the extent that an extra room had to be built on to the church. A new building was planned. Many people also committed (or re-committed) themselves to Christ: as frequently as three or four per meeting in May 1972.

The Rowleys opened their house to local people and were constantly inundated with visitors, many of whom came to Irene for medicine and vitamins. Portel was an insanitary place: dysentery and intestinal worms were common complaints to which the missionaries were not immune.

*　　*　　*

It was during this period that Irene's old prejudice against Brazilians began to be eroded. Gradually, as she became more at ease among them, she started to understand more about the people around her. She had always considered Brazilians merely shiftless and lazy, but realised now that she had simply misunderstood the reasons for their apparent apathy.

It was poverty and lack of hope that made them listless: the knowledge that nothing worthwhile could be gained from exertion made the people shrug their shoulders and stay in their hammocks rather than exhaust themselves to no avail. Extreme, strength-sapping heat made them sluggish and dozy - not any characteristic unwillingness to work. Irene could see that even an English person would become similarly lethargic, if forced to endure such unendingly dismal living conditions. It was only motivation that kept missionaries busy.

The Brazilians were not scroungers: they were sharers. Their attitude to possessions was different to that of Europeans. If there were two Brazilian families living as neighbours, and one family had two saucepans whilst the other had none, the needy family would ask the relatively wealthy family for one of the saucepans. The wealthy neighbour would not take offence at the request and would probably hand over the 'spare' saucepan without a murmur.

Irene had previously condemned the Brazilians' immoral lifestyle. It was common for there to be as many 'Papas' in a family as there were offspring - and 'Papa' was not necessarily expected to reside with 'Mama'. Incest was rife, adultery tolerated, and pregnancies in very young girls was far from rare.

All that was more readily explicable (if not accepted) in the light of the tedium of poverty. As Joe might express it, 'There's simply nothing else to do'. People become languid in humidity and heat, and self-discipline becomes relaxed. Added to that, there is no-one to correct the Brazilians' immorality. Many religious leaders turn a blind eye to unchristian behaviour - if they don't indulge in it themselves. There are very few ameliorating influences. Such as exist are like candles in endless night.

In retrospect, Irene also realises that many of her former ideas about Brazilians were no more than projections of her own prejudice. She had dispensed medicines to Brazilians and felt instinctively that the medicines would not be used as prescribed, but this supposition was based on her belief that the people were dull-witted, and not on genuine foreknowledge. Her instincts were flawed. The Brazilians were quite capable of following directions and usually did as they were told.

She had regarded Brazilians as dirty people, not appreciating the tremendous lengths many went to in order to keep themselves clean, in places where the only water came from a muddy river or a standpipe. Indeed, she was to discover that the British custom of bathing in a tub was regarded by Brazilians as unhygienic: Brazilians took showers.

She had regarded them somewhat haughtily from afar, witnessing their apparent ignorance of things English people took for granted, like healthy habits and hard work. Close to, she could observe that behaviour unaccounted for by environment could be explained by need: need of instruction, need of guidance, need of education, and need, above all, of the light of Christ.

Any residual personal pride inherited through the Batemans was also subdued by the Rowleys' son. It was impossible to remain lofty for long when seven-year-old Nigel was unexpectedly back-classed at school.

He obviously found schoolwork harder than did his peers, though at first Irene was inclined to wonder if the problem lay more with the school than with her son. Did AVA possess the resources to cope with Nigel's learning difficulties and provide the particular encouragements he needed? He had already received therapy in England (on their second furlough) which had improved his balance and co-ordination. Should the Rowleys return to England so that Nigel might be given the best possible care? Irene and Joe wondered if the upbringing of Nigel ought to take precedence over their other calling. They wondered if they should abandon their missionary activities and come home to England where Nigel's requirements might be met more fully. Anxiously, Irene and Joe committed their concern to God, who provided them with a surprising answer.

The back-classing that had so wounded family pride proved, within a few weeks, to be the very assistance Nigel needed. The effect it had on him was this: once Nigel felt he could cope with the teacher's demands, his increased confidence gave him a boost that accelerated his development. The back-classing that so discouraged his parents and sister had the opposite effect on the person most concerned.

Nigel was happy to be with his younger schoolfellows and did not share any of his parents' scholastic ambitions. Sufficient for him was to enjoy the affection of his companions which they offered him in abundance. He was a gregarious, smiling child who easily formed friendships and was popular with older children. Once he was allowed to find his own level, he could achieve his own potential.

Irene and Joe discovered that the care of their children need not conflict with their missionary call. God had not placed their calling in one part of the world and his care in another. He could provide for all their needs, wherever they were. If he wanted them to remain in Brazil, he would give them the means to do so. And he had.

10
1976-1980
PORTEL

Brazilian brothers and sisters

The prime location for churches in Brazilian river towns is on the main square, facing out towards the Amazon. In most Brazilian river towns, it can be taken for granted that this favourable position will be occupied by the Roman Catholics. In Portel, however, it was the Christian Evangelical Church that rejoiced in the prestigious site, donated to them by the local chemist whose late wife had been a believer.

This was Irene and Joe's new church, acquired through the need to accommodate their rapidly expanding congregation. The building was dilapidated and in need of virtual reconstruction, but there was a willing workforce of believers who contributed out of their often meagre income to the cost of bricks, timber and tools. The same Christians also laboured in the heat and humidity to construct a house fit for the worship of God. They were faithful and enthusiastic in their labour, and generous in all their giving.

It was a time of great blessing, but also of great testing for these new believers. In the unhelpful moral climate of Brazil they suffered many temptations to abandon their new-found faith. Some proved unequal to the spiritual battle. There were those who succeeded in creating new lives, and those who could not shake off the shackles of the old.

One such was Josias. He was married to a Christian and trained at the layman's ministry course (which Joe had helped to develop) with a view to becoming a full-time evangelist in Portel, following the eventual departure of the Rowleys. This idea had to be abandoned when he was accused publicly of immorality and was forced to resign. A different church gave him a second chance to bring credit to the name of God, but rumours of his past failings caught up with him and once more he was forced to leave.

There was Carlos, married to a lady who taught at the Sunday School. He was a convert, but dogged by a pre-conversion drink problem that frequently got the better of him. He appeared to gain control over his inclination to drink too heavily, but for some reason lost enthusiasm for his walk with the Lord. By 1980 he was making promises to the Rowleys that he would return to church, without ever getting round to keeping them.

Carlos had a cousin called Geraldo. Geraldo was an intelligent and thoughtful Christian, but almost blind, and a haemophiliac. He was physically weak and prone to infection. He taught at Sunday School though was often so sickly he could barely carry out his duties. Nevertheless, he attended the layman's ministry course and yearned to work for the good of other Christians. The mothers of both Carlo and Geraldo were involved in the occult.

Irene's closest encounter with the forces of evil occurred when she went to visit the house of a member of the congregation, whose daughter was demon-possessed. Irene pitied the girl and talked to her about the Lord Jesus Christ, then put her arms around the girl and her mother and prayed. She left the house after that, and, walking down the street, met another lady from the church. The lady needed help. She had many problems and was obviously in need of comfort.

Irene suddenly felt as if she could not help her. She felt indescribably awful, and could find no words of counsel or hope for this poor woman. She could not minister to her.

Another Christian lived nearby. Irene rushed to the house and begged her friend to hold her and pray that the dreadful, oppressive feeling might go away. The friend prayed, and at the words 'In the name of Jesus' the feeling suddenly left Irene, as if driven out by the words.

Joe later chastised her for having gone to the house of the demon-possessed girl without having first informed him, so that he could uphold her in prayer. He also rebuked her for making physical contact with the girl and her mother whilst praying. Irene never did it again.

*   *   *

The congregation of the Christian Evangelical Church soon numbered a hundred and fifty each Sunday morning, with twice that amount present at Christmas special services. There were frequent baptisms, and up to thirty men and women for each layman's ministry course, drawn from all over the region. Joe took on many responsibilities outside of Portel, serving on the AVA school board and on the mission field council, set up to discuss problems encountered by missionaries in the area.

There were many small difficulties to be resolved in Portel alone. There were argumentative Christians, sensitive Christians, weak Christians, domineering Christians, lazy Christians and foolhardy Christians. Irene and Joe were continually sorting out minor disputes and encouraging others to walk worthy of their Lord and Saviour. They had to cope with the discouragement of having their congregation decimated by falling attendance each time they went on furlough, or took a holiday: the Rowleys often wondered whether some church members' devotion to Christ was surpassed by their devotion to missionaries.

If they doubted the depth of some conversions, however, the testimony of others put sincerity beyond question.

Most notable among these was that of Zilda, a sixteen-year-old girl who was dying of a tumour. Her parents were Christians. Ten days before the girl died she trusted in the Lord for her salvation, and was born again of God.

Her mother witnessed a change in Zilda's demeanour as the girl faced death without fear. Zilda now displayed peace and repose, with a joyful assurance of eternal life in heaven. God also bestowed on her an added mercy, in that the terrible pain she had been suffering gradually lessened the nearer she drew to death: long before she died the pain had gone entirely.

There were many whose faith was proved by their works: the prostitute who left her soldier boyfriend and gave up her occupation: the many couples who married legally after years of cohabitation: the Christian girl who ran away to marry a non-believer and later returned repentant. All these lives bore testimony to the work of God.

Dale's Story

Dale was a believing friend of Nigel's. He was the same age as Nigel and from a Christian home, all the children of which had been named after missionaries. The family lived upriver and were ministered to by Heidi Anselm, a German missionary who was a friend of the Rowleys.

Dale had a wish: he longed, one day, to race his family's boat on the river with Joe's boat and that of Heidi Anselm. One day, Dale's wish came true: but not in the way he had dreamed.

It was late on a Saturday night when a messenger brought Irene and Joe the news that Dale had fallen on his hunting knife and had severed his jugular vein. Hurriedly, Joe gathered together a few medicines and rushed to his boat, turning it towards Dale's village. It was a long way to Ajara, and nearly midnight before Joe came within sight of it.

Joe heard the sound of hammering coming from the shore as he approached his destination. It was a particular sound that could only signify one thing in that place and at that time of night. The hammering sound could only mean that Dale had died, for it was the noise made by people constructing a coffin.

Joe landed his boat on the shore and went to the house. Dale's mother told him how her son had died in her arms.

He had been crying when he ran to her covered in blood, but had closed his eyes and become quiet as the life drained out of him. His mother started to weep when she realised he was dying. Dale must have heard her, for he opened his eyes and said, 'Don't cry, Mummy. The pain has gone and I can see Jesus, holding out his arms to me.' He died shortly afterwards.

The following day at five in the morning a short service was held for him, and the funeral party left Ajara by river for the cemetery. Joe and Irene had to catch a ship for Belem that day, so all three boats had to hurry: Joe's boat, Heidi's boat, and Dale's boat, with Dale in his coffin. It was almost as if they were racing.

*　　*　　*

Irene's mother died in May 1977. Irene wrote her sister: 'If I cry at all, it is because I have lost my best correspondent and one of the few who I could tell little things to (and they were important). I am praising the Lord that through my early years in Brazil I had Mum to write to each week. Now I'm old! and can cope for the most part without news from home. But she was a good mother and I only hope my children love me as much as I loved her.'

*　　*　　*

Irene spent a great deal of her time in Portel

nursing the sick. Certain patients are remembered vividly, like the man with the snake bite. The doctor at the hospital had wanted to amputate the affected leg, but the man had refused to allow him and went home instead to his dirty hut, to die. He permitted Irene to treat him, which she did for weeks until the wound healed. With horror she recalls a wound big enough to insert her fist, which she did every time she went to clean it.

Then there was the eight-year-old girl who had got her long hair caught on the prop shaft of a motor launch and nearly scalped herself. The girl recovered and, years later, still shows off her regrown hair to Irene each time she sees her.

Irene nursed with the help of God. She remembers the sawmill worker who was choking on a piece of meat and near to death. Irene found a catheter and poked it down his throat, hoping and praying that it would go down the right tube and dislodge the obstacle. It did. There was the baby in agony with a bean pushed deep inside his ear. All Irene had was some cooking oil and the power of prayer. She poured the oil into the baby's ear and appealed to the Lord that the oil might shift the bean. It did.

There were the tragic cases: the simple woman who did not have the mental ability to know how to care for her children and who consequently lost three in as many months, through inattention to cleanliness. Irene also recalls the baby who died of tetanus because the midwife's knife had been dirty.

Irene herself became very ill (the disease was later diagnosed as toxoplasmosis, and cured). She became exhausted to the point where she could do nothing at all except lie in bed and had no idea what was ailing her. Someone loaned her a book about a missionary who had died of leukaemia and Irene wondered if her own days were numbered. She was fearful. She reached rock bottom with depression and fatigue and prayed that the Lord would not take her.

Alone in the house one day, there came a knock at the door. She dragged herself out of bed to open it and greeted the wife of a deacon who was carrying with her a kilo of liver. Two more women arrived and they prepared the liver to nourish their patient, urging her to lie down and rest. While the meal was cooking they surrounded her bed. Shyly, one of them said: 'Dona Irene, we are going to pray for you because we don't know what else to do - and you are not to worry. The Lord will make you better.'

'How funny,' Irene remembers in an article she wrote later for a magazine. 'Here was the missionary, who usually does all the praying and encouraging, lying helpless while the dear ladies acted just as we'd taught them. They each prayed in turn - I was so very grateful. The youngest gave her baby to an older one to look after and stayed with me the whole morning, working around the house...No-one will ever know how much I appreciated the love shown to me by my three Brazilian sisters.'

This was clearly not the missionary of Cameta.

11
1981-1984
BELEM

(1) A New Idea

Irene and Joe returned to Brazil, after a furlough in England, in July 1981, taking up residence this time in the city of Belem. The district in which they were to work was a waterfront area know as the 'Old City' where there were many Roman Catholic churches but no Protestant witness. Protestants were generally unwelcome in the Old City, which was a middle-class quarter in close proximity to a shanty town.

As a rule (or at least in Irene's own experience) missionaries are reluctant to work alone in cities, preferring the security of a mission compound to the challenge of dwelling among natives. Spiritual and cultural isolation is aggravated by a close juxtaposition of Northern European and Latin.

The Rowleys, however, were prepared to resist their own herd instincts and live among those to whom they sought to witness. They were willing to go beyond mere neighbourliness and embark upon a venture that would hold down the draw-bridge of their Englishman's castle.

The concept of an 'Open House' had not been tested before in that area and was a leap in the dark for Irene and Joe. 'Home' had hitherto been Irene's refuge from the storms of missionary life: now she was to open it as a haven for other buffeted believers. All would be welcome within the Rowley's walls and at any hour of the day, be they visiting Christians from the Brazilian inter-ior or children from the dirty alleys of the Old City.

Joe advertised the missionaries' presence in the local newspaper, inviting callers. Brazilian neighbours regarded the new 'Americanos' with curiosity and wonder, but would they step over the missionaries' threshold and take up the Rowleys' offer of hospitality? A barrier of suspicion and prejudice might make them reluctant.

(2) Unwelcome guests

Three days after the Rowleys moved into their new house, one of Operation Mobilisation's two vessels, *M. V. Doulos,* came into port at Belem. The ship was carrying young people who jour-neyed from country to country distributing scrip-tures and witnessing to Christ. As soon as the ship docked, twelve young evangelists arrived at the Rowleys' door and asked for hospitality.

It would not have been correct to refuse them, even though Joe and Irene weren't entirely pleased to greet these first visitors to their Open House. In fact, they weren't yet prepared to be 'open'. They had only just moved in. They had only just been swindled by a builder who had overcharged them for work on their formerly derelict property. Still more damaging than the theft in Cameta had been the fact that the swindler had been a professing Christian whose dishonesty had become known to non-believers - and this in a place where Joe and Irene sought to bring credit to the name of Christ! The experience had left Irene and Joe with a sour taste in their mouths. They wanted to be left to lick their wounds in peace.

The visiting evangelists were not on holiday. They soon set to work in the Rowleys' neighbourhood, calling from door to door and sharing the gospel message with the locals in their varied dwellings. Irene and Joe might have regarded the young people as a hindrance, but they soon proved to be the vital link between the missionaries and their neighbours, for it was these unexpected guests that brought the Brazilians off the streets and encouraged them to cross the threshold of the Open House. Irene and Joe may not have felt quite ready to begin their work, but the work was ready for *them*.

Aided by this push-start from the *Doulos,* Irene

and Joe were able to establish, within weeks, a timetable of events: evening games and chats to the children, afternoon Bible classes, and a weekly prayer meeting for adults. Twenty-two boys and girls attended the second of the Rowleys' Friday afternoon sessions. Irene felt great elation some days later in the street when she heard those same children proudly repeating that week's Bible memory verse.

'Teacher!' they greeted her cheerfully, 'Ephesians chapter two, verse eight: "For it is by grace you have been saved, through faith - and this not of yourselves, it is the gift of God - not by works, so that no-one can boast." See, we know it already!'

Irene observed frowns of disapproval from staunch Roman Catholic neighbours and overheard their murmurs of discontent, but rejoiced none the less.

Joe organised evangelistic campaigns and continued to minister in the Brazilian interior. He preached at special meetings and was often absent from the home. He retained his involvement in the laymen's ministry course at Abaete and in 1982 was away for a total of twenty-four weeks. As a result, the welcoming face at the door of the Open House was most often that of Irene.

She held knitting classes for women and girls, helped initiate a Sunday School and a Thursday afternoon Good News Club, and held Bible studies with interested female neighbours. In addition, she took over the correspondence for the Transworld Radio programme *Manancial da Vida*.

Transworld Radio is a Christian broadcasting company, *Manancial da Vida* being put out by the Rowleys' own mission. Irene's job was to give out and correct Bible correspondence courses, receive and write letters, and keep in contact with missionaries elsewhere. It was all very time-consuming.

Joe started a football team for boys, and the house was very rarely empty of young people as he also taught English. Each activity was attended by at least ten of them, rising to thirty or so for Sunday School. Only two of these children were known to be Christians, but many would sit for hours discussing spiritual matters with the missionaries and asking profoundly challenging questions. There was an eagerness within these young people to learn Bible verses and understand the scriptures.

Irene and Joe prayed continually that God would shed light on his Word, but for years saw little fruit for their labour. Attendance at meetings and activities would fluctuate according to the time of year, whilst competition from Roman Catholic catechism classes would draw many away from the Open House. Only a few parents came to open evenings or went to Bible studies. There were only a few conversions.

(3) Family matters

Joe's health was erratic. He was prone to severe headaches, probably associated with high blood pressure. He had to take medicine and was occasionally debilitated. At times he was very ill, and suffered continually from a bad back.

Joanne took 'O' levels and learned shorthand and typing. She was baptised in 1982 at her own local church and became actively involved in its work, keenly attending youth camps and retreats. She eventually graduated from the Amazon Valley Academy and helped out there for some months before commencing a short course at the Word of Life Bible College in Recife.

She received unofficial nursing training at a local orphanage and considered following nursing as a career. With fellow students from Word of Life she ministered in the local church, visited the nearby prison to witness to inmates and guards, involved herself in house-to-house visitation, played the organ on Sunday and helped with the young people's work. Would she follow in her parents' footsteps and become a missionary? At least the burden of choice was her own. Her brother's future lay in others' hands.

(4) Nigel

Extract from a 1981 prayer-letter

'He has a low I.Q. He is struggling with a 'mirror image' (i.e. his left side is the stronger, but he is trying to write with his right hand) which apparently causes the confusion in his brain which hinders his speech, writing, maths and reading progress. We praise God for lots of things - he is no longer deaf, he climbs steps without fear, he rides a bike with ease and kicks a good straight ball with his left foot. He is very sensitive to spiritual things. We ask for your prayers in a very real way, that we all together may play our part in the creation of this person called Nigel.'

Extract from a 1982 prayer-letter:

'It has been discovered that he suffers from a rare metabolic disorder called Infantile Hyper-calcaemia (otherwise known as Williams' Syndrome, or 'Elfin Faces' Syndrome) which causes brain damage of varying degrees. Through contact with the recently set up Foundation we have got in touch with a clinic in Chester, the Centre for Brain Injury Rehabilitation and Development. They kindly studied a written history and recent school report of Nigel's, and although they felt AVA was the best place for him at present, they felt they could help more if they saw and assessed him. As Joe is to come to England this year, it seems to all concerned a God-sent opportunity to send Nigel with him. All seems to be slotting into place. Joe's expenses are to be paid by U.F.M. but we are seeking the Lord's help to supply Nigel's return fare and the necessary fees, as the clinic is a private one. Please pray for us...

I will add here a paragraph from the Foundation's letter to us:

'Hypercalcaemia produces a child who is quite aware and interested in life and humanity in general, but whose existence, though apparently sociable, is lonely and friendless, owing to an inability to establish any real friendship with a contemporary. Adults, though more tolerant, and amused and flattered initially by the child's polite and friendly approach, inevitably get bored with the rather endless chatter and over-effusive behaviour. The child therefore tends to be rejected by all age groups at a deeper level, though accepted socially for a limited time at surface level. Being by very nature sensitive, he/she feels this very much.

These children are very affectionate and compassionate to all those in trouble, and therefore have a lot to offer in the right place where they are appreciated and understood. But sadly the pace of life seems too fast for them nowadays, nobody has the time or patience to listen, and they get left behind in the general hurly-burly. Only those who have lived with an IHC child know how mentally exhausting it can be, and how necessary it is to have a break from time to time.'

We find all of this in Nigel and we want (before he is too old) to do as much as we can to help him live as normal a life as possible...'

Extract from a 1982 letter to Irene's father
'We had a gorgeous ten days with Joanne but after she'd left I was more depressed than I've ever been in my life. I couldn't snap out of it. Please pray too for extra strength with Nigel - there are times when I don't even like him any more. I know it's Satan attacking and I'm getting better again - but oh! it's hard at times. Especially now he's growing up and losing his baby ways.'

Extract from a 1982 prayer-letter
'We must share with you our great joy at the way the Lord met every need, and more! for Nigel's trip to England. It was so abundant a supply that Nigel still has an excess of finance (put on one side for his personal use) in case of other special need. Praise the Lord! Thank you too, those who prayed, as well as those who gave. The doctor discovered that Nigel is severely

brain-damaged and has great perception difficulties - but he was amazed at his reading ability which he called a miracle in view of the other problems he has. Praise the Lord! It was felt that with a daily home programme of exercises he will improve substantially.

It seemed, at first, as though we were at the foot of a very tall mountain with a long climb ahead, and not much energy to do it. Then the Lord gave me Isaiah 40:31 - "they shall mount up with wings as eagles" - and the burden was lifted. Eagles don't climb, they soar!'

12
1984-1990
BELEM

'Your friend and mine'

Lymm,
Cheshire
September 1984

Dear friends who pray,
Greetings in the Lord from beautiful Cheshire!
On June 12th, after a very good journey from
Brazil, we arrived in England. We were met by
relatives and friends and taken immediately to
this lovely house. Everything had been prepared
for us: nothing was lacking. We felt like royalty,
and know that we have the Lord to thank for this
great provision for our needs. Our 'home' church,
Lymm Baptist, found the house and prepared it
for us, and it is as though a banner has been
stretched across its roof, reading, 'Faithful is he
who promised, who also will do it'! It is complete,
even to roses around the door!

We have been busy visiting relatives these past
two months and getting Joanne settled into nurs-

ing school. Thank you for praying. Please uphold her as she tries to get into life in this country which has such different values to the one from which she has come. She is one of two Christians in her year and really needs prayer for her spiritual battle in this strange new life.

Nigel's first visit to the doctor in Chester was extremely encouraging. He has again improved a substantial amount on their scale of measurement. This is an answer to prayer and a matter for great praise.

Our news from Brazil is good. We have had several letters from the girls and young women. One especially good, telling of the conversion of Marina, one of our fourteen-year-old regulars. Praise the Lord...'

Irene and Joe were naturally delighted to hear that Marina had come to faith. They looked forward to greeting her in Brazil as a new child of God and deepening their relationship with her as they guided her through her Christian life. As a sister in the Lord she would be doubly special to the missionaries.

Irene and Joe did not predict *how* special Marina would be. They could not foresee *how* significant she would become to them in the future. Their relationship with her was indeed to deepen, but Irene and Joe could not have prepared themselves for the nature of that depth.

On March 17th, 1985 Nigel was baptised, to the great joy and gratitude of his parents. A teacher was found for him in Sharon Huggett, who would return to Brazil with the Rowleys in July. Sharon was a personal friend of Irene and Joe, and would help out at AVA for two years whilst paying particular attention to their son.

Irene and Joe eagerly looked forward to returning to Belem and seeing for themselves quite a number of new converts. The McAllisters (relief missionaries) had reported many blessings in the small fellowship, which appeared to be thriving in the Rowleys' absence. Happily, then, they boarded the plane at Heathrow, nothing daunted by the fact that Irene had had to undergo major surgery only six weeks prior to their departure. She was healthy now, and Nigel's needs (an ever-pressing concern) had been satisfactorily accommodated. Irene and Joe longed to get back into the thick of their exciting life in Brazil.

December's prayer-letter, however, brought news of trouble.

> Belem,
> Brazil

...We moved into our house in the 'Old City' on the 19th Sept. just one month after Irene's accident with the dog (she had been very severely bitten on the face). It has been hard. The sense of evil has been so strong and the attacks of Satan so blatant we have not known if we were on our heads or our heels! Praise the Lord that he is in control!

One of the attacks was through the children who have been coming to our meeting for years. They became jealous if we made a fuss of one more than another, and it grew so out of proportion that it became terrible! But with much prayer, and the co-operation of other missionaries in prayer, they all turned up one evening around Irene and asked for forgiveness - an almost unheard-of occurrence round here, but of the Lord!

Then there have been other difficulties with believers and pastors in immorality, both here in Belem and in the interior. Joe was called urgently to deal with one of the leaders in the church who had sinned with a brother's wife. Then there has been much sickness in the mission there, and as I write one of the lady missionaries is very sick and another in hospital, and another lost her baby last week. So it goes on. We can only hang on to the Lord and believe he has the ultimate say in what happens to each of us. Certainly we are living in the end times.

Through it all we have learned to trust in Jesus more and more. One of the most helpful verses given to us recently has been 'Is the Lord's hand shortened, that it cannot save?' Also, 'the battle is not yours, but God's'.

Blessing and opposition continued to walk side by side in the little church. In May, 1986 they wrote:

'...This letter is a little late, and we are sorry about this, but we decided to wait until after Irene had her surgery on her face, so we could tell you how she is looking. On the 8th April she had 24 hours in hospital and had 1½ hours delicate surgery to the scar. It was very well done. Praise the Lord for his goodness!

We seem to have been very busy since we last wrote. Abaete (the laymen's ministry course) in February was a great blessing with 69 full-time students and several day visitors. There were three graduates this year. Joe had to expel a demon during the second day from one of the girls, a very difficult situation indeed but the joy afterwards was tremendous.

During the month of February Irene and a few believers in the Old City decided to have early morning prayer meetings, and they were so very blessed it's impossible to tell you of the blessings, without writing a book! Mostly though Joe felt the power across in Abaete and it was one of the best courses they've had.

As there are so few actual believers who meet regularly in our house you can imagine that their problems become ours. So please pray for Angelica (baptised last August). She has a repaired harelip and open cleft palate. She is difficult to understand, very temperamental, and has a terrible tendency to depression. She is sixteen and often comes to meetings and cries the whole time and won't say why, or just gets up and walks out. These young people have awful home backgrounds, and they share some very sad things with us, which you wouldn't want your teenager to have to deal with.

Some 'regular' boys have stopped coming and they hang about on the corner of the street. One or two still come into Sunday School. Miguel, for instance, who is tempted to do wrong things and was recently in prison overnight for an attack on a man. He sits on the back row Sunday mornings and takes home tracts to read, then the next minute you see him talking with all sorts of undesirables on the street corner.

Last Sunday a boy came back who we haven't seen for several years. He was very restless throughout Sunday School and we felt he was a little deranged. We now know he's also taking drugs and has quite gone out of his mind. How sad it is. What can we do, except love them and pray for them? Our house seems more open than ever before.

Nigel is shooting up like a weed and as thin as ever. He has one noticeably shorter leg now; and we were able to buy an exercise bike for him to use each day hoping it will help a little. He seems to improve a little in his studies. Sharon says she is very encouraged with him. Pray for the staff at AVA as there have been some very unpleasant things happening there these days: burglary, and even rape of one of the maids. It is very hard for the folks who have to live on the property (and that includes Sharon).

We want you to praise the Lord for his faithfulness to us. In spite of everything he is faithful, you know. We do tend, as human beings, to look on the dark side and only see the worst in people and situations, but with the proper attitude before the Lord we can see his hand at work. It's a little like our back garden. Such a jumble of rubbish and old building materials, but we've planted a jasmine tree that has white, perfumed flowers, and then, after four years of waiting, another pink flowering tree had one bunch of fragrant blossom! It's just like the work in the Old City. In between the bits of brick there are purple flowers by the dozen and some azalea seeds thrown around have come up in unexpected places! Praise the Lord!'

Prayers were answered regarding church attenders. The Rowleys spent much time petitioning God for Paulo, a friend of Nigel. Then in December, 1986:

'...Remember Paulo? Nigel's friend, who came to speak English to him? Well, two Saturdays ago he walked into our front room at the time for the young people's fellowship and said: 'Good news, Dona Irene - I have asked the Lord Jesus into my heart, and I'm so happy!' So were we! We are especially happy as the Devil has been causing us discouragement about our work in the Old City. It is too slow, too small, etc., but then - Paulo accepts the Lord! Pray for him. He is already going through troublesome times. He has lost his job and is having difficulty finding another.'

Paulo was to have no easier a ride through the Christian life than did Irene and Joe. Subsequent prayer-letters report a long period of backsliding, followed by renewed commitment. Life for a believer at the Open House was evidently as much a matter of up and down as life for any believer anywhere else. There was light and shadow, high and low. Christians blew hot and cold in their devotion to the Lord and experienced blessing along with attack - just like anyone else.

Irene experienced her own very personal attack. It is noticeable that of all the people that were important to the Open House there was one whose name never got into the prayer-letters. Her name is significant by its very absence.

This one person was active, but her activities

were always omitted from public correspondence.
She was spoken of only privately, and then just to
a confidential few. Those few alone were ac-
quainted with the doings of the girl eventually
referred to simply as 'your friend and mine'. The
uttering of her title, combined with a certain wry
lift of the eyebrows, soon came to mean one thing
only: the next item on the conversational agenda
was Marina.

Marina

Some extracts from her letters to Irene following
'misdemeanours' (translated by Irene).

Dona Irene,
Mother - I am writing because it is very difficult for
me to speak. You know how I am, don't you?
Once more your weakness has won me over and
made me different. I know I did wrong. Look!
Excuse me, from the bottom of my heart. It is the
first time I'm asking to be excused like this. Really
if the truth were told I am feeling very ridiculous
having to write these things. Thank you for all this
you have done for me.
From someone who is a little rebellious,
Marina.

Dear Rowley family,
I would like to ask that you don't speak to me any

more. Pretend that you don't know me and I will do the same thing. It will be better for all of us. It isn't necessary to discuss this. I have already returned all that I had of yours. Ah! I prefer that it is like this, because I am very hurt and am no more a child that does not know what I ought to do. I have thought much about what happened and see this as being the best way to have no return and no fight.

Don't think I am going to come back like I have the other times - because this time you really hurt my heart by rebuking me. If you would stop and think what happened, you would see how much it hurts to have mistrust among Christians.

Thank you for your attention,
Marina.

Dear Irene,
I know that I hurt you and didn't ask forgiveness, but please be certain of one thing. I have tried to create courage to say that I am really sorry for all I did to you and Joe. I know I have wronged you greatly - and this was the worst thing I have done to you so far.

I know I am capable of being furious, hating all. You know, I didn't want to believe that I was wrong and ought to do something about it. But my heart told me that your love was true for me. It was difficult for me to accept this because you know what I'm like. But I'm certain that it was God who spoke to me - and spoke seriously!

I love you all. I want to thank you for receiving me when I returned without asking pardon, and I am sorry for what I said - I am truly sorry - really! You look on me as a daughter. I also think of you as a second family. You occupy a very big place in my heart.

Thank you for your attention and love,
Marina.

Dona Irene,
I decided to write this because I needed to say some things and can't get always to speak to you. Firstly, I want to say how grateful I am to you both. I recognise all you have done for me. To say thank you is not enough.

Do you know, Dona Irene? Perhaps I am being too proud, because I don't want to be like just any other person. I think that of all people I am the worst, and feel embarrassed about it. I think this because I have done so many wrong things in my life - I don't want to have everyone looking at me and feeling sorry for me.

Well, Dona Irene, I hope you understand. If you don't, then speak to me about it. I think this is all I have to say.

Thanks for your attention,
A kiss and a hug from Marina.

Dearest Dona Irene (I love you),
Now I understand how you were unhappy when I went and danced Carnival. I am really going to try never to make you unhappy again or God. Please pray for me. I know it's difficult. Please pray, OK?

    I love you,
    Marina.

*   *   *

Irene handed her biographer the above-quoted transcripts one June day in 1990 in Warrington, at the house where she and Joe were being accommodated on furlough. I had gone there to collect some more material for the preparation of this book, and was handed a sheaf of foolscap with the reluctant comment from Irene: 'These are some letters from Marina'.

'Who's Marina?' I asked. 'You haven't mentioned her before.'

Irene sat down in her armchair and burst into tears. I glanced through the transcripts and began to see the reason why.

'I don't know if I can face her again,' Irene told me. 'I don't know if I can face going back to Brazil.'

'Why?' I asked. 'What's she done?'

*   *   *

Marina conducts what Irene refers to as 'hate campaigns'. Marina once told all the children that their meeting at the Open House was cancelled. No-one turned up, so all Irene's hard work in preparation was wasted. Later, Marina entered the house and enquired innocently as to how the meeting had gone. Several days later all the children came in and apologised profusely for what they had done.

She is physically attractive and forceful, a natural leader for whom her peers have a certain respect. If she encourages them to be disruptive in a meeting, they will be disruptive. If Irene makes a comment about another child Marina will twist it into an insult and repeat it to the person concerned. She wields power over weaker individuals and bullies them, making them confused and miserable.

This behaviour is infuriating for Irene, and for Joe who once told Marina that she had a demon and was to leave the house at once. Irene, too, believed Marina to be possessed.

Joe is able to dismiss Marina's tricks with greater ease than can Irene, due to his less sensitive nature. Irene struggles with her own feelings of profound hurt, and tries to love Marina as the Lord would love her. It is extremely hard and wearying. One letter to Joanne reveals much of the problem:

'Have been perturbed by Marina.. She is evil. I was very cross with her today for taking a letter out of my Bible and reading it. I told her off and asked her to leave. She was furious. I even phoned her home to tell them I was very upset about it. Well, since then she's been 'paying me back' in various ways. She's called to say she's forgiven me - no apology, mind, but if looks could kill I'd be dead over and over. It's pathetic because she keeps making excuses to come to the house. Monday she came ten different times, but she gets others to do her dirty work and makes them tell lies as well. It is distressing. I'd prefer she'd stay away.

If I could I'd ask you not to write to her any more, as she uses your letters in wicked ways. I've been trying to get her to pray and read the Bible with me but all she says is 'Me? No thanks!' Pray I may be kept sane through it all. I need to get away from the house a bit.

Mostly I feel victorious about the problem, but I'm so sensitive. Keep praying. It has helped me to write to you about it.'

Another letter reveals:

'I don't know who is praying but he is hearing and I feel relieved. Yesterday Marina made a BIG FUSS of Dad (Joe) and ignored me but kept giving sly glances to see if I was watching or not, then she kept sending the others who were in the house to give me messages. I spoke normally to her and treated all the kids alike. One girl told me that Marina wanted to make peace with me, but I'm waiting for Marina to make the first step, as I've been OK to her. Anyway I kissed them all as they left, but Marina pulled away. So more than that I cannot do. She pulled Dad's finger out of its socket and today it's very swollen and sore.

I really need some time away. Still, God has promised me peace in this house. I'm going to print a verse in large letters and pin it up: 'GOD IS ABLE' - just to remind me! Aren't we awful? The things we allow to worry us! But he is going to give me victory in this place.

Marina has said she doesn't want to be a believer any more, and has gone off religion of any sort. I kind of wish she'd go off me! But I'm the only one who loves her unconditionally - and that's the Lord's doing.

I keep trying not to get mad at her. I will maybe write a book one day about all the things she has done to me...'

13
1990-
RAMATES

(1) The will to return to Brazil

In June, 1990 Irene felt that she did not have the emotional and spiritual strength to return to Brazil, because of her difficult relationship with Marina. In September 1990 she recorded:

'All year I have fought with the feeling that we ought not to return. I haven't kept it secret, and now Joanne's wedding to Mark has come and gone I must give myself to facing the possibility that we must. Joe is absolutely convinced we should return, so, as in the beginning, I will go with him and trust the Lord to give me peace. But I ask for more than peace: I need joy. I want to do God's will, not because I'm afraid that if I don't things will go wrong, but because I love to do God's will - whatever that might be.

Many folks have said things like: 'You've done your whack' or 'Twenty-five years is enough', or 'You're not getting any younger'. Perhaps we ought to be getting Nigel to put down roots in England with ourselves close by, to help him become more independent. My fear (and I'm ashamed of it) is that something will happen to Joe and I if we all return to Brazil, and Nigel will be left orphaned and lost in a country with no social set-up. But, as I write, I see I'm looking at earthly considerations. I tell myself: 'Haven't I always seen how God has worked for Nigel all these years? Will God forsake him now?' I have even said: 'Lord, take Nigel to heaven before me.' Is that wrong to do? If you have a handicapped child, you'll know that the child's death is the least of your fears as a parent.

But the fact remains: if our financial support comes in, we must take that as confirmation that we are to return. We have no real ties here - we didn't buy a house (as I'd hoped) and Joanne is happily married and settled. She has a house I would have cherished at any stage of my Christian life.

I look forward to Trans-World Radio work, but flinch inwardly at the thought of the Open House in Belem. Where has all my courage gone? I know I've been ill this furlough with my under-active thyroid, but that has been taken care of and I still cringe at the thought of taking up the fight again.

Maybe this is Satan's doing. He has always

tried to stop us from doing God's will, and more so in the Old City than anywhere. Maybe he's trying to get at my will. Well, with God's help I will go, holding his hand. I will wait and see how he deals with my fears and lack of trust...'

In November, 1990 Irene was given the courage to rise above her fears. She was given a driving force stronger than her self-doubt and stronger than her dread of facing Marina. Her new motivation had its roots in tragedy.

(2) Ramates

Somewhere in the Old City of Belem is a Gideon New Testament with his name signed against the printed declaration of commitment to Christ. Irene and Joe gave Ramates the New Testament when he was thirteen or so, though he was not baptised until the age of twenty-one, the year before he died.

Ramates was handsome and had thick, dark, unruly hair that Irene often trimmed for him. His own mother was often too busy to mend his clothes, so Irene did it. She also knitted him a woolly cap when woolly caps were the fashion, helped him with his homework, or sometimes just talked. She loved him like a son and Ramates visited her often, saying how much he enjoyed the atmosphere of peace in the Open House.

Irene warned him against the bad company he began to keep, saying, 'Ramates - if you don't stop going with these so-called friends I'll end up having to visit you in prison.' Whenever she said that Ramates just smiled, and told her he would be all right.

When Irene and Joe returned to Brazil after one furlough, Ramates stopped attending the Open House. Irene would often see him in the street and call to him, but he would merely wave at her and walk away. He had a girlfriend.

One evening he visited Irene with the news that his girlfriend was pregnant. Irene was sick at heart, even though he assured her he would get a job and earn enough money to help bring up the baby. When the child was born he visited her again, thrilled to be a father at nineteen, though with no intention of marrying the mother. Ramates resumed occasional visits after that and he and Irene had many long conversations about all sorts of matters. She told him regularly that she was praying for him to be put right with God and that she loved him, and that Jesus loved him too.

The Rowleys were preparing to come home to England for another furlough when two of Ramates' friends asked for baptism. Ramates had never been baptised, even as a baby, and it troubled him. He had considered the idea in the past, but then had strayed and put it off. Now, he became insistent, begging Joe to baptise him in spite of Joe's reluctance to do so. Ramates had never made an open confession of faith, and Joe questioned the real reasons behind his request.

Eventually, however, Joe's resistance was finally eroded. 'If you can confess Jesus Christ as your personal Saviour before the people at the church,' he told Ramates, 'then I will have to baptise you.' It was the day of the other boys' baptism service.

Ramates' face lit up. Radiant, he rushed home for a change of clothes and a towel, then dashed back to the Open House. While he awaited the hour of the service, Joe counselled him further about the cost of commitment to Christ. All three boys were baptised together and all three took communion in the Old House the next day. Irene's joy and gratitude to God was overwhelming.

In November 1990, Irene and Joe received the news of his death. He had been persuaded by friends to go to a party which had gone on late into the night. Returning home by car, the friends and Ramates had passed a pavement brawl and stopped to watch, as they knew the people involved. Someone in the fight had a gun. A shot was fired, missing its target and hitting Ramates as he sat in the car. He died at once.

Irene had prayed for him every day, almost

without fail, ever since she had first known him. She believes he is now with God and safe from further danger and harm. She and Joe are glad they baptised him before it was too late.

Was the death of Ramates a ploy of Satan, designed to discourage Irene at a time when other factors were already making her doubt her call to return to Brazil? It may have been so, she feels, but instead it has helped confirm the need to return.

Ramates' life was short: there was only a brief time allowed him to turn to God and find salvation in Christ. How many others, like Ramates, have only a few years in which to find new life?

Someone must go and teach them. Someone must lead them to victory over sin before they fall into eternal defeat. The need is urgent, and the time is short. Irene is eager to re-enter the fight.

Part 3
LOOKING BACK
AND
LOOKING FORWARD

14
1990
QUESTIONS TO A
MISSIONARIES' CHILD -
Joanne Rowley

Were you happy as a child in Brazil?
I was extremely happy! I knew nothing different.
I had lots of friends (mainly school friends who
weren't Brazilian) and I remember life being fantastic. I even remember saying, 'Why do grown-ups
have problems? I don't have any problems!' I
couldn't even imagine having 'problems'.

Did you ever long to be in England?
Never - because Brazil, with all my friends, was
always my home. England was strange, and I
knew no-one. English school was scary because
there were no Christians. I was used to having
Christian friends who thought and acted the way
I did. I didn't consider myself English. I saw
myself as an American girl in an American environment even though it was in the middle of
Brazil.

How did you feel about living with houseparents and away from your parents?

I first moved into the 'children's home', as we called it, when I was eight. I remember missing Mum and Dad terribly. I remember crying in my pillow at night. During the day I didn't feel as lonely because I was with others. I really looked forward to seeing my folks when they came to Belem every few months.

Living in the children's home was just a way of life for me. If I remember rightly, I lived with seven or eight different house parents. Some were fun, friendly and kind. Others were strict, unfriendly and unkind.

When we wrote letters to our parents every Sunday afternoon during rest hour after lunch, we weren't allowed to seal our letters. They had to be handed in. Then they would be put in a stamped envelope by our houseparents. We couldn't ever write anything negative about them because it would have been read. I suppose they wanted to know what we thought of them, so they would read our letters. I remember when I grew older I would seal my letters anyway and I would write what I felt. There was no way we could post our own mail because we never went near a post office. We only went to town on Friday afternoons and we were always supervised when in town.

We used to have 'room check' to check that our rooms were spotless. They used to even check under the mattresses for dirt! Not all of the parents were so strict, though. With some it was like being in a real family: with others we would just grin and bear it. It was much harder for me when my brother came into the home. I felt responsible for his discipline and his care because I felt (as his sister) that I knew him better than any houseparent. There were many conflicts and I felt I had to stick up for him all the time. I ended up shouting at him because I didn't want them to. They wouldn't let me wash him or supervise his showers because I wasn't allowed down the boys' hall, so he was just dirty all the time. You know what boys are like with showers! Nigel hated showers because they were cold, and he never combed his hair. I had to look after him. I even had to help him with his homework though I had plenty of my own. No-one else understood Nigel. He was different and special, and I'd grown up with him so only I really knew him!

Were you happy at AVA?
I loved it! I was always quite clever at school. I didn't find anything too hard. I don't remember studying a lot, either. I enjoyed playing the clarinet and I was really into sports. I was on the volleyball and basketball teams and the five-a-

side football team. We had lots of extra-curricular activities which were always great fun. When I was fifteen I had to do 'O' levels. I hadn't a clue what they were but I had to do them because I was English. I hated them! Who cares about Romeo and Juliet! I wanted to go to college in the States and I didn't feel at the time that I needed to do 'O' levels. Can you imagine sitting at a desk in a little office doing an 'O' level exam when all your non-English friends are out watching a soccer match? I didn't really work hard at them, so it's a miracle I ever got eight 'O' levels.

However, eventually I realised I would have the best of both worlds if I did do 'O' levels, because then I could either get a job in England, or, when I graduated at eighteen, I could go to college in the States. I sat Portuguese 'O' level and got an 'A' without doing any work - that was fun.

Do you recall any 'conversion experience' of your own?

Yes, I remember going to a Friday night service in the chapel at AVA where there was a guest speaker. I remember he told us we had to make a decision for ourselves even if we came from Christian families. I was too embarrassed to go to the front but in my bed that night I was saying my prayers and I asked Jesus into my heart. I was eight years old. I was crying and Aunt Molly (houseparent at the time) came in to tuck me in. She asked me what was wrong. I don't remember if I told her or not.

Did you ever consider missionary work?
Yes - I think most MK's (missionary kids) do. I was prepared to marry a pastor once but that was not to be. I never have had a real calling - just a desire - because I loved Brazil as a country. I still feel I could be a missionary, and a good one, because I know what it's like. I always imagine myself abroad somewhere, though not necessarily Brazil.

I suppose I'm just willing to go where I'm needed. At the moment I'm very happily married to Mark and he hasn't had any missionary calling as such. He feels he should dedicate himself to our church as the youth leader - that's being a missionary in a way because he relates well to the kids who attend the youth group. I would like to be more involved with the kids, but being a nurse and working shifts makes it hard to have any regular commitment. I don't feel I can give a hundred per cent to youth work when so often I have to work on Sundays.

Did you ever resent the fact that your parents' work kept you apart from them?
I remember being proud because I did 'O' levels

by correspondence which meant Mum and Dad could carry on with their work without having to go home to England with me, as some others were doing. I was the first Brit to do 'O' levels by correspondence, and the first to graduate at eighteen years old.

How involved did you feel in your parents' work?
I didn't feel involved with their work because I was so rarely with them. I hated going up river because I had no real friends there, and I stayed indoors a lot because (being blonde and different) people used to stare at me and point and say, 'There's Senor Jose's daughter!' I rarely went swimming unless Mum or Dad came because people would stare. Can you imagine living fifty yards from the Amazon and rarely swimming in it?

The town was very backward and Dad didn't like me wearing shorts or trousers. Only 'women of the streets' wore shorts! I didn't really enjoy my vacations because I hated the rough boat journey but Mum and Dad tried hard to make my stay up river bearable. They worked hard to make my bedroom nice and it was the first in their house to have a ceiling because Dad knew how much I hated bats flying around at night. I remember hiding a lot in my room when visitors came but I'd soon have to go out and be 'sociable'. They all wanted to know what I looked like.

Have you ever doubted your parents' ability to do their work? Did you ever feel they ought to return to England?
I was proud of Mum and Dad. I saw how much they were needed and how much they loved the Brazilians and vice versa. They certainly were able. The only time I thought they should go back to England was because of Nigel's education. AVA was not geared to special needs and I think Nigel would have benefited from some special education in England.

Do you think that your parents' work is valuable or important enough to justify the sacrifices they make?
Yes.

Are you better or worse for having been an MK?
I'm certainly the better for it. I've had so many different experiences that normal British kids couldn't imagine! My Brazilian past has helped me in all my interviews. The first thing I am asked is, 'Tell me about Brazil'! It's a great ice-breaker and I feel confident and positive about being 'nearly Brazilian'.

I definitely feel enriched by my experiences. They haven't done me any harm at all. They've done me good. I've learned to consider others. My only regret is that I wish I could have gone through the British system of education to see how well I could have done with 'O' and 'A' levels here. I regret not being able to compare myself with others, and also not having had the opportunity to do any 'A' levels. I'm sure I could've done them well.

Have your long periods of estrangement from parents made you less close to them than you might otherwise have been?

I can't imagine what it would be like to live with my parents, so I can't really say. I feel very close to them and when we're together, even now, it's really special. We certainly don't take each other for granted, even if my Mum thinks I do. I just became independent from an early age and learned to fend for myself sooner than others. I probably had a stricter, more disciplined upbringing than if I had lived with them all the time.

Would you rather live in England or Brazil?

If you'd asked me that six years ago I would have said Brazil, but Brazil to me is AVA and my Can-adian and American friends. They're not there any more. When I revisited AVA after having left, it wasn't the same because I only knew a few of the people there. It is part of my past. Home is where your heart is. This is true because when I was courting a Brazilian I was desperate to be in Brazil. Now that I'm married I feel England is my home.

I'll always have a special dedication to Brazil. When I'm in England I support Brazil's football team. I like watching Brazilian soaps on Channel 4, and I watch anything to do with Brazil. My accent is slightly American and this will never leave me, so my past is always with me. I love Brazil because of my memories: friends, the weather, beaches, and the friendly people. I like England because it's my home at the moment.

Which country is the most spiritually enriching for you?

Brazil - they are more attentive to the gospel. People are poor and needy and easier to witness to. Christianity is big in Brazil. In England, people don't need God. I work with non-Christians and they are just content with their lives. You're a freak here if you're a 'born-again' Christian.

How well have you adapted to English life? Do you feel different from those who have always lived here?

I have always adapted well to wherever I have lived but England was hardest. I wasn't used to Christians drinking, dancing and smoking. That was a real culture shock. I hated (and still hate) clubs and discos. In Brazil, Christians don't frequent those types of places because they are usually part of 'red light' areas. I never really went to the cinema until I came to England. Please don't think I'm slagging off English Christians. It's just that they have different standards than I have as an MK who has led quite a sheltered life.

I'll always feel different to those who have lived here all their lives. I have seen so much more than them. I have lived in a different culture and I feel happy and proud of my background. I'm glad I don't need to conform to be satisfied - for instance, I don't have to drink alcohol to feel I 'fit in'. I'm glad I haven't always lived in the same town. So many people know nothing different. They've always lived in a certain place and always had the same friends. I think they can become narrow-minded. My extremely 'sheltered' upbringing, as some would call it, has certainly not harmed me.

Have you ever seriously doubted your faith?
Since becoming a paediatric nurse I often question God. I see an awful lot of suffering in little, helpless children and I hear their parents asking 'Where is God? Why our child?' etc. There are no answers, though. We just believe, but sometimes in such circumstances my faith seems so pathetic.

* * *

Irene's counsel to Joanne
written to her whilst at AVA

'...I'm not surprised that you are feeling all mixed up - you will do, until you get down on your knees and say you're sorry to the Lord for leaving him out of things. I know though what happens, because it happened to me a few times, even here on the field.   But oh! the joy when you really stop what you're doing and turn to him.

Even when you don't feel like it, you must pray. Even if you can only say the Lord's Prayer and read the Bible. You know you should do it, but it gets too hard. Do you read your Daily Light?   I think that helps me to get into the right attitude, and I think that's what it's for. It's only a snack, but it's better than not eating at all!

Don't try and get *yourself* out of this spiritual 'low', as you call it.   Ask the *Lord* to do it, then carry on as you know you should, doing the things you know are right. Through it the Lord will make you a stronger Christian, but don't ever think you're all right, because none of us is: we need a new fixing-up and sorting-out every day. Sing a lot if you can't pray, and read hymns, because they're a means of praying. Play the piano, too. Play until you feel like crying, then ask the Lord to comfort you. He will! Ah! The times I've done that! It's like having a good wash...'

15
1990
SOME QUESTIONS TO IRENE AND JOE

What would you say to those who accuse missionaries of robbing Brazilian Indians of their ancient traditions and culture, thereby turning them into 'second-class Europeans'?

Irene: Prospectors for gold in Brazil have taken the Indians' land and riches and offered nothing in return but European diseases. Whole families in mining areas are dying from malaria and influenza and soon the Indian traditions and culture will disappear. Missionaries have no part in this - it is mere exploitation. The 'world' is taking control of the Indians and giving them nothing but death and destruction. Missionaries must tell the natives about Jesus, because there is otherwise no hope for them. Those of us who have hope for the future must share it.

To what extent would you ever co-operate with a Catholic, Mormon, Jehovah's Witness, or other non-evangelical missionary?

Irene: We have co-operated with a Roman Catholic dentist in an interior town. He came there to give one-tenth of his life to God, under the auspices of the Roman Catholic church. He discovered that the evangelical population of our rivers was greater, and in more need of a dentist, than the Roman Catholics of the town, so we sent him to live with one of our deacons up river for a few weeks. He had brought with him copies of a Roman Catholic Bible which we allowed him to distribute. He didn't preach: he just pulled teeth and gave out Bibles. The people loved him. After his time with us he went to a Roman Catholic village, and we heard no more from him. In Brazil we must be seen to be different from 'Rome'. We don't, however, preach against the Roman Catholic Church. We teach Biblical doctrine and let the Holy Spirit tell the Catholics what to do about it.

We've helped Seventh Day Adventists: they too have a social work that we can relate to. We haven't co-operated with Mormons apart from an American lady whose husband worked in the sawmill in Portel and who offered to teach Nigel at a time when I needed help. We teach our believers to avoid the other sects, though they find it difficult to do this because they are naturally kind and will accept literature at their door because they feel sorry for the person offering it.

Should missionaries run hospitals and schools for those with whom they wish to share the gospel, or should they aim solely to plant churches?

Irene: In Brazil it's not easy to have mission schools and hospitals because of the laws of the land, so in that case I would say 'concentrate on preaching the gospel. Help socially when you are able'. To do an effective social work you'd need endless finance from outside and it would take over all your time. We can only help socially in a small way, for example, with our neighbours. Brazil is more or less organised to do its own social work - not that it does it though!

We try and preach the whole gospel, that is, to love your neighbour as yourself. We therefore encourage believers to help one another socially. Brazilians have an inborn kindness, even as non-Christians, and mostly do their best for other people.

Can you describe Brazilian spiritism/peculiar aspects of Catholicism/voodoo etc., if any of these occur to your knowledge?

Joe: When the Portuguese discovered Brazil five hundred years ago they forced the Indians to accept Catholicism or die. Many died, while others used their discretion to survive, accepting Catholicism but not forgetting their own proud beliefs in ancestor worship.

The Portuguese brought African slaves to Brazil in their thousands. Africans were also forced to accept Catholicism but they maintained their spiritism, their black (and white) magic, etc. Therefore, throughout the centuries there has been this mixture of culture and religions. The vast majority of Brazilians would class themselves as spiritualists and there are also those who are led by witch doctors - both among the Indians and the descendents of slaves. European Brazilians have also been caught up in the occult. Their lives are dominated by black magic. Most communities have their temples from which you can hear drumming throughout the night as they go through rituals of cleansing, spells, counter-spells, healings, etc. Demon-possession is an everyday event - a natural consequence of dabbling with the satanic.

The Brazilian calendar has religious Saint's days; civil celebration days such as Independence Day, Flag Day, Declaration of the Republic, etc; also commercial days such as Mothers', Fathers', Children's, Students', Teachers', Valentine's; then the occult days honouring the various deities in the black magic hierarchy - for example the Day of the Dead, and Carnival. The Christian missionary uses 'religious' days to have special meetings, retreats, conferences, seminars and so on. Evangelicals will not compromise and celebrate superstitious feasts but will use them as opportunities for outreach, tract distribution, open-air meetings etc.

Do poor Brazilians ever resent the fact that missionaries in their community may be wealthier than they are themselves?

Irene: Poor Brazilians would not respect poor missionaries. They expect you to be better off than them and wouldn't like it if you looked poor. Missionaries should not flaunt their wealth, however, but ought to appear clean, thrifty and comfortable.

Brazilians have a tendency to be bad managers of their money and could often be better off if they were less wasteful. They are prone to credit debt.

What have you observed of the destruction of the Brazilian rain forests?

Joe: In the early seventies, Brazil offered land to the many thousands of homeless and landless from the south of the country. Unfortunately these poor folks had to borrow money from the government agency involved in order to buy the land.

Once there they burned trees and planted their crops, but found the soil was very poor. The crops failed and the new farmers fell into terrible debt, so had to sell their land to rich cattlemen who made use of the already-clear land for the planting of grass.

Thousands of square miles of forest have been flooded by hydro-electric schemes involving the damming of rivers. Mining of iron ore, manganese, uranium and gold is causing terrible destruction as well as river pollution. Vast areas of the forest are being burnt to provide charcoal to fire the massive steel mills in the heart of the Amazon.

The summer months brings the burning season, when you can fly over the burning forest for hours in thick smoke. Chemical pollution in the rivers includes that from mercury used in prospecting for gold.

One of our churches has lost all its fishing and mussel-farming industry because of pollution. The fish and mussels all died and the people are now reduced to working for rich cattle-men, cutting grass with their jungle knives. They have become desperately poor.

Poor folks have fished and farmed for thousands of years, but now the chain saws, high-powered machinery and boats have turned paradise into the largest timber and livestock resource in the world. The poor folk are no better off, but even poorer now that the habitat of wild animals and fish is being destroyed. Deer, tapirs, turtles etc. are stalked and killed in vast quantities, and fish are caught in massive nets that leave nothing behind for later.

Most of the forest is owned by city-dwelling landowners who sell lumber rights to the poor tenants who have to give fifty per cent of what they produce back to the landowner. If a tenant is unsuccessful the landowner will sell the land to someone else who will then refuse hunting or survival rights to the poor locals who might have lived in that area for generations. They cannot expel people that live on the land, but they can fence them away, which results in them being forced to leave anyway. There is no justice for the poor.

Prospective missionaries often fret about whether it is fair to expose their children to the possibility of danger or disease abroad. What would you say to those parents?

Irene: Missionary children overseas are usually very healthy. In a boarding school situation they rarely get ill and of course are well fed and enjoy plenty of sunshine and fresh air - all of which goes to make large, healthy children. I would say to parents who worry about such things that if you are sure God wants you overseas, be assured he will provide for your children.

Do you believe (as some missionaries do) that all Christians should serve abroad unless specifically called to remain in their country of origin?

Irene: No. I believe you should serve God at home and only go abroad if you absolutely cannot do otherwise. Please don't go because you think you ought or because you think it's a worthwhile thing to do. Serve God wherever you are, and if he compels you to go overseas then go. Be open to God's leading: it is most important to be in the centre of God's will. You will have enough heart-break to contend with just by being abroad and away from familiar things without the terrible pain of knowing you're not in God's will.

It would appear from my experience that the tropics (or any missionary situation overseas) brings out the worst in you. The layers of your personality get peeled away and you are left very, very vulnerable to *everything*. Only if you are sure of God's call and presence with you can you cope with some of the situations that occur, especially with colleagues who have also been peeled down to the core personality-wise. It's no joke being a missionary.

If you have a call or conviction you can feel the arms of God in any given situation and know that whatever is happening to you at the time is all in his plan for you. That is how you cope with leaving your children in boarding school: you may go into the toilets and cry your eyes out after saying goodbye, but God gives you a peace and comfort that compensates.

Concerning the attitude of those in Great Britain to missionaries, what reaction do you get from your supporters as you give talks in churches? Are they interested or apathetic, insular or broad-minded, concerned or indifferent?

Irene: Those who financially or prayerfully support us in a committed way are usually very knowledgeable about us and interested. They are also deeply concerned about us, our health, and family matters, as well as being concerned for the individual Brazilians we mention in prayer-letters. A lot of supporters ask about individuals by name as though they know them personally.

If we don't keep in touch with a church or visit very infrequently a large proportion of the congregation won't know us and therefore will seem less interested. Personal contact really helps.

It frightens me to think what will happen in a few years time, when a lot of our most faithful and interested prayer warriors die off. Who will take their place? The young folk don't seem as 'prayer-minded' as their older counterparts.

I think the general church attitude is one of indifference. They've seen so much on TV that they've become immune to need. Also, because we aren't specifically 'social' missionaries but 'only' preach the gospel, they kind of 'cool off' towards us.

Did you ever become disillusioned about Christians or Christianity through your experiences of personality conflict on mission stations and elsewhere? If not, how?

Irene: I never became disillusioned because I knew that all it was personality conflict, and nothing more. I knew that God loved everyone in spite of their faults and that I had sometimes to deal with my attitude. It wasn't always easy, but I tried to change myself to fit in with other people rather than expect them to change to fit in with me. I don't mean that I never got angry or said what I felt, but I always tried to make the peace again. I couldn't bear unrest or disturbance and always tried to live peaceably with all men (and women!) however much it cost me.

In what ways has God repayed you with a hundred times as much as you sacrificed in his service?

Irene: I have always had a house to go to at the end of each day, except when I have had to travel overnight. I've counted over fifty addresses so far, though there could even be as many as a hundred, including holidays and weekends away. I've stayed in lovely houses in Warrington and

Lymm, and disgracefully shabby ones in Brazil, though even then there's always been furniture and a roof over our heads.

I gave up close physical contact with my 'Bateman' family, but the Lord gave me everyone back, rolled into the three others that make up my 'Rowley' family. Joe was father, mother and brother at different times over the years and has been the most faithful and loving husband one could wish to have. I praise God many times over for not letting me go out alone to the field, but as a married woman. We have shared joys, sorrows, sickness and health, laughter and tears. Only a loving God, who knew me better than I knew myself, could have given me such a partner who ably filled all the roles he was called upon to play.

Our children, also, as they grew up, reminded me of one or other of the family. Their facial expressions at certain moments were precious reminders of Mum or Dad or a sister or brother. As they came to faith in Christ personally, they also aided me more specifically in their understanding of my spiritual needs. Because of his condition Nigel has spent more time with me than Joanne and has become a true brother in the faith. He will hold my hand and pray with me whenever I feel the need for a joint prayer-effort. His prayers are simple and to the point, and he believes in a prayer-answering God. Often his faith puts me to shame as I potter along in my own untrusting way. He is used by God to sort me out and puts things into perspective.

Other brothers and sisters God has supplied in abundance, in our missionary colleagues with whom we have shared joys and sorrows. It hasn't mattered that we are of different nationalities. It's just mattered that we were together, loved Jesus, and understood and loved each other. I've had sisters by the dozen to compensate for my own: sisters to cry with, laugh with, shop with, reminisce with. Our children have been given uncles and aunties by the score, be they American, Scottish or Swiss.

I thought there would be no-one in the world to take the place of my mother, and for years there wasn't until I met Dona Sebastiana. She was dark-skinned, small, wide-hipped, with black curly hair and brown eyes - the complete opposite, physically, of my mother. But her chin was long and flat, just like Mum's, and she passed her tongue over her lips in a way that reminded me of Mum. When Nigel was very small she took him off me for a day and night just so I could shop and sleep. She comforted me when I was discouraged and she'd make me little presents. She was, and still is, a blessing to me.

Once the Lord gave me a promise: 'All your children shall be taught of the Lord, and great will be the peace of your children' (Isaiah 54:13). I have so many children in Brazil I can hardly keep count. They all have different personalities and gifts, and some are born again, others not yet. I love them all, grown up ones and little ones, and children of colleagues from different nations.

I exchanged cool, temperate England, with all its beauty (which I love) for hot, tropical Brazil, which the Lord has made me love. I've seen things of incredible beauty, and places and flowers so beautiful they defy description. How to tell of the exotic sunsets - a different one each night - that we watched in Portel? How to tell of the sound in the warm night of frogs croaking, sounding like an orchestra tuning up to play a symphony? How to tell of the sound of waves crashing on the shore near Belem, and the waterfalls and crystal rocks of Minas Gerais?

Is God not good? How could we ever doubt him?

LOVE ALL

"I wanted to write a funny, sexy book. And sex is the funniest thing of all, so that's what it's about."

MOLLY PARKIN

Molly Parkin is one of this country's most beautifully outrageous ladies. Ex-fashion editor of *Harper*, *Nova* and the *Sunday Times* she has now written her first novel. Light-hearted with slick witty dialogue, it is one shameless romp from beginning to end.

"LOVE ALL is mostly about sex . . . In seven days she fellates her father, takes on board her two regular lovers, sleeps with her ex-husband, is half-raped by a homosexual, has her anus enlarged by an adroit French restaurateur, sleeps chastely with a Lesbian ex-lover, picks up a buffet-car attendant, and is back for more . . ."

TIMES LITERARY SUPPLEMENT

"Written with the lightest of touches, and a mirthful exhilarated sense of its own libidinousness . . . quite the funniest novel I have read in a long while."

DAILY TELEGRAPH

"At last puts on paper a lot of people's fantasies."

LIVERPOOL DAILY POST

LOVE ALL

"I wanted to write a funny, sexy book. And sex is the funniest thing of all, so that's what it's about."

MOLLY PARKIN

Molly Parkin is one of this country's most beautifully outrageous ladies. Ex-fashion editor of *Harper*, *Nova* and the *Sunday Times* she has now written her first novel. Light-hearted with slick witty dialogue, it is one shameless romp from beginning to end.

"LOVE ALL is mostly about sex . . . In seven days she fellates her father, takes on board her two regular lovers, sleeps with her ex-husband, is half-raped by a homosexual, has her anus enlarged by an adroit French restaurateur, sleeps chastely with a Lesbian ex-lover, picks up a buffet-car attendant, and is back for more . . ."

TIMES LITERARY SUPPLEMENT

"Written with the lightest of touches, and a mirthful exhilarated sense of its own libidinousness . . . quite the funniest novel I have read in a long while."

DAILY TELEGRAPH

"At last puts on paper a lot of people's fantasies."

LIVERPOOL DAILY POST

LOVE ALL

Molly Parkin

A STAR BOOK
published by
the Paperback Division of
W. H. ALLEN & Co. PLC

A Star Book
Published in 1975
by the Paperback Division of
W. H. Allen & Co. PLC
44 Hill Street, London W1X 8LB

Star edition reprinted 1977, 1979 (twice), 1980, 1984

First published 1974 by Blond & Briggs Ltd

Printed and bound in Great Britain by
Anchor Brendon Ltd, Tiptree, Essex

ISBN 0 352 30080 9

Love All
especially Patrick

"Lick it," he said. That's the first thing he said. Not even hello when he'd opened the door. Just stood there with nothing on, lay down on the cold lino, legs apart, and said "Lick it." I was holding my handbag, but he looked so strained that I didn't wait to put it down first.

Afterwards everything was all right.

"Cup of tea?"

"Would I!" I said. "Nearly caught my death at the station. Twenty minutes' delay."

"I thought you were never coming. Toast? See you've brought a new pot of jam."

I patted my hips. "Not for me, thanks. Got to keep an eye on it."

He took his teeth from the mantelpiece, put them in his mouth, and started eating on his own.

When I'd crossed the street I turned round and waved goodbye. He parted his net curtains, but other than that made no sign. Round the corner I took the first taxi I saw. It dropped me at Brighton Station. I was lucky—a London train was just about due. When I was on I went straight to the buffet car. I really had meant to ask for tea.

"Brandy, right?" asked the man behind the bar.

"Do I look that bad?"

He gave me the miniature and a plastic glass. "No better cure!"

It was a good suggestion. I sat in the deserted carriage at a corner table and twirled the brandy, taking small sips and staring out of the window. I knew the landscape by heart, could tell at which point telegraph poles gave way to trees, ordered streets turned into fields. I'd seen it through all seasons—every Monday.

"She's dead," he'd said. That had been the start. No tears. Helpless.

"But I'll come."

7

"She's dead."

"Yes." After that impossible to say no. Anything he'd have asked. Anything to melt the numbness of his face, to kindle up a spot of life. To make him as he'd been before.

The train drew into Victoria where I took my clothes from the locker and changed in the ladies' lavatory. Then I went to collect my car. The shops were still open so on the way home I stopped off to buy a new lipstick. There was nowhere to park, so I left the car right outside on the double yellow. The store was very hot and highly perfumed and the assistant who served me was sexy and young with lots of false eyelashes. "I'm not wearing mine today, but I do usually."

She didn't answer. So I bought three lipsticks instead of one, but I needn't have bothered. I went through to Lingerie. Hard to resist a new bra. Uplift is right, in every way. All the display stands were stacked with breasts. Cups A to D in black, white and flesh.

"Anything scarlet?" I asked.

The saleswoman shook her head. "No call."

"Violet?"

"Never. Flesh. Flesh is what they like now. These, not a seam in sight. For under see-throughs. Many of my older ladies buy them for bed. Swear that under a nylon nightie not even their husbands would know."

"I think I'll try black. I'd never wear a bra in bed anyway."

"As you say. For those who can get away with it."

"But they do look very good so I'll try a flesh as well. Sure to come in handy."

She followed me to the fitting room.

"Thank you," I said quickly, and tried to shut the door.

"Nothing like the advice of a trained corsetière. I received my first certificate in 1932. Now I am the most highly qualified in the whole department."

I took off my coat and prayed God my deodorant hadn't given way as I pulled my sweater over my head. She undid the bra I had on.

8

"This has seen good service."

"An old favourite."

"Now then." She stepped back to get a good look.

"Children?"

"Yes."

"You're very lucky. They've held up well!"

She caught hold of a handful. "Bend over. Best way is always to drop them in. That's it. Perfect. Just a minute." She lightly squeezed one straying nipple into place. "This little piggy went to market. Tut, tut. Should always be perfectly central."

"Thank you very much," I said. "Perhaps I won't bother trying the others on. This seems fine."

By the time I'd got out my car had gone. A window dresser tapped on his side of the glass. "Towed away," he mouthed. "Thank you," I mouthed back. And smiled as if it didn't matter.

It was two hours later than I'd thought by the time I got home, but it made no odds—there were no calls anyway. The children were already in bed and asleep. Their father had been and gone and the au pair, Françoise, was preparing to entertain up in her room. She was loading a tray with ice and tonics and the last of the gin.

"May I?"

My heart sank, a very big gin and tonic was just what I could do with. "Of course, have a nice time."

She winked and went upstairs. As she passed I smelt my favourite perfume. For the next half-hour the doorbell rang at regular intervals. High-pitched excitable French voices drifted down from the hallway. All girls. Then silence. God knows what they got up to in that room. In the morning I'd pass one on the stairs again and both of us would be embarrassed and look the other way.

There was hardly anything in the fridge. The children must have had cornflakes for supper again because all the bottles of milk had been opened, with the creamy tops gone. But there was one bottle of champagne. I looked at it, wondering whether to or not. Other than that, all the drink shelf offered was a bottle of Win-

9

carnis which someone had brought me at the time of my abortion, the remains of some extremely sour Algerian wine and a miniature coffee liqueur. Tomorrow I'd stock up again. The cork popped out and hit the low ceiling, adding to the other cork marks already there. Time soon to have this room repainted, and most of the others, come to that. I unplugged the portable television and carried it and the champagne to the bathroom, turned on the hot, undressed and settled down in steamy luxury to drinking.

I was still in there when the phone rang. I didn't hear it because I'd fallen asleep but woke when Françoise banged on the door. "Coming," I said. The water had gone cold, the champagne bottle was empty. A clergyman was talking to himself on the television. I'd lost all sense of time.

The voice at the other end of the line was thick and blurred. At first I didn't recognise it, then I did.

"How are you after all this time? Just passing through London, been to a ghastly business dinner. Tried to ring you earlier. Did you get my message?"

"No," I said, still sleepy.

"I say. Well, what about it? Me popping round just to say hello. Quick night cap, that's all."

"How awful of me. I'm afraid I've run right out of drink."

"Leave that to me, little lady. Now jog my memory, what's the address again?"

When I'd put down the phone I looked at the bedside clock. It was half past twelve.

I thought I oughtn't to be in a nightie when he arrived, so I put on a clean pair of black tights, my black suede high-heeled boots and my new black bra. Looking in the full-length mirror I thought what a shame it was that I had to put anything over the top at all. The champagne I'd drunk made me feel incredibly sexy. I smelt my shoulders and ran a hand over each breast, adjusting the nipples the way the shop assistant had done. I smoothed my bare midriff and watched in the mirror one hand straying between my legs. "Not yet," I thought and turned away, deciding what to wear. I chose a pair of silky trousers, full in the leg but very tight around the hips. On top I wore a skimpy long-sleeved shirt with three buttons from the neck. I left them all undone. I did my face, lots of gloss on the mouth, lower lashes, perfume splashed—nothing left to do except lower the lights and put on a record. Then I sat and waited.

At half past one I remembered glasses, so I went and got two from the kitchen and filled a container with ice, in case he was bringing whisky, and took them back to my room. It had originally been two rooms but, when we'd bought the house, my husband had knocked the dividing wall down and made it one. At one end was my double bed—it had been ours—at the other was a large low table and an arrangement of easy chairs. Sitting-room style. The colour television was in the middle and could be swung in both directions, but I usually looked at it in bed. At two o'clock he still hadn't come, so I fetched the miniature coffee liqueur and drank it in one go. Then I undressed and went to bed. I left all my make-up on and one light, in case.

When I opened my eyes I felt something falling on my cheek. The lashes from my left eye. He was standing by the side of the bed, undressing. There was a brandy bottle, black and opaque, Napoleon I supposed, on the bedside cabinet and two full glasses. He was very drunk. I put my lashes carefully in an ashtray and sat up to say hello.

"How did you get in?" I whispered, surprised.

"A couple of Froggies were leaving as I arrived, and how's the little lady, got waylaid, sorry, so sorry."

Still wearing his shirt and tie, but nothing else, he fell on the bed and went straight to sleep. I got up and went to the lavatory. When I came back I took the lashes from my right eye, put them with the others in the ashtray, got in my side and started drinking one of the brandies.

He was flat out, snoring, so I lifted his shirt to look at his genitals. It was a particularly slack set. The penis lolled unhappily, like a stranded fish, slightly to one side. I fingered the balls, their bag was far too big for them. Never mind, he had nice legs. So, concentrating on those I rubbed myself off, then covered him with a spare blanket and set the alarm clock. I put it at extra early to get him up and out before the children came down. That was always what I did. Mornings and me was for them, nice cuddles and breakfast in bed for the three of us. But by the morning he'd gone anyway. Apart from the brandy bottle and two empty glasses—he must have drunk his when he'd got up, something I couldn't ever quite face myself—there was nothing to show that he'd been there at all. An hour later a dozen red roses arrived. The note said, "Apologies, little lady. Better performance next time. Promise. J."

I don't know why, but I felt particularly wonderful. Not that these days I ever really felt anything but. Divorce over and done with. Money now paid neatly, banker's order, every month. At first, before everything had been finalised, we used to have a different arrangement. Paul gave me housekeeping every Saturday, just as if we'd still been together. He'd ring in the morning. "Meet me for lunch. I'll give you your money." "Thank you, Paul," I'd say gratefully. As if I were the guilty party. In the restaurant, with the children looking on and both tables either side, he'd count it out in one-pound notes, holding each to the light to make sure they weren't forged. Always a couple short. "Just missed the bank."

My lawyer was appalled. "Calculated humiliation" was how he put it and told me off for lack of dignity. I privately felt pleased to get anything, whichever way it came, but I agreed it did seem rather weak. It was much better now this way. More civilised to have things cut and dried. But it didn't have any closeness.

The children snuggled up, one each side of me. Two small girls, their bodies slippery and simple. Uncomplicated by breasts or hair growing other than on their heads. Impossible to remember when I had been like that. I held them tight and tickled them and we were all still laughing when Françoise came in with the breakfast tray. She looked slyly at the brandy and two glasses so I got it in first.

"Nice party last night?"

She shrugged. "My best friend, she did not come."

Oh Christ, she'd be moody for days. "Oh dear, what a shame."

"But I ring 'er and she say tomorrow."

"We must remember to buy some more drink then."

At that she brightened. "Scotch whisky, very good." "Yes, it's a nice drink," I said, and made a mental note to buy wine. Not mental enough.

"Scotch whisky and gin tonics and Bloody Maries. But wine in this country, not so good I think."

"I'll make a list today," I promised, defeated.

She'd warmed to her subject. "But more I like champagne—"

I interrupted briskly. "So do we all. Don't be late for your classes now." But I smiled to soften it.

"Here I go." She blew kisses to the girls, who blew kisses back, covering the bed with crumbs.

They were very fond of her. She was sweet really. It had taken a lot of doing, the final deciding to have a stranger share the house. But more than that, to have one share the children. We'd never had anyone when Paul was still here. I don't know why quite, except that I may have been put off by stories of other husbands ending up in the au pair's bed. But I wouldn't have admitted to those thoughts then. Nor to any thoughts of infidelity on his part. Looking back I see I was half-baked. Later I knew differently.

Now, looking at his daughters, I saw how much like Paul they were. Strong straight hair, very fair, green eyes—pale like gooseberries. Long lashes. Later on I'd teach them how to darken those with dyes, and apply thick coats of mascara. Look much better. Like him, they were beautiful.

Breakfast over, I drove them to school. On the way the youngest, Fanny, said, "Daddy said on Saturday he'll take us to the zoo."

"You'll like that, you'll be able to ride on the elephant."

They squealed excitedly. Harriet was named after Paul's mother, always a sore subject. After all, my mother was dead, if we had to go in for family names why not hers? "What, Violet?" "Well, why not?" "Too common!" And that had been that. Harriet said, "You didn't say good night to us. Daddy did."

She pulled her mouth down and stared accusingly and by doing so managed to look incredibly hostile. Fanny copied her immediately. It occurred to me that when they were grown-ups they might not like me at all, well, or me them for that matter. We'd look at each other all the time then with that same hostility.

We'd reached their school, I turned the engine off. "You know on Mondays I'm very often not back in time," I started to explain. But they weren't listening any longer. They'd spotted friends and were already shouting at them and clambering out of the car. "Have a nice day," I called. They both turned shining faces full of love. And mine shone back. Years away from any worry.

I drove home, past other mothers just like me dropping their children off at equally expensive so-called progressive private schools. Masses of them in that area. All more or less the same waste of money. My view, not Paul's. State schools later on. If I could fight it out. I turned into my street. It was a marvellous morning. Spring in the air. A still cold sun shone on immaculately clear windows and novelty brass door knockers. Budding daffodils in window boxes matched the colour of front doors. Mine included.

"'Morning, miss! Lovely day. Like the front sweeping?" Same question every week. Same street sweeper for the past five years. He'd already got his broom in the tiny paved front garden, and was bearing down ferociously on a small piece of torn newspaper which had blown in. "If you could, thank you very much," I smiled as I dropped a coin into his waiting hand. But inside me I went all hot. Playing the gracious lady. Paul would have been proud.

It was Tuesday, the week was beginning, the hours stretched ahead like an empty harbour. I loved it like that, no one in the house till late afternoon when Mrs. Bowen would arrive to clean and before the children were collected by Françoise on the way home from her classes. Well organised, considering how chaotic the household arrangements had once been.

The phone rang. "My darling." Charles. The lowered, hurried voice. Phoning from home, wife out of the room? Phoning from the office, secretary in the outer one? "Can we possibly switch tomorrow to today?"

"Of course."

"One o'clock then. Ah, documents here, Miss Dean."

I smiled as I replaced the receiver. The office!

I opened the windows and looked to see if I should change the pillow-cases. He was very particular. Mine seemed fine. As I was putting a clean one on the other, the phone went again.

"Good morning, gorgeous."

"Sam," I said.

"Got tickets for tonight. Great play. Think you're going to like it."

"How lovely."

"Right, I'll pick you up at seven, we'll have a drink there and eat afterwards. What are you wearing, honey?"

"I may wear long or perhaps trousers."

"Now, I mean."

I laughed. "Not wearing any, only tights."

"Whore!" he said. "Mad about you. How was yesterday?"

"Fine," I said. "Much as always."

"You and your social work. See you tonight. Be ready, slut."

By five to one I was in my dressing-gown, the bedroom looked beautiful, curtains closed. Phone off the hook, hidden in the cupboard. All chaste and warm and welcoming. At the last minute I remembered the vase of roses but it was too late. Charles was at the front door already. He stepped in quickly, nervously glancing towards the street as he did so. He double-bolted top and bottom.

I put my arms around his neck. "It's quite safe," I soothed. "No one can possibly come."

We went into my darkened room. A shaft of sunlight gleamed through where the curtains weren't quite together. He took off his glasses. "Now let me look at you." We laughed, it was an old joke that we both felt safe with.

"Nice day for a picnic," I said and we laughed again. Another old one.

He put down his carrier bag, Fortnum's. "An exceptionally fine claret and duck pâté with garlic to your liking, madam?"

I moved forward to kiss him on the mouth, but he was already looking around for his coat-hanger. He never was one for kissing much. I still couldn't get used to it. And he was shy about undressing too. But that I understood more, so looking the other way I quickly took off my dressing-gown and waited for him in bed.

The first was always far too quick, no sooner in than over, and the second which began almost immediately was only marginally longer.

He lay back. "How was that for starters, madam?"

"Perfect," I said, though as usual I was feeling stranded and up in the air. But the wine soon sorted things out, and the pâté, so that by the third time it was just about as good as it ever could be.

Afterwards I was desperate for a cigarette. I'd known I would be. That's the effect our loving had on me. "I wish you wouldn't." He watched me lighting up.

"Sorry, Charles, I have cut right down. I'm giving it up soon."

"A filthy habit. Besides which I worry about your health. Don't you ever? Don't you see how irresponsible it is? What would happen to the children? You seem to forget you're a mother."

I changed the subject. "How's Deirdre?"

He sighed and began tidying the remains of the picnic back into the Fortnum's carrier bag. "Napkin? Here, give it to me. Is that the cork there? Would you like me to wash these glasses out? Pass me the bottle, done in, isn't it? Right, I'll get rid of it all on the way back. Wouldn't do to leave traces."

"How is she?"

He sighed again. It was his favourite topic but even so he liked several prompts. "Oh, my darling. Why do we ever mention her name? When just to be with you is such perfection. Why spoil this heaven—how is she? She's unbearable. She's everything that you're not. She's insensitive, selfish, extravagant, stupid, vain. We're neither of us happy. We hate our life together. But will she admit it? No! And there are the children. She knows I can't leave whilst there are the children to consider. Do you know what she said to me this weekend?"

16

"No, what?"

"She said, she actually said, 'Charles, if you left me I'd see to that you'd never ever have access to the children for as long as you live.' How could a man in my position leave anyway?"

"She's no right to say that."

"No right! She said it, my dear. Oh yes, she said it."

"Legally, I mean. She couldn't enforce it."

"But it shows the thinking, you understand. It illustrates so clearly the vicious character of the woman. Doesn't it just! She knows perfectly well that there isn't anything I wouldn't do for those children. Why, that boy of mine—as bright as two pins. Almost walking now, you know. Not bad for eighteen months, eh? Clever as a cartload of monkeys. Be sitting on a horse in next to no time. You should see his sisters, both of them show-jumping standard. Deirdre takes them for a canter before breakfast every day now. Oh yes! I've got to hand it to her, fine woman in the saddle. Pity she isn't the same on the ground, or bed for that matter. You know the latest development, don't you?"

"No, which one is that?"

"This sleeping apart malarky, separate rooms now. That's grounds alone, isn't it?"

"Restitution of conjugal rights, I think."

"Something like that. I tell you if it weren't for those children and my constituents—"

"What would you do, Charles?"

He'd heard his name, the conversation changed course again. "Good Lord." He glanced at his watch. "This won't do. Tempus fugit. Got to give an address tonight. Have the speech to write. And a hundred other pressing appointments. Cocktails at the House."

Still talking, he got out of bed and started dressing. In the darkest corner of the room. With his back to me. When he'd finished, he put on his glasses and carefully combed his hair. Then the vase of roses caught his attention. "Particularly fine blooms." He frowned. "Not another admirer, I trust." And he laughed at the idea.

ng of your buttonhole, but I bought a bunch to ce," I said.

on the bed and held my face in his hands. "That's onderful thing I've ever heard, my darling girl." He even sed me.

When he'd gone I took the phone out of the cupboard and replaced the receiver. I rang the off licence, the grocer and the greengrocer to order stuff. At each they reminded nicely that my bill was overdue. "Tell me the amount and I'll give a cheque to the delivery boy," I promised and apologised profusely. It wasn't even as if I hadn't the money. All that was lacking was organisation. I was appalling at accounts—anything of a financial matter. Bills came, like letters, and lay unanswered, just hanging around till they got lost. I liked the phone much better than the post—more immediate, talking to people, more involving altogether.

The three deliveries came all within ten minutes of each other. The first time I answered with just my silk dressing-gown on, but as I was writing out the cheque I saw the grocer's boy staring at my nipples. He was very young, he couldn't have seen many. I don't know who was more embarrassed. I was meaning to have a bath, there was no point getting dressed but even so, when he'd reluctantly gone, I went and put on my bra and knickers under the dressing-gown to write cheques for the other two. Funny that, shy at my age.

In the bathroom, running the water, I put a face pack on. Honeymask, it had a marvellous smell, meant to be on for fifteen minutes. "Follow instructions carefully for maximum satisfaction." Best to obey instructions. I'd only taken to going in for skin care and all that quite recently really, but from the look of me it was paying dividends. I hadn't bothered so much when I was married but that was because Paul had been so adamant. Though he'd seemed to approve of women when we were out who I thought were dreadfully done up. "But you're different," he'd say. "It's not your style. There'd be no point!" By the end, of course, there hadn't been. But now I'd come to love it, the

18

pampering, applying oils and creams and perfumes. The private swooning at the secret smells of me.

I poured lots of costly bubble from a bottle into the full bath, then got in carefully so as not to splash my setting mask. Near me on the shelf was Paul's expensive badger shaving-brush and the old-fashioned razor he'd left behind, anyway he'd switched to electric. But I liked shaving with them on my legs and under my arms. I loved to work up a good lather. The soap I used was household and smelled slightly of carbolic but you could get the best lather of all with it, bar proper shaving sticks of course. It reminded me of my father, and of the first boy who I'd ever let touch me down below. He'd washed his hands with it after. I hadn't much growth to shave off anyway but I liked to catch it before it got to the bristly stage. I'd once known a man who claimed to have had an orgasm on the train to Edinburgh from sitting opposite a woman with hairy legs, and the story had so impressed me that I'd gone all summer not shaving. He was a vegetarian. The bubbles in the bath had almost disappeared, I still hadn't managed to find a make which lasted through to the very end. The water was very silky though—I could feel it doing my skin good—and the surface when I lay perfectly still was shinily unbroken like summer seas abroad. I started at the tap end, left to right, sometimes I did it the other way around. Searching with my eyes, otherwise not moving a muscle, for those infinitesimal dark brown dots floating on the surface. A childhood habit. My mother would catch me scratching—"She's got fleas again. That means the last of the hot water." Only way to catch them was to drown them. Me in the zinc bath in front of the fire. Everyone crowding round. Whoever happened to be there—usually a neighbour, always my father, an auntie good on gossip, my sister. All joining in. "There it is!" "No, that's dirt!" "A tealeaf!" "See if it cracks between your nails!" "Stay still!" "Got it!" The satisfaction of seeing it squashed, pinprick of blood, my blood, staining the nail. Its belly full, emptied. Dead legs coming out at all angles.

Thirty years on and I'm still looking. No chance of a killing these days. Life was far too sanitary, except at Brighton. The fifteen minutes was up. Time to rinse my mask off. Tingle, tingle. Tight-pored. Perfect. On sheer impulse, I started washing my hair still sitting in the womb-like water. All the wrong way round, of course, because now the dripping shampoo and the steamy hot from the shower attachment was opening up all the pores which I'd just taken such trouble to close. Oh well. Drying myself, I thought I heard the front door click. Much too early for Mrs. Bowen. I called out quickly but there was no answer. Nobody. It was irrational I knew to be so resentful of unexpected intrusions when for so much of my life home had been an open house. Perhaps that's why—why I now took such childish delight in my separate existences. No area overlapping any of the others. Only me knowing exactly what was going on with whom, where and at any one time. None of it was by chance.

As soon as Paul and I had broken up I'd started thinking about how my life should be. The very day the divorce came through I gave a party for as many people as I could think of. A form of farewell really, because the next evening, when the sourness of my hangover had subsided sufficiently for me to be sure of my judgement, I sat down on my own with the guest list and a pencil. And started striking off all the people that I knew I never wanted to see again. Lots of them were married friends who'd only come to the party as a nice gesture, but with divided loyalties. They were no good. For them to feel comfortable I had to be married too. They were people Paul and I had gone to the theatre with or stayed with for weekends, all of us together with our children. Others were single girls, old enough to think themselves on the shelf, defeated creatures, ones I'd tried to pair off hundreds of times. I put a line through those too. It depressed me to think that now they might consider me one of them. The last thing in my mind was to turn into a loser. I'd seen too many women sitting together in restaurants, hair set specially, selecting out of season strawberries, flirting decorously enough with the waiters, but inside manic for a man. That brought me to the bachelors. There were a lot of those. Some I knew I'd never see anyway whether I struck them off or not, where Paul had been the appeal.

By the time I'd gone through everyone I was surprised to see how few were left. A small kernel of friends, close, but not to be thought of as confidants. So that was it. Time to start again. It was much easier than I'd expected.

Who had I met first? Charles, I think. But then again perhaps not. His face by the time I met him was so familiar to me from television anyway. Tortoiseshell glasses, carefully combed hair, beautifully cut suit—tailor's dummy. "This vigorous young politician." Later on in line for who knows what. Party Leader? Tory, of course. Not my type, not one bit, too much of the schoolmaster. And I'd had enough of Tories. But obviously I hadn't. We met at the dentist's of all places. In my time I'd spent a small fortune on my teeth, most of them capped now. They started going, two, three at a time, when I was about thirteen. All those sweets. Paul had ordered me to Harley Street. The first time I'd opened wide the dentist had called his partner to come and look. "Ye gods," is what he said. Since then it had been regular visits.

I was done up to the nines the day I met Charles. The receptionist showed me into the waiting room and there he was. I'd been shopping in Knightsbridge, had bought, just like that, a lovely dress I'd seen in the window of an expensive little Madam-type shop. Normally I wouldn't go near those places—I don't like their sales pressure—but I'd fallen in love with the dress. They'd only just put it into the window, so they said, and tried to palm me off with other things. But I insisted, funny for me. They took it out so that I could try it on. It fitted perfectly, wasn't tight but clung discreetly and made me look very curved and enticing. It had long sleeves, full ones which buttoned tightly at the wrists with tiny buttons, four or five of them. They were grey, sort of gunmetal like the dress, but the material was a jersey silk which changed colour in the light, sometimes pale like a pigeon's chest, in other places sharp and silvery. It ended just below the knee and was the most expensive thing I'd ever bought. But then I was due for a change. "Perfect for cocktails, the theatre, dinner," they said in the shop and purred approval as they took the price tag off. It was ten o'clock in the morning. "I'll keep it on, thank you," I said and walked out feeling fabulous. I went straight down the road to Harrods. An hour and a half later I stepped out grey from top to toe. Huge silver-fox hat, soft suede gunmetal handbag, gloves, stockings and suede high-heeled boots. Loaded with carriers containing what I'd originally been wearing. I didn't like to think what it had all cost but at that time I still hadn't got used to having money in the bank. "Do you mean to tell me you actually have no idea at all of your husband's income?" the lawyer had said irritably. "It didn't seem important somehow." "It does now, however." When he told me what I would be entitled to I was flabbergasted. I could see my stupidity get on his nerves.

The commissionaire sprang forward to hail a taxi. "Harley Street," I said. I could have said Buckingham Palace and he wouldn't have batted an eyelid. Clothes maketh the man. Me too. The dental receptionist gave a gasp when she saw me. Normally she was a miserable old trout troubled badly with arthritis. She'd wave towards the waiting room with her stick and let me open the door myself. But today she actually straightened up and pulled her shoulders back as if we were in some sort of competition. "Mr. Bruce isn't quite ready for you yet. His last appointment arrived a little late, I'm afraid." Charles looked up from his *Country Life* as I walked in. I recognised him right away. "Good morning," I said and gave a charming smile full of enchantment and subtle promise. I'm good at those when I try. Looking as I knew I did I could have taken anything on. "Love at first sight"— that's what he'd said afterwards. Oh yes, he had his romantic side. My own feelings were far more complicated. The second I set eyes on him he became a challenge. To be seen out with someone so well known for a start. But it never had worked out to be that. "Far too risky, darling." Since then all he'd seen me in was a dressing-gown, twice a week, whenever he could manage, but not evenings and never weekends. Served me right really.

The second had been Sam. Well, not the second, there had been others in between but not ones that were suitable for my stable. I'd been playing with the kids, it was their bedtime but we were pretending we were all three going to a party. They were wearing my shoes and old mini dresses which on them came down to the floor. Fanny had on a pair of elbow-length evening gloves which reached her shoulders and a long cigarette holder with a sweet cigarette in it. Harriet had found a wig which I once used to wear. I made up each of our faces. I put crimson polish on all our nails. Lots of black and violet eyeshadow. We'd sprayed behind our ears and were just dabbing extra down our cleavages, which they found very funny, when Paul rang. "What are you doing?" he asked in his abrupt way.

"Putting the children to bed."

"Rather late isn't it?"

"Only seven-thirty."

"It's ten past eight, they should both be asleep by now."

"Oh dear," I said, "well, they're just dropping off anyway."

"I've got a do on tonight. Advertising Executives' Guild. Dinner-dance thing. Would you care to go? Means being ready in half an hour."

I knew what it meant all right. Whoever it was had let him down at the last minute, too late now to find another fill-in. I looked at myself in the mirror, well I certainly was dressed for a party and what was the alternative—washing my hair and an early night to be fresh for Charles in the morning. I hated those advertising do's—smooth-tongued Hooray Henrys, corpulent balding chairmen, dieting bitchy wives.

"Why not?" I said. I was just in the mood to get drunk.

I tore Françoise away from the television to put the girls to bed. I promised they could wear their nail polish to school if they pretended to be asleep when their father arrived. Then I kissed and hugged them good night.

I looked pretty startling, even I could see that. Hell, I thought, and why not. I'd been too many times before, with Paul, discreetly playing the dutiful wife, drab as a shadow. I'll leave my eyes as they are. They looked enormous already, violet shadowed and mascara'ed, but for extras I put some lashes on as well, heavy black ones top and bottom. I powdered my entire face almost white including the lips. Then I gave them a coat of gloss to make them very shiny. I wound round my head a long black silk scarf till it looked like a turban and hid every bit of my unwashed hair and I pulled it right down to my eyes over my whole forehead. It looked like some religious order. I had two long black dresses, one was very bare about the shoulders with tiny shoestring straps, the other had tight sleeves to the wrist, a narrow skirt and high neck with a tightly fitting bodice except that it was slit in the back from the neck to the waist which meant you couldn't wear a bra with it. Out of curiosity I tried it on back to front. It looked incredible, a startling strip of creamy skin and cleavage, everything self-supporting and in its place. But did I dare? It seemed to be asking for trouble. But then that was what I was looking for after all. I could hear Paul's car outside and in last-minute panic loosely tied a floor-length black feathery boa round my neck so that it hung centrally and hid the possibly offending breasts. Then I went to open the door.

He looked at me critically in the dim hall light. "Anybody I know? Put my name on the wreath if so."

"Everything else is at the cleaners," I said. "The girls are asleep, I'll get my bag!"

"Won't people think it funny me coming with you?" I asked in the car.

He turned on the car radio and started swivelling the programme dial. Ear-splitting snatches of husky continental crooners, American country-style music, pontificating pundits and highly charged dramatic dialogue ripped my ears off. I knew it would annoy him so I said it again, this time yelling at the top of my voice. "Well, won't they?" I hand it to him—he has the most delicate wince in the world.

"Not if they're civilised," he said quietly in a momentary hush. Then he found Wagner and for the rest of the way steered with just one hand and with the other conducted an imaginary orchestra in the loudest performance of their life. I was glad when we got there—it had been just like being married.

Our table was worse than I'd feared. My place name put me off for a start: Miss G. E. M. Shottie-Green. The man on my left must have got there first and memorised all the names. "Daughter of General Shottie-Green, by any chance?"

"I'm actually Charles's ex-wife!" For the rest of the evening he introduced me as "General Shottie-Green's first wife. Have you met?" The man on my other side turned his back after the first five minutes. "Which branch of the business are you involved with?" he asked. "I'm a Media Director myself."

"Oh, I'm more a housewife." The electric light switched off immediately. "Which automatically puts me at the consumer end." I knew the jargon by heart.

"Quite."

I'd managed on the way in to down three gin and tonics in a very short time. I was actually hoping to get a fourth in but I hadn't moved quite quickly enough. Charles had his eye on me.

"Go easy."

"That was only my first," I protested.

"Untrue."

It was easier at the table, I think the wine waiter had got my number. Charles was seated far enough away for his frowns to seem a bit of a fake. By the fruit salad I was just beginning to glow. But I had no one to talk to. I looked across the dance floor and all around the banquet room, the band was assembling, plucking, strumming, tuning up. In a minute I'd have no one to dance with either. Everyone else was still seated so I stood up to make sure of being seen and made my way to the Ladies'-Room. As I reached it there came a sudden silence preceded by the banging of a gavel and a pompous voice announcing "Ladies and Gentlemen, our President." Hell, fancy missing the President. When I came out he was still speaking. I could see between the ornate pillars which separated the banquet room from the long bar where I was that everyone was entranced, hanging on his every word.

"Jesus Christ! What a crap bag! I tell you, kid, you've got beautiful bowels, they moved you at the right moment. I'll tell you something else, you're no chicken but you're the best-looking broad I've seen tonight."

He caught my hand, walked me to the deserted bar, took two brandies from one of the loaded trays and held them up. "To both of us."

"To both of us. And to my bowels," I supplied.

That was Sam.

We stuck together from then on. We drank and danced and danced and drank until in the end we could hardly stand up. Everyone was staring, not just at my scandalously spilling breasts but at the splendour of Sam himself. He was a huge man, built on the lines of Orson Welles, and he was wearing a white dinner jacket and black and white check trousers which straight away set him apart from the formal suits of all the other men. Paul approached us at one point, mortified and mad at me for making an exhibition of myself, I could tell, but towards Sam he was as smooth as silk.

"Departure time I believe."

All I did was giggle. Sam slipped his massive arm around my waist and kissed my ear.

"Departure time is my department, right?"

"Right," I said.

Paul turned on his heel in time to hear Sam growl, "Who the hell was that prick?"

"Only my first husband."

"Who's in line for your second, kid?"

"Who knows?" I said and kissed him in the middle of the crowded floor.

We left in the end because we were asked to. That became the pattern of all our outings—spectacular exits. Always the centre of attention. There's no doubt about it he was a drinking man, and an eating one too. Meals with him lasted three times longer than with anyone else, so did other things. "Climb aboard," he'd command, "and work me over." Lying back on a double bed he all but covered it. There was no question of him on top. "Cause of death—smotheration." He rarely if ever got an erection, but we had a lot of nice times trying. If he was troubled, he never showed it. We put together a whole library of tantalising pictures to see if that could get him going. He'd prop himself up with a pillow and

26

study them carefully while I stroked and kissed and licked his huge erogenous zones. A few times there was a flicker, but no more than as if a tadpole had swum through the sea. I was always the first to fall asleep—after two or three hours I found it pretty tiring work. I couldn't have kept it up every night as he would have liked. And I couldn't have kept up with the drinking either, I would have minded too much being an alcoholic as compared to just liking to drink. What he got up to when he wasn't with me I never asked. I knew there were ex-wives somewhere, still in America I supposed. Neither had children. And I knew that he lived alone now, though I hadn't been to his home.

"What the hell a man like me is doing out with an old woman like you, Christ knows," he'd keep grumbling. "Jesus, people are going to think I can't get it up any more. Nubile nineteen-year-olds is what I'm used to, not a rat bag with two brats in tow. C'mon now, open my pants and take a peek, at your age you've gotta be grateful." Then he'd bellow with laughter and give me a bear hug. We understood each other.

By the time Mrs. Bowen arrived to clean I was down in the kitchen making tea for the girls. Cauliflower cheese, one of their favourites. She came straight in and sniffed.

"Nasty smell of them old caulis. Goes right through the house. I never have them myself."

My stomach tightened, I'd dealt with Mrs. Bowen's dark Welsh gloom for five years. Today I could tell she needed more than normal cajoling. "I'll open these windows, that will clear the air." She took off her coat and shivered. "Very cold today, I should have worn my cardi."

"Have a cup of tea, that will warm you up," I said and plugged the electric kettle in. "I'll have one with you."

"Oh no, not for me. Too much hoovering today! No time for sitting with tea in my hand."

Piss off then. "Later perhaps."

She didn't answer, just went "Phew," stared accusingly at the cauliflower and waved the air in front of her nose. Minutes later

27

I heard the hoover droning on the floor above. As a sound it depressed me more than any other. That and ballet music. I gritted my teeth and grated a crumbly lump of pale orange Cheddar on to a yellow plate. Lovely colours together. The sound came closer as Mrs. Bowen started on the stairs. I slowly stirred the grated cheese into the smooth creaminess of the sauce and watched it melt. My mother had gone out cleaning. When I was very small she'd taken me with her. "Sit on that chair and don't move till I tell you." Hours of staring at mantelpieces crammed with family photos and china dogs and brass candlesticks, all being carefully spat on and polished by my mother. Trapped on an island, scrubbed and dusted and swept around. Then back home where nothing of that sort went on at all. To my father sitting by the fire with his cup of tea and bad chest. Pensioned off at thirty-three.

I strained the boiling water from the cauliflower taking care to keep it intact, and removed it to an orange ovenproof dish. Then I poured the thick sauce over it, dotted the surface with butter and a fine layer of cheese crumbs and popped it under the grill. Seconds later the girls arrived and the house came to life.

After I'd given them tea we looked at television together. Françoise had a drink. She was lit up before it touched her lips, just from seeing so much of it on the shelf.

"This is to see us through the month," I said warningly.

"Un mois." She pursed her lips and lifted her eyebrows. I could tell she was trying to translate it from French to English in terms of evenings in her room. Mrs. Bowen came in to say she'd see me tomorrow and caught Françoise with a glass in her hand.

"Would you care for one?" I said quickly.

"Me? Me, I never touch the stuff. You know that. The sherry you gave me last Christmas made me bad in the night. I was up all hours. No. I'll be off now for my bus. Let's hope the queue's not like it was last night."

"Say good night to Mrs. Bowen, girls," I said.

"Good night," they chorused, but neither took their eyes off the screen. So I stood up and saw her to the front door to make up for it. Halfway down the path she turned round frowning.

"Those children are getting to be real madams." I thought she wouldn't let it pass.

As I was shutting the door I saw Paul's car draw up. There was a girl sitting beside him in the front seat. I saw him switch the engine off and bend towards her in conversation. Before they could see me I closed the door and went quickly into my room. When the bell rang, the children, expecting him always at this time, ran to answer it.

"My poppets," I heard him say. I peeped through my curtains at the girl in the car. She was about seventeen, eighteen at the most. Blonde, very pretty, groomed like a poodle. Money.

"Is your mother here?" I heard Paul ask.

Fanny fumbled at the door handle. "Mummy, Mummy."

It swung open wide. Without knocking Paul walked in, snapping on the light. "What on earth are you skulking in the dark for?"

Now I felt caught out.

"Don't tell me you're attempting to economise on electricity for a change."

Once I would have turned to tears at that. The critical stare, the curt voice—now I just laughed, which made him worse. He frowned.

"Yesterday," he said coldly, "I made a promise to the children. I mentioned Regent's Park Zoo. However, circumstances have altered. This weekend I shall not be in town. I have to fly to Munich on business."

Blonde?

"That's all right," I said, "I'll take them to the pictures instead."

"The cinema isn't the only alternative."

"No, but it's the nicest."

"Yes, yes, yes," squeaked the girls.

"I'll try smuggling them into an X film. They could go in as middle-aged dwarfs."

"Could I have a moustache?" shouted Fanny.

"And me a hunchback?" said Harriet.

"Perhaps," said Paul, the light of battle in his eye, "Mummy

29

could take you to the ballet. You'd love that wouldn't you? Harriet? Eh, Fanny? I'll arrange the tickets tomorrow."

"Ooh," they both sighed, silenced.

The bastard.

"How wonderful," I said sweetly. "Three tickets for the ballet. Say thank you, Daddy."

"Oh, Daddy, Daddy, thank you. You're a lovely daddy."

"That's settled then," I said brightly. "Saturday the ballet."

I stepped past his satisfied smile and shouted, "Françoise, ballet tickets for Saturday—you and the girls, isn't it exciting? Thank you, Paul, good night."

An hour before Sam. Time to try a dozen things on. Whatever I wore he always noticed. "Shock 'em, honey," was his way. On one occasion when I'd met him at a restaurant, I came wearing black stockings, a black dress with tiny white cuffs and collar. "Christ," he'd thundered when I took my coat off. "People'll think I'm eating with the waitress." And he'd sent me home to change. When I came back I was wearing just the same but with a frilly white apron tied round my waist. This time the rest of the diners took a dislike but from Sam I got ten out of ten. "That's my gal. Why how you're learning!"

By ten to seven I was ready and went to kiss the girls goodbye. Françoise whistled appreciatively and gave me one of her winks.

"You look like a man," Fanny said and rolled on the floor in a giggling fit.

"Are you going out like that?" said Harriet doubtfully.

"Why not?" I said and looked in the mirror.

"Won't people stare?"

I had on a crimson satin trouser suit, very tailored, and under it a bright red satin shirt with a red and white spotted tie. On one lapel I'd pinned a scarlet artificial poppy. I combed my fringe to reach my eyes, the rest of my hair I'd pinned into a tight little knot at the back. "Stare? I hope so," I said. "What's the point of dressing up if people don't stare?"

"Your mummy," said Françoise, "she have very good taste. She know which goes with what. Me I stay safer."

30

"So did I at your age—now, girls, bath time. Can you see them up, Françoise, please?" They all three pulled a face. "You can use my best bubble stuff if you go this minute." They got up right away, Fanny chasing Harriet.

Françoise lingered. "And for my bath too yes? I have a new friend, she come later."

I sighed inwardly. "Don't use it all. You only need a drop to do the trick."

She smiled and nodded and wrapped her arms around herself. "It make me feel so sexy, so silky, smelling sweet in the bath. All the time I am thinking naughty things. I am—"

"I'd see how the girls are getting on—they could be drowning by now."

She gave herself a final reflective squeeze, grinned conspiratorially and went upstairs.

Sam arrived in a taxi which he kept waiting. He pressed the bell with one finger and kept it there till I'd opened the door. "Where the hell were you? In the middle of a shit? Been standing here hours—" He broke off in mid growl. "Jesus, you look great—what are you trying to do, you cunt, outshine me?"

In the back of the taxi he slid his arm around my shoulders. "Missed me? It's been two days you know."

"Not at all."

"Bitch, don't expect anything from me tonight. I been balling all day with a Bavarian sex bomb. Thighs like a giraffe, tight little titties like golf balls. No nipples on 'em, though. Cul-de-sacs. Two blind alleys." He slid his other hand under my jacket and squeezed. "Not like these." I caught the taxi driver's eyes. So did Sam. He leant forward. "The wettest little pussy in the world. Aren't you proud to have that as a passenger?" And he slammed the partition up and lay back roaring.

When we got out I made a point of saying good night to the driver as Sam was paying him. He didn't look up but as he steered away from the kerb he yelled back, "What do you feed it on—fish fingers?"

"Great guy," said Sam. "Great sense of humour."

31

"Where are we?" I asked.

"We're behind the Hilton, Park Lane, London, my little flower, about to refresh our souls with several stiff martinis and endanger our minds and moral fibre in social intercourse with several of my accursed compatriots," he said in his W. C. Fields voice.

We stepped through smoked-glass doors into a discreetly lit, carpeted hallway, complete with porter. As the tiny lift slid smoothly up, Sam cupped my chin with his hand.

"Don't leave my side, you faithless girl. These men are movie moguls. If one of the fuckers offers you a contract I wanna be there for the percentage. They're looking all over for someone to replace Rin Tin Tin." He patted his pockets. "Theatre tickets—"

"Are we still going?"

"Nag, nag, Jesus. Play it as it comes—see how we work out, kid."

We stopped opposite a stainless-steel door with a shiny microscopic eye in it. Sam pressed a large black bell on the wall, a second passed while someone the other side was obviously scrutinising us. Then, soundlessly the door slid sideways, and we stepped in. Everything was black and white. Ceramic tiles, set alternately on the entrance floor, shiny black patent leather walls. All-white paintings hanging at regular intervals. A white marble gravestone angel, wings outspread, holding in her praying hands a big black city umbrella. Open above her head.

"That's bad luck," I said, "to open a brolly indoors."

"Bad luck, design, taste, idea, a crap film set—mindless," Sam rumbled.

He moved into a long low-ceilinged room, still all black and white, another film set, this time with full cast assembled. A black man in a white suit sat at the white grand piano playing Cole Porter, while a white man in a black suit, shirt and tie rushed towards us shouting out, "Sam's here." Suddenly we were surrounded. Someone thrust a martini in my hand, I took a gulp and within minutes felt the first kick, starting first in my stomach, then at the back of my knees. I remembered that apart from Charles' pâté I hadn't eaten all day and decided to pace things a bit otherwise I'd be flat on my face within the hour. It had happened before. I looked at Sam, he was already taking his second. We'd be lucky to reach the theatre, that was for sure. Most people's faces seemed familiar to me, but I didn't know a soul. Sam was too busy talking to introduce me. Like all parties, the first ten minutes was the worst. Gradually from being the centre of the group I found myself at the edge. Time to flick through the gramophone records or examine the books on the shelves, pick up small assorted objects as if I was interested in where they came from. Ivory carvings, jet-black geometric puzzles. Clear perspex boxes, crammed with cigarettes. I took one out and looked round for a light.

"Allow me," said a woman's voice, while a hand weighed down with jewelled rings flicked a flame towards me.

"Thank you very much." It was the first time I'd heard my voice since I'd arrived. It sounded forced and artificial, over-careful.

"Enjoying the party?"

"Not yet," I answered, "but I expect I will."

She laughed, "Happy optimist," then drifted away. I watched her go. She must have been about fifty-five, I could tell by her neck, but her face was smooth and unlined like a teenager's and her body was slim and straight with extraordinarily high breasts. I wondered when she undressed how many seams and tucks there'd be. None, if she was clever with her lighting, that anyone would see. Except with their fingertips.

I caught sight of myself in one of the many mirrors and saw with surprise how very much at home I looked. Sophisticated, slightly bored, suitably beautiful. It didn't please me, not one bit. Too unfriendly. My glass was empty, time for another and to join the attack. I drank it in one go. A handsome young man at my elbow watched in amazement. "Darling, was that wise?"

"Terribly unwise," I said and, because he was still looking, reached for another.

"Well, if it's that sort of night, I'll join you," he said and did the same.

33

I clinked my glass with his. "Why not?"

From then on it was plain sailing.

"You're divine," he said. "Where did you get your suit?"

"Yves St. Laurent."

"Where else?"

"And yours?"

"The same."

"Of course!"

"Who does your hair, darling?"

"I do."

"Why not try Vidal?"

"I have had it cut there but now I'm growing it, so I wash it myself."

"But that's madness. Why grow it? Go to Roger, get him to cut it all off, except the fringe. And have that dyed red or better still green. Be divine!"

"Do you think so?"

"Of course! Everyone's having it. I'm going to tomorrow."

"You're not!"

"Come with me. They can do us together. Be fabulous, darling."

"Well, I might have it cut but I don't know about the colour." I was thinking of Charles. "My children mightn't like it."

"You can't have children. But you're so young."

"Child bride," I said.

"How chic."

"Divorced now, of course."

"Who isn't? Where do you live?"

"Chelsea. Where you'd expect." And I told him the street.

"How grand. Flat or house?"

"Whole house, but it's very small."

"Bijou," he corrected.

"Whole house, but it's very bijou."

"Oh you are funny, darling. Do you know everybody here?"

"No, do you?"

"Intimately. Alas. At one time or other!"

34

"And where do you live?"

"With whoever I'm with. Currently I'm between engagements. Last summer I was in Rome. I spent Christmas in Tunisia. I was hoping for this spring in the Seychelles but instead I'm staying with my mother."

"Oh, where's that?"

He lowered his voice and looked around. "Can you keep a secret?"

"Of course."

"Streatham Hill!" He held up his hand. "Now I know what you're going to say—parts of that are very nice—don't bother. We both know it's appalling." And he gave a beautiful shudder.

He was amazingly handsome, too much so by half, with a long lean body and the sort of teeth you read about, very white and even. And very thick brown hair with sunburnt streaks. But his mouth was too full and sort of babyish, it made him look as if he'd cry easily. I liked him already. I wanted him to feel that everything was fine and that he didn't have to try so hard. Something of it must have crossed my face. He leaned forward.

"I'm glad we got together. To tell you the truth I was feeling a bit low when I arrived. I'm Rupert."

"Rupert Bear," I said.

"Adore him too. What's yours? No, don't tell me! Let me guess. Rowena? Rebecca?"

I shook my head. "How about Myopia?"

He gave a scream of delight. "What a marvellous name. That, darling, is what I shall call you. Myopia. You're not sensitive about your sight? I mean, you don't wear lenses or anything?"

"Perfect eyesight. Can see for miles."

"That's it then, Myopia. Come on, let's try it out on someone."

He looked around excitedly then stopped and put his hand on my arm. "Before we lose each other, what are you doing tomorrow? Because, apart from having my hair done, I've promised to go to Joe Garibaldi's fashion show. You'd adore his clothes—would you like to come? Do say yes."

"What time?"

"Lunchtime at Animals. It's divine. Haven't you been there? Oh you must have. Everything leopardskin. Even the plates."

"How horrible. Does the fur get in your mouth?"

"Printed plastic, silly. Joe's taking over the whole place. Champagne and smoked salmon."

"How lovely. I think I'd love to come. I've seen his clothes but only in magazines."

"Dauntingly expensive, my dear, but such panache! You'd look a dream in them."

"I think I'd feel uneasy spending that much."

He laughed and flicked my fringe. "What a sweet child you are, get a boy friend to foot the bill. That's what they're for, darling." He lightly fingered his superbly cut lapels. "My dear, you don't imagine I paid for these?"

I gazed at him for a second and then looked across the crowded room at Sam. "I don't seem to be very good at that," I said. His eyes followed mine and seeing Sam he sighed.

"Now that's the sort of money we all need."

"Sam? He's who I've come with. But I think you're wrong. He's not very rich."

He let his jaw drop. "You're joking!"

"No I'm not. I've been seeing him for ages."

He leant forward eagerly. "He bought you the house."

"Don't be silly. He hasn't bought me anything, except dinners and things. Honestly."

He drained his glass and groaned. "Darling innocent, you're sitting on a goldmine picking daisies. I can't bear it!"

"What do you mean?"

"What I mean is that Samuel Gregory Jr. is Contemporary Films Incorporated. He owns it all now. His father died last year."

"Oh, he said his father was dead, and his mother. My men are usually orphans."

He groaned again. "Don't tell me they're all millionaires too. You probably wouldn't know. Darling, I can see you need taking in hand. My God, Myopia is nearer the mark than we'd imagined."

"I've gone all dizzy," I said. And I had too.

"Quite understandable, darling. So should I have in the circumstances."

"I think it's the drink. They're very strong these martinis. I'd have been safer on gin and tonic."

He took the glass from my hand and shepherded me to the door. "Squat a while in the loo, darling. Much the chicest place to collapse! I'll see you when you come out. The party will still be here."

I sat for what seemed like a month on the open oval lavatory seat. From time to time people discreetly rattled the door handle, but I couldn't move. I tried to focus on my feet. There were four of them. My satin trousers flopped in concertina folds around them all on the floor. When at last I stood up I saw in the mirror, by twisting round, that the seat had bitten into my buttocks and left a ludicrous red frame around my hole. All it needed was the artist's signature. I pulled my tights and trousers up—and fished around in my pocket for a lipstick. After that my flat slim compact. A spot of powder and I felt fit to face the world. I didn't have any money on me at all. If Sam had gone, Christ knows how I'd get home.

He hadn't and nor had anyone else, come to that. If anything, it was even fuller. Perhaps I'd only been in there minutes, after all. It does that, drink. Robs you of all sense of time. So does pot, of course, but much more so, floating for centuries when in fact it's only half an hour. Both at the time seem a way of getting through life more quickly, what they do instead is slow it up.

Swaying slightly, I looked around. I couldn't see Rupert anywhere. I liked the idea of the dress show. I hoped I hadn't lost him for good. Sam was still surrounded, he was astonishingly popular but thinking about it, if what Rupert had said was true it was hardly surprising. At that moment he looked up, towering above everyone else, and caught my eye. His face broke into an enormous grin and he beckoned. I didn't attempt to go towards him, just grinned back and waved. His smile froze and turned into a frown. He beckoned again, but this time angrily. He was drunk.

"You'd better go to him, darling," said a voice behind me. Rupert's. I turned round with a dazzling smile.

"Why?" I was drunk too. "Kiss me."

Rupert's startled eyes and anxious mouth were the last things I saw. What I heard was the smashing of fine glass, the rip of expensive satin, and an animal roar from Sam as my head whammed against the wall. It took the full strength of five men to hold him off. Numbed as I was, with bells jingling in my ears and soaring specks of light looking uncommonly like stars before my eyes, I still was all for hitting Sam back. But restraining hands kept me where I was, on the floor. I slowly lifted one foolish finger and touched the egg which was swelling on my head. My shoulder was completely bare. I looked down at it with surprise, at the fringed edges of the torn beautiful jacket and the shredded shirt beneath. Then I looked at Sam. His neck was dark red, his eyes glaring down at me were wild and bloodshot. Sweat was pouring down his face. It was a terrible tantrum!

"Sam," I said weakly. "That was very silly. Serve you right if you have a seizure."

There wasn't a sound in the whole room except from the pianist who had switched from Cole Porter to Noël Coward *Mad About the Boy*, that's what he was playing.

People helped me to my feet. I shook their hands away and walked the few unsteady steps to Sam. The five men tightened their grips and Sam, blinking hard, flinched as my hand came up to his face. But all I did was lightly touch his mouth. Very slowly I undid his tie, unbuttoned his collar and with two hands tore as hard as I could till there was no shirt left at all. Then I kissed him. The laugh started in his stomach just as it did in mine. He looked me up and down, saw that half my jacket was still intact, took hold of that sleeve and ripped it from its socket. We were convulsed. The astonished rest of the room began to giggle from nervousness. Sam undid his flies. "Dare you, cunty." I grasped a handful of trouser either side and pulled as hard as I could in all directions. Every seam went. What was left slithered down his legs to the floor. Tears of appreciation ran down his face. With one swoop, wearing now only his jacket, tie and underpants, he picked me up and slung me over his shoulder.

"Great party," he boomed between laughs. "Sorry to leave, folks, but we gotta go."

As the lift went down I caught sight of Rupert's face white and excited. "Animals at one. Bring Sam, he can buy you a new suit!"

When I woke in the morning my head ached hellishly. The egg was still there but the whole of the left side of my face was now puffy and painful. More than anything I was terribly hungry—we never had got round to eating the night before. It was raining by the time we'd left the party and Sam was all for walking round to the Hilton for dinner just as we were. The hall porter wouldn't hear of us walking anywhere. Said we'd be sure to be picked up for indecent exposure. He insisted on ringing for a taxi and made us wait in his little office whilst he did so. As it was, when the taxi arrived, several residents passed us in the hall and all made a point of looking the other way at Sam's "Mind now, darlings, enjoy yourselves" said in a silly English accent. Sam held on to me very tightly, as much I suspected to support himself as anything else.

"You've not to come in tonight," I said. "You're to go straight home when you've dropped me."

"You're mad at me, you bitch."

"I'm not at all."

"You're mad at me because I whammed you, and I only did that because you were out petting with some guy half the party."

"I wasn't. I was in the lavatory."

"With some guy. Honey, I saw you go. What are you trying to say—I'm blind, for Jesus' sake!"

"What, Rupert? Don't be silly. He's not like that."

"You mean he's a fuckin' faggot? That doesn't fool me, not for one minute. I know faggots, I know one faggot who's a grandfather, for Christ's sake. What do you make of that? He's got more in his trousers than a chocolate éclair."

39

"Sh, sh, calm down, Sam. You're marvellous. You know I think you are. I'm not mad, not a bit, but now I'd like to go home and to bed. My head is hurting, that's all. Please." I took his hand and held it tightly to my mouth.

He stroked my hair. "Shall I see you tomorrow, honey?"

"Ring me in the morning."

He looked anxiously in my eyes. I started to laugh. So did he then.

"Hey, what do you suppose they thought, that set of wankers?"

"Disgracefully bad behaviour?"

"Livened the evening, though. What do you suppose they're doing now, talking about us?"

"Tearing each other's clothes off?"

He stopped chuckling and touched my shreds. "You looked so gorgeous tonight. You know that. Tomorrow I'm going to buy you another of these. Not just one—ten, twenty—anything you like. You're not much of a screw but you're a bold little bugger."

I got up well before the girls and Françoise. I made some tea for myself and took a couple of aspirins for the pain. Then I splashed the puffiness with iced water and skin tonic which seemed to make it go down a bit. My hair was agonising to brush, each stroke set my scalp going, so I gave it up and instead pulled on a little purple silky cap which covered the whole lot. The hairdresser's, having it cut or coloured, was out of the question today. I found a pair of purple sunglasses and a favourite old dressing-gown, striped pink and purple, and went down to the kitchen to make breakfast. By the time Françoise came down everything was ready. Freshly pressed orange juice, ice in each glass. Boiled brown eggs with everyone's name written on in red biro and a whole dishful of golden buttered toast cut into narrow strips for dipping in. I heard the girls shouting to find my bed empty. "Mummy, Mummy." "She's not here." "She's gone." "Where is she?" I turned the radio on extra loud to give them a clue and they came running down and tried to climb up me, one on each side. Françoise was delighted to see everything done.

"Special treat," I said in case she thought it was the start of a new régime.

"Why, Mummy, why?"

"Just because."

"I like just because," said Fanny banging her egg with a spoon.

"I like just because too," said Harriet carefully slicing hers with a knife. "I like it because the breakfast is nicer."

"That's not true," I protested. "Françoise makes lovely ones." I could see her face.

"I try to do good for you, Harriet."

"Yes, but you burn the toast and then you scrape it but I can still tell by the taste. Mummy's is much better."

"Ah," I said, "but I can't make coffee and Françoise is very good at that."

"You always drink tea, though, Mummy."

"That's because I can't make coffee as well as Françoise. Eat up before it gets cold." My head was beginning to thud again. "I'm going to a dress show today," I said brightly. "Beautiful clothes being shown off by beautiful girls."

"Little ones? Will there be anything for us there?"

"Models. Grown-up ones."

"Mannequins," corrected Françoise. "My friend in Paris she is a mannequin for Dior. I know her all my life. She have very bad hacnee—acknay? Many plackheads and pimpoles. Open paws. It's horrible! Ugh!"

"How did she get the job at Dior?"

"She get it because she have very thin elbows and no front and back and she have a tall neck like a chimney—"

"Does she smoke?" Harriet asked, and spluttered egg all over her orange juice.

"Don't be silly, Harriet," I said. "That's rude. Françoise was still telling us about her friend. Go on, I love hearing it."

Fanny was all eyes, she'd put down her spoon and was examining her elbows and feeling her front with both hands. "I've got one, haven't I, Mummy? And a botty too," she added sadly.

Françoise went on as if there had been no interruption at all. "She show me many photographs of herself. Because of her tall neck she is modelling the beautiful hats of Dior, but always from the back."

"Oh dear, but perhaps that's the best angle for hats. Lots of them have bows and things there."

"Not so at all," said Françoise triumphantly. "If she face the camera she would break it. I count once how many plackheads she have and it take me—"

"Poor thing." I stood up. "That's a lesson to wash your faces, girls, isn't it? Up you go. You too, Françoise! I'll clear these."

I piled everything on a tray. Going up the stairs Harriet shouted down, "Thank you for breakfast, Mummy," and then to Françoise, "How long did it take you?"

The answer drifted down. "It take me the all of a week—"

I'd driven the girls to school.

"What are we having for tea?"

"You only just had breakfast."

"I'm hungry."

"You can't be."

"She is. And so am I."

"Perhaps you'll have nothing then, if eating makes you hungry."

"We're not a bit hungry. It's a joke."

"Very funny."

"Can we have cake and buns and chocolate biscuits like other people?"

"What, all at once? Which people?"

"Chubby. She brings buns for playtime."

"So does Podgy Olive, she eats them on the lavatory."

"If you want to be called Chubby and Podgy, I'll stop off now and buy you some buns."

"Podgy Olive has got lots of dimples," Fanny said wistfully. "I haven't got any."

"Later in life you'll thank me." I kissed them goodbye. "But I know it's hard to see now. When I was your age I was called

Fatso and Jumbo and Piggy, you couldn't see my face for dimples. But it wasn't anything as nice as you think."

When I got back the phone was ringing, but as I reached it, it stopped. Hell! I went up to run my bath, I had the first foot in when it rang again. One wet footprint all down the carpeted stairs. Man Friday.

"Hullo."

"Darling, it's me!"

"Charles. How lovely."

"Must be brief. Friday. Friday evening. Paris. Back Saturday. What do you say?"

"For the night? But, Charles, how can you? You never can in the evenings, let alone a night."

"I'll explain later. Now, yes or no, darling?"

"Let me think. Well I suppose so. Françoise will be here but Saturday is her day off."

"We'd be back before breakfast, darling. I've got to be."

"That's all right then—oh how lovely. I love Paris. What a wonderful surprise, Charles."

"Settled then. I'll telephone you in the morning with further details. If time allows I'll drop in later in the day. Good morning to you." His office voice all of a sudden. He replaced his receiver briskly. Click.

"Good morning to you too, sir," I said and replaced mine.

I ran up the stairs two at a time but slowed down when I felt it doing my head no good. Friday. I'd be better by then. Well, I felt better all ready. I loved a journey. That's what I liked about Mondays as much as anything. Getting on the train. Being on the move. Paris in the Spring. . . .

* * *

"Let's save up and go, it'll be smashing. All those sexy French men. They love English girls. They'd go mad about us!"

"Don't be so daft, Jean. I'd never save that much."

"You would. You could work all Easter holidays on the Palace

43

Pier and then we could go just for a week before term starts. Anyway you've got your grant."

I laughed at that. She had no idea, Jean, of what grants were. She thought they were some sort of personal allowance like the one she had from her father. She was by far the richest girl in my lot at college, but for all that never looked very much. "It's these glasses. When you're saddled with glasses there's no point in trying. Do you know, I've never been out with a boy! No one has ever asked me." From then on we were friends. Well, I thought it was such a shame, because she was lots of fun and her figure wasn't at all bad. And it wasn't as though she wasn't keen. Keen as mustard. Much more than me. But then at that time I was recovering from a broken heart. It was because of my broken heart that my mother said, "Go. Paris is just what you could do with, love. If you can get the money together." I think she was sick of me mooning about the place. Later, I heard next door telling her, "Ooh Vi, them frogs. 'Ope she don't come back wiv no big belly." "She's a sensible girl," was my mother's reply.

I got a job on the Palace Pier, well more under it really, in the arcade beneath the prom. About ten strides from the Gents; it wasn't too pleasant for the first day because the wind was blowing my way. But in the end it proved all to the good. It was a wonderful Easter weekend financially. It rained from morning to night which brought everybody, all the trippers, down into the arcade for shelter. They were so drunk most of them that they didn't know what they were spending on. Mr. Pilsky, who owned the café where I worked, said he'd never known such bumper takings. It was his wife, Ruthie, who'd taken me on.

"Experienced waitress?"

"No, but it won't take me long to learn."

"You don't learn on my time, dear. Out of season different matter. With the Easter crowd I need speed. Right then, washer-up?"

"Thank you," I said. I was in the windowless passage they called the kitchen for about five minutes, I'd already slipped once on the greasy floor. Chef, he introduced himself as that, had

44

dropped a whole pan of boiling fat by forgetting to hold it with a cloth. Already it had formed a fine white coagulating skin. He was a frightening-looking man, covered in sores all up his arms and over his face. His collar where it met his neck was stained with old pus and fresh blood.

"Wouldn't get too close if I was you. Best fish fryer in the business but riddled with pox. We don't touch his food here, kid, I bring me own sandwiches. If you're cute you'll do the same," whispered the friendly counterhand.

After the five minutes Mr. Pilsky had come in. He looked me up and down, turned me round and pinched my bottom.

"Who are you?"

"The new washer-up."

"Madness! Ruthie, who put this kid in the kitchen?"

"I did, David. Did I do wrong?"

"Wrong? Where's your business sense, girl? What, this kid? Knockers like hers, that face? Should be out front for the customers to see. Pull the fellas, you fool!"

"She got no experience, David. She don't—"

"Experience! Experience! Showmanship, Ruthie! We set up a counter outside—soft drinks, ice-cream, chocolate, anything! Get it?" He put his arm round my shoulders, right round so that his fleshy hand pressed hard against one bosom. "What have we got for the little darling to wear?"

"The overalls are in the cupboard, David. Take your pick," said Ruthie, but the way she looked at me!

"I'll see to it, all under control. Now you get it set up outside. We're here to make money, girl," and to me, "Student are you?"

"Yes."

"Thought so. Can always tell a student. Flat shoes and no make-up! Right! But you're a good-looking kid. Should make more of yourself. Don't you wear no jewellery—earrings, I mean, and suchlike?"

"No, but I could get some at the end of the week when I have my wages."

He opened his wallet and peeled off a note. "Get yourself some

45

on the way in tomorrow and while you're at it a bit of lipstick at the same time."

I looked at the note and said innocently, "Will this be enough?"

A strange look passed over his face. He came closer and cupped one of my breasts, his other hand he put between my legs. "Don't come that line till you've done something to earn it, kid. Please me and I'll please you." Then he turned round and started sorting through the clean overalls in the cupboard. "Ahhah, this one will do a treat. We had to have it made special for a girl last year. Very small she was, like a child you might say. Get it on."

I held on to the sleeve of my jumper and pushed it through the short arm of the stiff white overall, then tried to do the same with the other arm. "It's too small," I said.

"Rubbish."

"It is. I'll never do it up."

"Get your jumper off then. Go on."

"Is there anywhere to change?"

"Here's all right by me. And get your skirt off too. You need a nice tight fit on an overall."

I felt like crying, which was silly. I put my mind to Paris which was the only reason I was with this horrible man. What a time we'd have there Jean and me. I thought of good-looking French boys with black hair and nice brown hands. I thought of dancing and afterwards kissing by the Seine. I kept on thinking all that and then I turned my back on his disgusting face and slowly took my jumper off. His voice rasped through what I was thinking.

"You walk around half naked—where's your brassière?" He spun me round to face him—my arms involuntarily came up to hide myself. He pinned them to my sides and took one step back. "Bloody hell, they're the best titties I've ever seen. Why wear a brassière with that lot? You got some sense, girl. Ruthie, come 'ere, Ruthie. What do you say to this pair? Long time since you saw some like these, eh?"

Ruthie came through and stood there speechless, so did the counterhand and the two waitresses and last of all Chef, skidding on his greasy soles. "Phew." "Blimey." "I could pay more than me rent with them." "She'd make a fortune on the game." "Worth spending a bit to set her up." The counterhand caught my eye but I could only just see her. Jean and I were strolling down the Boulevard St. Germain. We were approaching Les Deux Magots. We sat down at one of the tiny pavement tables and ordered two Pernods. "Scott Fitzgerald might have sat on this chair." "Or Hemingway." But it must have been raining because everything was blurred and shiny. My face was wet and there was a salty taste in my mouth.

"There you are, you coarse buggers. You made the poor little sod cry." The counterhand came forward. "Don't take no notice, love. It's all in fun. It's just you're not used to it."

"Ooh, listen to Nelly."

"Yeah, listen to 'er—she'd be the first to get your drawers down, kid. You like a pretty girl don't you, Nell?"

Lots of laughter and cat-calls.

"Shut up, you lot," Nelly said fiercely.

Ruthie stepped forward and put her hands on her big hips. "David, am I wrong? Is this a café due to open in five bloody minutes or is it a fuckin' striptease?" and to me, "Decent people, girl, do not go round without undies on—or don't they teach you that in college?" She spat it out. Mr. Pilsky let go of my arms. I snatched my jumper up and held it across my front. I stopped crying but my face and chest were still splashed with the tears that had just been.

My turn to spit, I spun round on Mr. Pilsky: "And decent people don't go round undressing other people just for a chance to see their body. Not that is unless they're dirty old men. If you want to know, my brassière is in the wash!" But I ended childishly "So there!" And I stuck my tongue out. Nobody said anything. The waitresses looked uneasily at each other. Chef became interested in how his greasy soles were sticking to the dirty lino. Nelly muttered, "Good kid, tell them." Ruthie was glaring at her husband. I'd gained ground. They were all pathetic.

"Well," I said gaily, "would you like one last look before I get ready for work?" I dropped my jumper, quickly unzipped my skirt, stepped out of it and did a twirl around. I twanged my knicker elastic towards Ruthie. "Undies, see?" Then I picked up the ridiculously small overall, buttoned it up and pulled the belt as tight as it would go. "Should get in a bit of business, Mr. Pilsky?"

I didn't tell my mother, she'd have had me out of there in no time. Paris or no Paris. But days later I told Jean.

"I'd have walked out."

"Where to?"

"There must be other jobs."

"Not this late, everything had gone on the Palace Pier and the West Pier. I tried."

"But aren't there jobs in the hotels on the front? What about the Metropole or the Grand?"

"Not for three weeks, you fool. They want you for the whole season. Anyway, all there was was chambermaid and my mother said no."

"Why?"

"Because she said my father had said I wasn't to. He told her that these hotels are full of dirty old men who get the chambermaids into bed when they bring the tea in the morning. And then don't even leave a tip!"

"He'd go mad if he knew about old Pilsky."

"Pilsky is no trouble now. Anyway Ruthie is there keeping an eye on him. She doesn't let him out of her sight. To tell you the truth I play up a bit now, you know, bending over a lot and leaving a button undone. He goes all hot and bothered. It makes her really mad."

"Aren't you awful," Jean said, but I could see she was impressed.

"Yes, I could turn into a terrible flirt, just like that."

It was true. There was something infectious about the arcade. Everyone on holiday, paper hats, pop bottles, candy floss, beer. And I'd got used to the revealing tightness of my overall. It was filthy after the first day from heaving cases of fizzy drinks and bending over the dusty fridge fishing out ice-creams. But all the grey patches did was emphasise on the white starched cotton what curves lay underneath. The Hourglass. That's what they called me.

"You should get entering for the Bathing Belle contest. They're running heats this week on the end of the pier," said Lottie, one of the waitresses. "Shouldn't she, Mave?" she said to the other.

"Yeah, you'd win hands down."

"Oh, I wouldn't. I know I wouldn't. My legs aren't long enough. You have to have very long legs for that."

"Well, love, you want to get out of them ballet slippers for a start. What do they call them? Pumps. They don't do nothing for you. Do they, Mave?"

"Hopeless. Get up the road to Tip Toes. They got smashing high heels. Ever so cheap. Nice pair of white ones. Really smart. Only ten bob. Make your legs look like Rita Hayworth's."

"That's all you need, love," said Lottie, looking at my legs.

"And a nice perm," supplied Mavis.

I thought seriously about the shoes but not about the rest of it. I'd rather have died than parade about in a swimsuit. Anyway my father would have put his foot down. He didn't approve of beauty queens any more than chambermaiding. Besides, how would I have time off? Only ten bob. I had ten bob. The change from old Pilsky's pound. I'd bought the earrings, huge brass gypsy rings from a shop near the station. They'd cost five bob. Another five bob had gone on a lipstick, Sun Kissed Orange (refill: half-price), and a thick soft black eyebrow pencil which I rubbed on my eyelids with Vaseline to make them dark and shiny. I always washed it off before I went home and I didn't show them the earrings either. "Tarty." I had half an hour's dinner break each day when Ruthie relieved me at my little kiosk. I was always pleased to see that at those times the till showed hardly any sales at all. "Oh," I'd say glancing at it, "a quiet spell." She never bothered to answer.

This day I skipped my sandwiches and ran as fast as I could to Tip Toes. Half an hour later I was back in my first ever high heels. I'd walked in them all the way down the prom. Shoulders back, head high, careful steps, only way to keep balance. Twice I turned my ankle and nearly fell. Some silly boys started marching alongside. "New shoes?" Lots of titters. But I took no notice. Nothing since, no dress, or fur or piece of jewellery, has made me feel as glamorous as I did that day. I wore them home when I'd finished work.

"Now you're talking," Lottie had said approvingly.

"That's more like it, kid," said Mavis. "What did I tell you? Rita Hayworth."

Even Ruthie sniffed. "Nice to see you smartening up, about time."

"Haven't we got a high stool for her to sit on, Ruthie? Show the legs off a bit?"

"No, David. We haven't."

But my mother wasn't too impressed. "Shoddy, made of cardboard. You'll be lucky if they last a week. What do you think, Dad?"

"Make her legs look funny, too long or something. All out of proportion. Take them off."

I took them off but in my bedroom I practised walking for hours with them until in the end I'd perfected a wonderful hip-swinging cross between a slink and a wobble. Jean was terribly jealous, she went straight to Tip Toes and got herself exactly the same ones. White, slingback, peep toe, high stiletto heel. I didn't mind at all but I said to her, "Jean, that's silly. You've got the money. You could have got real leather ones. Much nicer."

"But not so sexy. Come on, show me how to walk."

She kept her shoes at our house; if she'd taken them home her father would have burnt them right away.

Time was drawing on. Already I'd been at work ten days. About ten more to go. The first week had been frantic. Sometimes we hadn't shut till twelve o'clock at night but that had been Easter week. It meant a long walk home for me because by the time we'd cleared up my last bus had gone. But it was worth it, for the extra I earned. Then it fell off altogether, the weather had changed for the worse. Brilliant sunshine. The beach was packed, but people were bringing their own picnics. We did quite a turn-over with beach tea trays and my lukewarm ice-cold drinks, the lollies and ice-creams, but the café was half-empty. People didn't fancy heavy fries in that heat. Takings were down by a third. Mr. Pilsky was sunk in gloom, he didn't even have the spirit to ogle me any more. By eight at night there was no point in staying open—sometimes we even shut at six.

"At this rate I'll never have enough saved," I moaned to Jean.

"Perhaps the weather will break."

"Pray."

She must have, because two days later when Paris was beginning to appear as unlikely as Paradise, it poured all day. I shortened my bra straps to give a bit more cleavage, got round the front of my kiosk, pretending to clean it as often as I could, to show off my legs. And by midday had sold out of ices. At one point Nelly came out for a smoke.

"Hope you're making up your money, love."

"Oh yes, I've been non-stop. Sold out on ices."

"That makes no odds. Ices they check on." She looked over her shoulder and jerked a thumb at Pilsky who now was on top of the world. "That's what you fiddle, love." She nodded at the ice-cold orange, a circular glass tank full of acid-looking orangeade with a plastic orange floating on the surface. "You keep the colour going but dilute it right down with water. Fifty per cent you forget to ring on the till." She winked. "Use your loaf, love. Believe me, we're all at it."

Two hours later I'd made ten shillings and felt as guilty as hell. My pocket bulged with coppers and sixpences. Nelly caught sight of me and darted out. "Shove it in the till and take it in notes, you little fool." Then she winked again. "Atta girl."

I was at it every day after that.

"Four fizzy lemons, miss."

"Why not try the ice-cold orange? Really sharp and tasty."

"Try anything once—"

Lots of them spat it out on the spot, leaving the remains in their waxed cups still sitting on the counter. Pouring it back? Lightning wasn't half as quick. By each night I was making at least two pounds extra. "That's what you call private enterprise," Nelly said. But the day after she said it, old Pilsky caught her in the act. She was sacked on the spot.

"Don't go giving up," she whispered on her way out. "Just go careful. Got it?" A final wink and she'd gone.

I couldn't have given up anyway, it was like a drug. I came to understand what excitement a real burglar must feel. Five days before I finished I sold my first pair of earrings. Just like that, off my ears.

"Smashin' earrings, darlin'. 'Ow much?"

"Oh, I wouldn't sell them."

"'Ow much?"

(Quick sums, hundred per cent profit.) "Well, I paid ten shillings for them."

"I'll give yer fifteen. Do lovely for the missus."

"But I don't want to sell them."

"Pound?"

"Right!"

On the way in next morning I spent the whole pound on four more pairs. That's where being so near the Gents' came in handy. They used to spill in there straight off the charabancs, come out and then catch sight of me. And my earrings. Twenty-five pairs I sold by the end, with me paying less than five shillings for them. I got my own price knocked down for buying in bulk, but I still charged the full pound.

They were sweet on my last day. Lottie got quite tearful.

"Ooh, we will miss you. Won't we miss her, Mave?"

"Don't be so soppy, the kid's going to Paris. You should be saying bon voyage. It's very romantic. *Paris in the Spring*—"

"Toujours l'amour," Lottie sang out.

"Up against the back door," sang Mavis back, and went into peals of laughter. Then she was serious. "Have you done it yet, kid?"

"What?"

"Give it away, I mean. You're not a virgin, are you?"

"Sort of."

"Blimey, what's sort of?"

"Well, I had a boy friend. But he couldn't find the hole."

"Bloody hell. Was he blind?"

"Actually, yes. Yes, he was born blind. But he doesn't see me any more. I'm just getting over it."

"Cripes, you don't want to hitch up with no blind bastard. Not at your age. I wouldn't let no daughter of mine. Play the field and then pick the best. Somebody who's going to make a bit. But if you're going to come up with the goods, for God's sake see they got a french letter on! If you're caught short and they haven't, mind to have a wipe round with a soap and flannel after!"

"My sister had it off with a French sailor once," Lottie sighed. "At the back of a pub in Portsmouth. Said she'd never known anything like it. The different things he did."

"That's right, kid. A bloke who knows what he's doing, believe you me, can get goosepimples growing on your eyeballs!"

Ruthie was relieving Chef when I said my goodbyes. I was quite glad that he wasn't anywhere around. I was afraid he'd want to shake my hand with his sores or, worse still, kiss me. How shocking to go to Paris with the pox! She stood at the chip machine, sweating in a cloud of blue smoke. Half of them were burning as usual. "You're off then," a wave of the fish slice, and a turned back. Good riddance to you too!

Old Pilsky paid me off taking as long about it as he could. Finally he handed me the full amount and pressing it tightly in the palm of my hand said thickly, "You're a very silly little girl. You could have made ten times this if you'd used that," and he pushed a podgy knee between my two. Afterwards I thought of all the witty things I could have said back. Some came at the time but I let the moment pass, I don't know why but I didn't even pull away.

He came terribly close, was getting very excited, pressing up against me. I could feel it in his trousers, thick and bulging down the side of one leg. We were in what he called his office, a partitioned-off space no larger than a cupboard. It was the end of the evening but I was going off an hour early to pack and get ready for tomorrow. The day's takings were in a tin box on his small table. In my high heels I was taller than him. His bald head was about level with my breasts. The rancid smell of his greasy scalp whiffed into my nose. He'd taken his jacket off and just above where he'd rolled his sleeves up I could see the week's sweat stains on his shirt. He was sweating again now, his face was wet with it, dripping on to me. I was still in my overall, thank goodness. Both arms around me now, knee working furiously prising mine apart, he whispered hoarsely, "Come on, girl. What are you saving it for? We got time now. Come on quick. I'm crazy about you." I made no reply. Suddenly he broke off, reached towards the tin box and took out a five-pound note. I still stood there not moving but my heart was going like mad. He stuffed the note down into my brassière and keeping that hand there forced his fingers in towards my nipple. With his other hand he drew one of mine between his legs. I half-heartedly tried to pull it away. Why so half-heartedly? Was it the money? It wasn't really, because with all my fiddling and earnings on the side, not to mention my over-time, I now had much more than enough. But I'd got greedy. I wanted the fiver as well. I felt it stiff and scratchy against my skin. I'd put that aside for presents. Jean and me on the last afternoon, into Galeries Lafayette. Scent for my mother or a string of beads or a square silk scarf, views of Paris printed on it. Socks for my father, red, or braces, canary yellow, to show off and lots of those miniature liqueurs—he'd like that. Initialled handkerchiefs, French cigarettes, belts and shiny handbags. A tiny baby's dress, white, edged with broderie anglaise for my sister, expecting next month. He was undoing his flies, forcing in my unprotesting, lifeless, fingers. Jamming them round his swollen clammy thing, squeezing and rubbing up and down. I could tell by the feel what colour it was, putty and slugs, underdone pork. On my very first day I'd buy some new shoes, very high, suede perhaps, toffee-coloured. Pack a tin of elastoplasts in case they made blisters. The smell of him had got right down into my stomach. I kept swallowing hard and trying to breathe through my open mouth. Why was I letting him? Why on earth? Because of the danger that someone, Ruthie, any of the others, could come in at any moment; because he was pathetic and I could make him do anything and I felt sorry for him; because he'd given me the money; but most of all now, because his excitement was becoming so unbearable to him, so highly charged and quivering that it was exciting me too. There was no doubt about that, I actually liked his fingers clawing in my brassière. My nipples were stiff and sticking out like anything. And between my legs I felt all sticky and sort of tingly. Throbbing. If a doctor were here he could place a cool finger in and take my pulse from it. "My God, my God, my God," moaned old Pilsky, and letting go of my hand he quickly pulled a dirty hanky from his pocket and plunged it into his flies. "See what you've done, you bitch! Get out! Go on! Go." He shut his eyes and sat down heavily on the small table, still holding his hanky in, moaning softly to himself. Was it hurting or what? He seemed in pain.

"Do you think he was then?" We were sitting on the boat train. The carriage was empty.

"I didn't wait to enquire, Jean! What on earth have you done to your hair?"

"Isn't it awful? Mummy took me to her hairdresser yesterday and made me have the ends permed. I look a sight, I know."

"I've got a pair of nail scissors. Would you like me to cut them off?"

"What, now?"

"When we get there. This train is too jerky."

"Yours looks nice. Lovely and shiny."

"I ironed it, that's why. It makes it very shiny. And straight. I hate my hair curling. Do you know, I was up at five ironing everything. I had to wash all my clothes last night to get rid of the stink from the café, I swear it's even got into my shoes. I put a bit of blanco on them to hide the scuffs. My mother was right, they haven't lasted very well."

"You've brought mine?"

"Do you want them now?"

"Yes let's, come on—put yours on too."

55

They looked awful away from the arcade, very cheap, terribly tarty, but it got us in the mood.

"Have you done what I told you, Jean? The glasses."

"Shut your eyes, I'll put them on." She scuffed in her handbag. "All right, open! What do you think?" she said anxiously. She sat on the edge of her seat, frizzy-haired, pigeon-toed like a child, wearing on her face an enormous pair of sophisticated dark glasses. I started laughing, I couldn't help it. They looked so out of place. Her mouth went down at the edges. "Well, you said to get them." There was a small break in her voice. I went on laughing.

"Oh Jeannie. They're lovely. They really are. That's why I'm laughing. You look like a film star."

She stood on tiptoes, the slingbacks slipping off her ankles, and looked in the mirror above her seat. "Do I? Do I really? You're not making fun?"

"Well," I said. "Stand here. Let me see. The glasses are film star but now we've got to fit you round them. Perhaps I better cut your hair after all now. What about having it really short? Will your mother mind?"

"She'd have a fit, but it's got a week to grow a bit. Go on, do what you like."

I left about three inches all over, it was almost a crew cut.

"You'll have a shock when you see it," I warned. "But before you look, let me put some lipstick on you." It was a pleasure painting her mouth. It was a very big one, full, wide, and went up at the ends. I felt like kissing it when I'd finished, coloured bright orange it looked such a happy thing. Before I let her look, I replaced the dark glasses. Without the silly frizz around her shoulders her head was a beautiful shape. It narrowed into a vulnerably child-like sweet little neck, her ears were tiny and close to the scalp. Completely exposed, her jawline was sharp and perfect. "Now look." I'd made her beautiful!

We stood together at the mirror. She couldn't say anything at first. "Is it me?"

"Can't you see in those glasses then? They've got your prescription lenses, haven't they?"

56

"I can see perfectly, it's a bit dark that's all, but I can see as well as with my others."

"That's all right then."

"What do you think?"

"Smashing!" I said. "You look like a bird, like one of those bush babies with the big eyes, or an owl. A sort of sexy owl— I can't describe it really."

"But sexy?"

"Oh yes, with that lipstick. It draws attention to your mouth. I should think the whole of Paris will be trying to kiss it."

She kept on looking in the mirror, turning her head slightly this way and that and running her tongue lightly over her upper lip.

"Don't do that, you'll lick it all off."

"It's got a funny taste, like peardrops."

"It's only a cheap one. We'll buy nice ones when we get there, ones with more oil in which makes them shinier, more expensive of course."

"What would your father say if he knew you wore lipstick?"

"Kill me, what would yours?"

"Kill me too."

"It's a wonder they let us come you know."

"But then they can't guess what we're going to get up to, can they?"

I didn't answer, just looked out of the window thinking, then, "Jean, what are we going to get up to?"

"Wait and see," she said. In many ways she was much bolder than me.

We arrived at the Gare du Nord at five to four. Everyone was talking in French.

"They're all talking in French."

"I know, isn't it funny?" We stood on the grey platform with our cases in our hands, cocooned in our own Englishness. Completely lost. My mother'd be putting the kettle on now. "Jam or Marmite?" to my father.

Jean cleared her throat and took control. "We'd best change

57

your money first." She'd got her francs already, her father had arranged it all through his bank. "Go and ask in the post office, see if they'll do it!" mine had said.

A young porter seeing us standing there rushed up and seized at our cases. "Non, non," Jean said and added, "merci beaucoup." He shrugged. "Okay, pretty girls. You no want I help," and putting his bunched fingertips to his puckered lips gave a big kissing noise. We started walking towards a sign which said Bureau de Change but we had to go quite slowly because of our shoes.

"We should have practised walking with the cases," Jean said.

"Just go carefully and try to relax. Keep your shoulders back like me." My hips swung easily left to right.

"I am," then after a minute, "What are they all staring for?"

I had to admit people were staring, or so it seemed. Men. Men walking towards us, gazes directed first at our feet, travelling swiftly up the legs, hovering at suspender level, taking in the waistlines and particularly above, fastening on the mouth, fixing finally on the eyes. Bold looks. To make you blush.

"Assessing," I said.

"Undressing more like." I could hear the excitement in her voice.

"Go easy, Jean. We're not even out of the station yet."

"No, but it makes you see what it's going to be like. Come-to-bed eyes everywhere!"

We had no idea where our hotel was in relation to us. However close, our cases were too heavy to walk. The métro seemed too confusing by far so we took a taxi.

"We won't do too much of this," Jean said as soon as we were in. "We'll find men with cars and they can drive us round," and she added, "We won't spend on food either, because we'll get taken out for that."

I looked at her, she was bubbling over. Back home she always was on the boil but it was a bit too tomboyish, had too much of the giggly schoolgirl to fascinate. Here her high spirits had altered mysteriously to a sort of radiance. She still looked mischievous; but ripe. That was it. Ripe for the plucking. Beside her I felt tired. The last three weeks had been a harder slog perhaps than I'd thought at the time. "We'll have an early night, I've just worked it out, I've been up twelve hours!"

She lifted her dark glasses and peered at me in short-sighted horror. "On our first night?"

"Well, if we have a good rest tonight we can get going to-morrow." It was Mother talking!

"Don't be silly. Tonight we're on the town." She looked through her glasses at me and frowned for a second. "You look a bit tired I admit." Then she brightened. "But after a bath you'll feel much better."

"But—" I was going to say I had my bath last night. In Jean's house they had one every day. Her father had chosen the hotel, arranged the bookings, or rather his secretary had. "What will it be like, the hotel?"

"If Daddy's had anything to do with it, safe and respectable. Suitable for two nice girls. I thought perhaps tomorrow we could move."

I lay back and laughed, from sheer weakness.

"The first thing I'm going to do is treat you to a Pernod. How about that?" Her grin stretched from ear to ear. Like a cat about to lick the cream.

"Whatever a Pernod is I'll love it, in fact for all of tonight I put myself completely in your hands." I leaned forward to see more out of the window. There was a slight drizzle and the damp-ness shone in patches on the peeling buildings. Everything was grey, a dull pink, a depressing shade of dung. Thronged with people who looked much the same. The whole thing matching. It had a strange look to it, the colour of a pigeon, I thought. But something about it affected me strongly. The atmosphere, the shuttered windows and unexpected alleyways, small streets, balconies, signs and fading notices, cafés, bars, bright lights. It made me think of holding hands, forbidden fruits, darkened doorways, getting in at all hours. Romantic. That was right. A fine thread of excitement circled slowly in my stomach, increasing in speed until it formed a tight and unbearable coil. I sat back and looked at Jean. "I hope we're nearly there," I said, "I think I'm getting diarrhoea!"

*　　　*　　　*

I didn't know where Animals was so I took a taxi. "Animals? New place, isn't it? Behind Covent Garden. Lots of weirdos." His eyes flickered from my pale face and parma violet lips to my matching long false fingernails. "Yes. That'll be it."

"I expect so," I said and got in. We moved off, heading towards Hyde Park.

"Mind you, by my recollections they only open at night time."

"I think you're right," I shouted back. "But today they're putting on a fashion show." We slowed down for red lights and he twisted round to look at me.

"You a model then?"

"Oh, no, nothing like that."

"In films?"

I laughed. "No."

"You should be. I could swear I seen you on the telly."

Must be my day, I thought. Sam had rung.

"How're you doin'?"

"I've got a head the size of a house, and one side of my face is completely paralysed."

"Hypochondriac! Have you sewn that suit up yet?"

"It's in the dustbin."

"What! What in hell's name sort of woman are you? A little tear, you throw a good suit away. Move that sexy rump and go get a needle and cotton or I'll come round with a horse whip. Come to think of it, that's one we haven't . . ."

"I'm just going out."

"That's right, you're going out," he imitated. "With me," he added.

"Well, in fact, I'm going to a fashion show at a place called Animals. But I . . ."

"Meet you there. What time?"

"At one, but Sam . . ."

"What now, for Christ's sake? I'm a busy man, get off this fuckin' line, can't you?"

All I hoped was he wouldn't be rude to Rupert.

I needn't have worried. In the end Sam didn't come. We saved a seat for him, Rupert and me, but as the show was about to start he telephoned. The receiver was handed to me in some awe.

"Honey, I can't make it."

"What a shame. I've kept you a seat."

"Worse than that, I'm flying back to Rome right now. Back tomorrow night. Save it for me, huh? And try to be good."

"Of course. I'll see you then."

"Whose clothes are you gawping at? Do you like 'em?"

"Joe Garibaldi's. Oh yes, they're beautiful."

"Right, put him on the line."

"But . . ."

"Sweetheart, I'm just paying that pimp a fortune to design what amounts to five pinafores for one of my movies. Is it too much to ask him to come to the telephone?"

I handed the phone over and escaped back to my seat.

Rupert was all excited. "Darling, what did he say?"

"He can't come, he's flying back to Rome, he'll be back tomorrow and he wanted to speak to Joe Garibaldi," I whispered.

"Here he comes now," he whispered back.

"Who?"

"Joe."

"Oh, is that him?"

A tiny, smiley boy walked carefully towards us. Lots of people started clapping and he acknowledged it by lifting his narrow hands and extending the fingers just like Royalty. He slipped into the empty seat we'd saved for Sam. Close to, I could see he wasn't half as young as I thought. Fortyish, I'd have said. He was wearing tight black jeans and a black polo-neck cashmere sweater, with plimsolls. Like a dancer, there wasn't an ounce of surplus anywhere. He looked at Rupert through his black lashes. "Rupert!" And Rupert looked steadily back. "Joe!" They obviously knew each other very well, or had done at one time.

"Well," he said, turning to me. "And who's the lucky girl today? Mr. Gregory, patron saint and bless his drip-dry soul, has ordered à la carte for you, my dear. The whole collection if madam so desires. His very words."

"Sam's? For me?" I gasped.

"Well, not exactly his very words. You no doubt are as familiar with the gentleman's vocabulary as the rest of us but that was what we took it to mean."

Rupert was beside himself. Well, so was I, but inside me I heard my mother's voice. "There's nothing for nothing, remember!"

"Do you think I should?" I said out loud.

Rupert gave a low moan of anguish, and did his jaw-dropping act. Joe didn't bat an eyelid.

"Look upon it as payment for services rendered, my sweet."

I permitted myself a worldly smile. "Well, put like that I'm delighted to accept."

"Don't do that, Myopia. You made me quite ill for a moment there."

I patted Rupert's hand, the show had started.

I couldn't see a thing. It was pitch black. There was a funny noise going on. A sort of faint hissing like escaping gas. I sniffed. A crowd like that, we could have been dead in minutes. Who'd look after the children? It got louder as if a lot of people were blowing softly into tin whistles, which they must have been because from being very soft it gradually got unbearably shrill and finished off all hell let loose with bloodcurdling screams and bongo drums and fierce trumpet blasts and God knows what else. Spotlights, dozens of them, snapped on out of nowhere, playing round and round on an exquisitely sequinned human artichoke unfolding on the floor. I hoped they'd dusted. Every segment was a different dazzling colour. With each fresh blast of brass one broke away—emerald from top to toe, or purple, deep turquoise, a delicate glinting pink—and danced a solo round the whole. The audience was in raptures. I looked at Joe, expecting satisfaction, but instead he sat tensely on the edge of his seat staring into the heart of the artichoke. A look of horror on his face. As the final girl unfurled, he covered his eyes with his hands. "My God, I can't bear it. The whole effect ruined. She's wearing the wrong tights. Petunia! They should be petunia, petunia. Not, not PUCE!" Unable to bear it any longer, he sprang up and darted away.

"Oh darling, there'll be hell to pay for that," Rupert whispered to me.

"He seems highly strung, I must say."

"We're better off without him if you're choosing what you want. Otherwise he could take awful umbrage over the ones you don't tick. You've got your programme, darling. Here's a pen. Oh, isn't it a thrill!"

"You must help choose, Rupert."

"Thought you'd never ask."

We were both over-excited by the end, pointing and nudging, deciding and ticking. There were about fifty-five outfits, but each came in at least three colourways.

"Oh, it's so you," Rupert kept saying, or "No, rather too," or "You'll die if you don't have that." We agreed on everything except two all-white things.

"I'm not very good with white. It shows the dirt."

"Darling, you must have *something* white. Don't be ridiculous."

"But it would only do for the summer."

"Why?"

"Well, I'd have to be brown to look right."

"I'm ticking them for you. Give me your programme. Where are they? 'Snow Siren'—Ivory crêpe de chine lounging pyjamas, batwing sleeves, stiffened face-framing collar. Crystal beaded loose tie belt and matching skull cap. Perfection! Where's the other? 'Ice Maiden'—White glacé kid ankle-length trench coat, with tailored, matching kid trouser suit, gauntlet gloves, and shallow-brimmed pull-on hat. Divine, darling!"

"Oh dear, I've no notion how to clean white leather. It's dreadfully impractical, Rupert."

"What are you planning to wear it for—washing the car? Do stop being so *hum*drum. It doesn't suit you one bit."

"It's my mother coming out again."

"She," he sighed, "has a lot to answer for."

"Let's do a count-up. How many ticks? Two, four, six—help! Fourteen, I make it."

"Fifteen, you're forgetting the suede dinner dress. Cherry Ripe. You've got to have that, it's the only halter neck."

"Rupert, it's much too many. It looks so greedy."

"I lose all patience! I really do! The whole collection if madam so desires, that's what Sam said."

"Yes, but half the stuff I haven't got anywhere to wear them."

"First rule of life. Never underdress, otherwise you end up sitting at home. Two, look as though you ought to be *somewhere* grand and soon you'll find you are."

"Sounds pretty trite to me."

"Trite but true, dear heart."

"Anyway . . ."

"Anyway. Grab it whilst the going's good. It isn't always there. Well, look at poor me—stranded at Streatham Hill. At my age!"

"Rupert."

He turned a tragic face. "Myopia?"

"Here comes the champagne. Let's drink to an early release."

"And then we'll pin down Joe and present him with our choices." He'd snapped out of it already.

"When do you think I can have them?"

"Depends."

"On what?"

"Well, on whether the glossies have photographed them yet or not. Whether there's another show for clients or another for overseas buyers, lots of things. You can't take them off the models' backs just like that, darling."

"How disappointing. I'm going to Paris on Friday. I was hoping to have something new for that."

"Paris, how divine. For long? Oh, I *shall* miss you."

"Just for the night."

"Oh naughty! With Sam or am I being indiscreet?"

"Yes."

"Which?"

"Indiscreet."

"With another! Oh, my dear. You must tell me who."

"Perhaps I won't."

"Spoilsport! Is he rich too? Oh, what a silly billy question! You don't know."

"Actually I don't. But as far as I know, not."

"In that case, he's rolling. Or famous?"

"No, honestly, Rupert."

"Sure to be!" He held up a hand to silence me. "Let's find Joe."

We found him but he was surrounded.

"Aren't they ghastly, these sycophants?" Rupert murmured.

"Well, at least we're here on business," I replied smugly.

Joe caught sight of us. "Ah, here she comes." He waved us in, people turned to look and make way.

"Well, my sweet, did anything at all catch your imagination? Tell me, which shred would you consider shrugging over your shapely shoulders?"

It was a tricky moment. Rupert came to the rescue.

"There wasn't one that she doesn't simply die to wear. We managed to whittle it down to a mere fifteen—but is it possible, do you suppose, Joe, to go further and duplicate all those in black as well?"

There wasn't a moment's hesitation.

"Black. Black sequins, satin, feathers, silk, black chiffon, cotton, leather, lace—magical, my angel." He snaked a sinewy arm around my waist. "What an utterly awful scamp, she glances at my collection and already predicts what my next will be." Then he shrugged and laughed. "No secret any longer. Let me see what you have chosen."

He cast a practised eye down the list and gave a gurgle of pleasure. "All my favourites. Oh, I couldn't be more pleased.

Each a statement. Pure drama on you—what more could I have hoped for?"

He turned to an astonishingly well-groomed skeleton at his side, whose face, despite its glossy henna'ed hair and bright red mouth, brought "beasts of the field" to my mind. Something about the fierce, wet, rolling eyes and long upper lip.

"Moo, my pet." "Here's your answer. A superlative stroke. What could be more appropriate than to photograph my collection on this gorgeous girl. After all, the clothes will be hers. My latest client. 'Personal Choice'—how about that for the heading?"

Rupert gave me a small shove. "Myopia, this is Moo Moffat-Paw, the editor of *Chic.*"

She held out an icy claw, covered in sparkling rings, and drawled, "Myopia! What a charming name! An invention?"

"Well, I'm actually called . . ."

"I'm certain I'd prefer Myopia! It's a frantically bright idea, Joe. No need to look further. Impossible these days to get Dietrich. Elizabeth Taylor's far too fat. I myself am bored to distraction with black girls, however beautiful. It's about time we launched a new look. Gilbert shall do the face. You have beautiful bones, my dear. Are you Russian?"

"Willesden Welsh," I said quickly. "But I do know about photos." I could feel nervous perspiration exploding out of every pore. "I always look dreadful in photos. Everybody says so."

Everyone stared at me appraisingly. I sucked my stomach in as much as I could.

"Ideal," said the awful Moo. "Not too young, not too old. An age for our readers to identify with."

"Well, Moo, and which photographer?" said Joe.

Rupert pinched me. "Myopia's off to Paris in a day or two, so you'll have to fit around that!"

He was pushy! As if I spent my whole time flying around the world!

"Lopasto's in London. He was working for *Vogue* yesterday. We could try him."

"Or Pustansky?"

"Oh, I don't get on with Germans, not at all," I said. "And they never . . ."

Joe snapped his fingers. "We need womanly warmth, the elusive aura, sensuality."

Moo's liquid eyes began to leak. "Mystery, Mother Earth, and her Modern Wardrobe, no—not Earth Mother—the Mood of the Moment. Garibaldi—clothes for the Gadabout Goddess. Oh, it writes itself, Joe."

"A woman photographer, that's what it needs, Simpatico. Strength. Moo! How about Jan Crump?"

"Frightful creature. Far too butch. Makes everyone look like a lorry driver. Oh no! But you're right. A female." She tapped her teeth with a crimson talon. "Tammy Sprigg. A new girl but too pop. Lawn Adone—too fey, far too."

Joe threw his hands in the air at exactly the same moment as Rupert. They looked at each other and burst out: "Damson!"
Moo looked at me dubiously. "Ought we to?"

"Ideal," they chorused. "Exactly right!"

"Why did that awful woman say 'Ought we to'?"

"Darling?"

"Rupert, you heard."

"Who, Moo? That rhymes: Moo Who! Who Moo!"

"Why? What's she like, this Damson?"

"Divine. A fantastic photographer. Uses animals a lot. Myths and legends stuff. She'll probably pose you being ravaged by a pig or with bees swarming on bare breasts."

"What—in my new clothes? I don't want them spoilt."

"Or I'm not sure she's not passed on from animals."

"To what?"

"Well, you'll soon know on Friday. They're frightfully lucky to get her. She works all over the world now. Must be fate that you're both going to be in Paris on the same day."

"Yes, but I wasn't going till the evening. I'm not sure what who I'm going with will say to travelling separately. I mean, that's half the fun of it, the going together, isn't it?"

"Don't be silly, darling, you can meet him there. You mustn't start having second thoughts now. You'll be famous after Damson's photographed you. Everyone always is. Don't you remember the ones she did of Princess Margaret?"

"Why did Moo say 'Ought we to' then? Because of the animals?"

"Just one dyke distrusting another, my darling. Nothing for you to worry your beautiful head about."

When I got home there was a telegram waiting for me. Unsigned, but I knew who from. "Paris cancelled. Deirdre dead." It was in the early editions of the evening papers. "Saddle Tragedy." "Political Hostess Dies Hunting." "Broken Neck for Earl's Daughter." With snaps of Charles hurrying from the House of Commons looking grief-stricken, when, by what he'd said to me about her, he was probably overjoyed. Oh dear, what with one thing and another! I thought about going to bed with a cup of tea to think about things but there seemed too much of it to take in at one go. So instead I left a note for Françoise and walked up the road to the cinema where I wouldn't have to think at all. It didn't even matter much to me what film was on. It was the getting in there I liked most, the seedy glamour, the scented warm, the comfy seats, sitting in the middle of a crowd and getting lost. It never worried me either if I went in halfway. I always stayed to see it through again anyway. That's where going with other people spoilt it. Always, "Come on, let's go, this is where we came in."

I paid my money and went to the cheapest seats, right in the front row, between two teenagers and an old-age pensioner. Swallowed up by the screen, in the thick of things. A tear as wide as a river flowed from a bright blue eye, the soundtrack was very sweet, lots of strings with a sob in them. The teenagers were kissing like mad, and the old-age pensioner was snoring so I knew it must be a Romantic Love Story. Just my sort of thing, especially if it all went wrong. That's what pleased me most. One of them killed off. Like Deirdre. Except that now thinking about that, which

68

was what I was trying not to do, I wasn't pleased a bit. It had a feel of crisis to it. Things to be decided upon. Resolved. Oh well.

When the interval came, I ignored the calories and bought an ice-cream but after the first mouthful my mind flew to Friday's photographs and to wondering whether I'd fit into the clothes or not. So I stopped eating and put the almost full tub carefully under my seat. The old-age pensioner had woken up and was watching. I stood up and headed for the Ladies'. When I came back he was licking his fingers, the empty tub rolling by his feet. I nodded and smiled.

"Nice stuff, ice-cream."

"What?"

"I say, it's very nice, isn't it?"

He stared at me as if I wasn't all there.

"Ice-cream, the taste. But unfortunately fattening."

He was terribly thin. I was still blushing when the lights went down.

I walked home slowly, stopping now and then to look in shop windows. The delicatessen had trapped a fly for the night in a large cheesecake. The upholsterer's was full of nude sofas, calico coloured, waiting to be loose-covered in an assortment of fabrics, customer's own choice. The TV shop had all its tellys on with the sound switched off. Several people stood on the pavement in front of the flickering screens, lip-reading and laughing at the jokes.

I crossed the road. The nice old-fashioned chemist's had had a face-lift, all its frontage ripped out and replaced by sheet glass, top to bottom. Inside they had a fitted carpet. One half of the window was devoted to cosmetics, seductive photos of sullen girls with sly eyes. The other presented the alternatives. Hot-water bottles, laxatives, weighing scales and dietary aids.

Life in the launderette was in full swing. Oh, I would have given my eye teeth for such a meeting place in my bedsitter days! Taking your pick as you're packing in your undies, smouldering away all through the second wash, exchanging shy smiles at the dry-spinning stage. Afterwards a nice walk home, dropping in for a drink in the pub on the way. Not, I suppose, that I would really have found it so nice then. After all, my sights had been set on higher things—night clubs, sports cars, meeting men with cultivated tastes like that.

The chandelier shop was adrip with diamond lights. I'd been passing the place for years, identical arrangements, nothing ever changed. How the hell did they keep going without selling, unless it was just a front for shadier dealings? I had a soft spot for chandeliers, very big ones the size of a small room. Nothing in it but that—if you could spare the space. With electric fans to keep it on the tinkle. And a feather duster tied to a broom handle for reaching the top.

My toes were beginning to ache, well it was ages since I'd eaten. I could do with a drink, I thought, as I reached the top of my street. And a steak and two sliced tomatoes icy cold from the fridge, then getting into bed with a bottle of wine and a book. Three cigarettes left, I worked it out, from my ten-a-day discipline. Not bad going. I smiled at the comfortable hours ahead. A passing neighbour, whom I'd never spoken to, smiled back. I looked at my watch, eight o'clock, time to catch the girls before they fell asleep.

Paul was a marvel at precision parking. His car, just so, sat evenly cheek to kerb, mine in urgent need of a wash, one wheel on the pavement, sprawled wantonly behind it.

Françoise rushed to the door as I turned the key.

"Your 'usband he wait hours." She rolled her eyes and pointed to my room. My heart lurched, but I said calmly, "I'll say good night to the children first."

The television was on in my room, swivelled round so that it faced my bed.

"You can go out if you like, Françoise. I'm staying in tonight," I said.

"Oh yippee. I go right now."

Paul's eyelids flickered as she slammed the front door behind her. He was lying fast asleep across my bed, hands folded neatly like a knife and fork on his long flat stomach. Upstairs, our daughters, also asleep, looked exactly the same. I'd kissed them both, but they hadn't stirred. I wouldn't risk it with him. It was three years since I'd kissed him last. And then, without any heart in it. More hate than heart. Which as far as the kissing went and what came after was all to the good. But it had made bed a violent greedy playground. Full of guilt on his side, and seething suspicion on mine, softened only by the pillows. Nowadays with sexual indifference set like cement between us it was all very hard to recall. But he had a big one. On that my memory served me well. A mighty sword! The size to confound King Arthur! John Thomas the Terrible. Perhaps that's why he'd needed others as well as me. To help empty the outsize tank. An unpaid team of pumpers.

I laughed out loud, mirth had replaced misery, and he woke immediately. Irritable like a child.

"What's there to grin about? I nodded off. You were out," he added accusingly.

"Yes." I was about to explain but why the hell? "Yes, I was out. It's true."

He lit a cigarette, coughed and ran his fingers through his hair.

"Ooh," I said, "it's starting to recede."

"Don't be cruel."

"It happens to everyone. I'm sure mine is too."

He rubbed his eyes and yawned. "God, I feel awful."

"Go and have a wash. That will wake you up."

"I'll have a drink instead. What have you got?"

"Everything."

"Jack Daniel's?"

"No, I haven't got that."

"Glenfiddich?"

"No."

"Just whisky, any will do," he said wearily. "Lots of ice. I assume that's not asking the impossible."

"It's foolish to assume anything with children in the house," I said annoyingly, as I went out. Hell, I thought, it ought to be possible to be more pleasant than this.

71

I handed him the brimming glass, ice clinking invitingly, and managed to spill some on his trouser leg.

"There. Take a swig of that." Perfectly pleasantly.

He mopped his wet leg with a pristine handkerchief.

"It's remarkable how accurately you combine the sailor's barmaid jargon with the expected degree of slap-happy service."

All right then. Right. "I think I'll light up," I said. "Now where are my fags?"

"Would you care for one of mine?" He leaned forward over-politely and snapped open his Asprey's gold case.

"What? Gauloises?" I said coarsely. "Give shocking halitosis. Where I was last week a man emptied the whole bar with his bad breath. He was smoking Gauloises. No, I'll stick to my own. Less anti-social."

We both of us stared somewhere over the other's head. He cleared his throat and coughed, again.

I looked at him. He swallowed hard.

"Is something wrong? You're clearly nervous."

He sighed heavily and said sarcastically, "Since when has the need to expectorate indicated neuritis?"

"Oh. Well, you can spit in the ashtray if you want to."

Another silence. Then, "Is it deliberately done to irritate?"

"What, Paul?"

"This assumed vulgarity. Is it for my benefit alone?"

I thought for a moment. "You've twigged it. Yes, I think it is. And your offensive pomposity. Is that for mine?"

"Possibly so. I apologise."

"That's all right. Don't apologise. Just say sorry. Your glass is empty. Would you like another?" Whenever was he going?

"Sorry. Please. I'd love a second."

We both spoke as I was pouring.

"What . . ."

"What . . ."

"Sorry, you go."

"No, you, mine's not important."

"Well, in that case, I was wondering what your plans for dinner were."

"Who, mine?"

"There wouldn't, unless my eyes deceive me, appear to be another person present."

"You're at it again."

"So I am."

"It's a bad habit. Is that how you speak to everyone now?"

"I need you to puncture me. I always have."

Whatever was he working up to?

"No plans, really. Except an early night. Yes, you're better deflated."

"I hadn't meant to make it late myself. I just have several matters to discuss. Best done over dinner. Where would you like to go?"

"Would have to be near. I've just given Françoise the night off."

"Near or far, what difference does it make? It's highly improbable that you'll be able to perceive the house from your plate or for that matter hear piteous infant screams, should they occur above the chomping of surrounding Chelsea jaws."

"Are you pleased with that?"

"Modesty prevails," but he allowed himself a small smile.

I laughed. "Come on then. But I'd still prefer nearer. If the house burns down, it'll look better if I can say I was out posting a letter."

We were in bed by the time Françoise returned. I heard her switching the lights off as she went up the stairs, listened to the gasping lavatory cistern, and in the silence that followed, looked at the illuminated hands of my alarm. Paul lay fast asleep in my arms. Half past twelve. We'd been there exactly an hour. He was still in me, slippery and warm, as soft now as the tongue in my mouth. Yes, he was still there. His cheek lay on my left breast, the happy damp nipple resting between his open lips. Like a baby, fallen asleep in mid-feed. I smiled in the dark. The sort of smile that model mothers do when they're selling washing powder on the television. Indulgent, understanding, ever-loving and very kind. Which was exactly how I felt. Oh, I wouldn't have at one time, even so much as up to a year ago. But now I had more than one egg in my basket. That's what made the difference. I stirred slightly and stroked his head. He clamped his lips together and started sucking, his hand on my other breast, slowly tightening, relaxing, then tightening again. No. I would have been cold and resentful at even the sign of an approach. Well, he'd tried before and I had been exactly that. I'd thought, "Being made use of, after all that's happened, he still wants to make use of me." But tonight it had happened quite naturally. Without any fuss. Truth was we'd made use of each other. Equals. He'd caught my eye, over the carré d'agneau, but in fact had been consciously courting me all through the avocados. He'd caught it and wouldn't let go.

"It says everything, that look," I said at last.

"What does it say?"

"It says animal lust."

"Oh, I'd put it more daintily than that."

"There's no need. I can read."

I still hadn't made up my mind by then.

"You're trying to seduce me."

"Because you're so seductive."

"Am I?" I said. "I'm not trying a bit."

But by the end of the crême brulée, I'd decided, as well he knew. I looked round the restaurant, everyone was at it, all couples holding hands, bending heads together, whispering. Thrumming with love. Very catching. Our legs lay lightly touching underneath the long tablecloth. Mine were stretched out and crossed at the ankles. His were either side of them, tightening all the time.

"Do you do it the same?" I said. "Or have you learnt lots of new tricks?"

"Brandy, darling?"

"I've learnt some. You'll have to tell me after if you see a difference."

"Hardly romantic."

"Oh, I don't like that any more. Sighing and stuff. People only do that when they can't think of what to say. It's a question of age. It's normal to be inarticulate when you're young. But by our age you can get closer with words."

"Though not necessarily comparisons." He took my hand and kissed it. "This feels the same."

"There you are, that's a comparison." I was hot and getting bothered down below, sipping my brandy. I sat on my chair, my insides lurching around impatiently. For two pins I'd have stripped everything off there and then. Stood up, stretched over and stuffed both breasts in his mouth at once. Pinned him down with a naked knee, unzipped him quick and yanked it out . . .

"Oh dear," I said in the end.

He squeezed my fingers. "Anything up?"

"I've got a feeling I'm oozing. Preparatory lubrication. Quite beyond my control, my genitals are one jump ahead."

"How extraordinary. So are mine. Slip your shoe off quickly, you can feel it with your foot."

"That's all very well," I said with some concern. "But I just hope I haven't leaked through my dress. Don't laugh. They're very funny at the dry cleaner's. They won't take stains they don't understand."

Paul. I lay there cuddling him, thinking fondly of Sam and Charles. It's easy to love men, all of them, when one is asleep in your arms. It's when you haven't got any that you hate them. I'm like a pond, I thought, with sun shining or rain falling, grey mists or just dark blackness and these are things which happen to change my surface. But at the bottom, it's solid, solid earth which is never affected at all. A fish pond. These men, my children, they were fish who happened to be swimming through me. One day I'd be empty, but not until I dried up altogether.

He woke suddenly, bathed in an unexpected fine sweat. I put a low light on at the side of the bed and he buried his face in my shoulder.

"Paul."

75

"I'm boiling. There's no air."

I threw the bedclothes back and in the sudden movement I lost him. He'd slipped out leaving a purring, sticky space. His long body glistened palely all over.

"You're all of a sweat. It's pouring off."

I slipped a finger underneath his arm, then sniffed it.

"It's got a lovely smell. Very fresh. Like young cats."

He squeezed me. "How do you feel?"

"Rather philosophical. And fanciful. I think I've gone a bit funny."

"A cup of coffee?"

"That might pull me round."

"I'll do it, shall I?"

"Everything's in the same place. Can you remember?"

I sat up and lit a cigarette. How friendly it was! Friendlier than for years. Just because I'd given in—gracefully—or rather, grabbed what I'd wanted. But when he came back he said, "We haven't talked yet."

"So we haven't."

He didn't look at me. "I'm thinking of getting married again."

The coffee slid smoothly down my throat, just the right amount of milk in it. "When?"

"Next Monday morning. Will you be free? I thought it would be nice if you brought the girls."

Now he did look at me, anxiously, like a child who's not quite certain how the adult will react.

"Is she expecting?"

"Good Lord, no. Nothing like that. I've made it quite clear I don't want any more!"

"Have you known her long?" All the time I was asking I was trying to think how I felt. Wise like a Mother Superior. Being begged for a blessing. Very heady, ego-boosting. They had some perks in their business, those nuns.

"Long enough."

"And how long is that?" I was in fear of overdoing it. Too much concern and knowingness.

"About three weeks."

"Ah," I said, all understanding. "Love at first sight."

He kissed my lips, took the coffee cup from my hands, put it on the floor and held me tightly. "Will you come?"

"Well now," I said in a businesslike way. "Monday, I can't because of Brighton."

"How is the old bastard?"

"Getting older," briefly, "but the girls could. I can get them ready before I go. They will have broken up for Easter."

"That's the other thing. I'd thought of flying off somewhere and taking them too."

"What? On your honeymoon?"

"It'll kill two birds with one stone. I've been promising them a holiday for ages. I'd thought of Greece."

"What does she say?"

"Oh, she's not politically minded."

"About the girls coming."

"She'll love the idea. She's seen them from a distance and adores them already. She's mad about the house too," he added.

"Is she? Are you thinking of moving in?"

"Why? Do you feel like a change?"

"I hadn't. But you never know. Anything could happen, couldn't it?"

He kissed me again. "That's what I admire about you. Your attitude to life."

Next morning with the sun streaming through every window and the house inside humming with hilarious excitement, I wondered exactly what my attitude to life was. That was the trouble. I didn't have one. Just an awful eagerness to please.

Françoise was on the phone to France. I was paying her fare and she was going home for a fortnight. On Monday. Everything was happening on Monday.

"Will we be bridesmaids? Shall we have special dresses? And carry flowers? Is she pretty, Daddy's wife? I'm going to call her Mummy."

We got to the school just as Harriet's teacher was walking in.

"Good morning, Harriet," I heard her say stiffly.

"My daddy is getting married on Monday. I'm going to be his bridesmaid."

"Are you indeed? And where is your Good morning?"

Old misery!

I bought all the papers on the way back to read about Charles. Now an eligible widower, of course. I was just settling down to it when he rang. I couldn't think what to say.

"I was just reading your name. Isn't that funny?"

"You got my telegram."

"I did. How are you feeling?"

"I must see you."

"Of course. I'm here."

"This evening?"

Sam was back by then. "No, I'm afraid not tonight."

"Surely you can." He was cross.

"No, I don't see how. It's a bit short notice. Sorry."

"Tomorrow then."

"Oh dear, I shall probably be in Paris after all, tomorrow. You see, I'm doing sort of fashion shots . . ."

"Fashion shots?"

"Yes, for *Chic* magazine."

"Really, darling. I'd rather you didn't. The whole situation has changed now, don't you see? You'll have to start being a little more responsible for your actions. You must remember I'm in the public eye."

Everything was on roller skates, flashing by, going far fast.

"They'll be very respectable, honestly. Not in the nude or anything like that. She's a marvellous photographer." I thought of the animals and stuff. "She's done Princess Margaret."

"What time will you be back?"

"It depends how long it all takes."

"Here's a number to ring. I'll expect to hear from you at about five o'clock tomorrow to say which plane you're catching."

"All right. But Charles, how are you feeling?"

"I'll talk to you tomorrow. But . . ."

"Yes?"

"I'll tell you something. I need you very much."

Oh dear. Would I let him down? I walked round the house, opening the windows. I felt suffocated. In the children's room, I started sorting through their clothes. "Go to Harrods," Paul had said, "for anything they'll need. Put it on my account." Kneeling on the floor I began a list. Sandals, swimsuits, knickers, vests. No, not vests, not in Greece. I crossed vests out. Summer nighties, sleeveless towelling beach robes. Do as dressing-gowns when they got back. New toothbrushes. Who would see to it they cleaned their teeth? Will they be all right? Will you be? you mean. Two weeks alone. I lay flat on the floor and looked at the ceiling. It had looked wonderful when it was done. Bright red. Fiesta, that's what they called it on the colour chart. I'd have liked it all through the house. Now it looked tired and old as if all the life blood had been drained away. The fiesta had flopped. It needed doing up, the house, needed licking with soft brushes and coaxing with hot coats of colour. That's what I could do, get the decorators in. I sat up, then slid back again. But not if I wasn't going to stay. I wouldn't mind a move, the more I thought about it the more I could see that I wouldn't mind. And this time wherever I went I could have whatever colours I wanted. All black or gold or silver. An emerald green from top to bottom. Like my sequinned dress from Garibaldi. God, I promised to ring Moo Moffat-Paw.

I made a cup of tea and took it to the phone. "*Chic?* Miss Moffat-Paw, please. Oh sorry, Mrs." How could she be Mrs. if Rupert said she was a lesbian?

"Myopia? Well, all set for the morning, my dear?"

"There's been a slight alteration. In actual fact, I won't now be going to Paris."

She screamed so loudly that I had to hold the telephone right away from my ear. When I put it back she was still gurgling. It sounded like a death rattle. What an hysterical creature she was!

"Just a minute, I haven't finished." I spoke calmly as if to one of the children. "I mean to say that I am still free to go but I'd like to have it clarified as to who will be making all arrangements and meeting the expenses." I enjoyed saying it. Very hard and businesslike.

She screamed again. A ghoulish attempt at girlishness. What a difficult woman to live with!

"My dear. These are minor matters. My minions will deal with those. The important thing is that you're free, to go to Paris of course, I mean. We have four glorious colour pages depending on you. Now, what time today will you be coming in? I'd like to try everything on and choose which outfits we'll take."

I hadn't thought of it, but of course she'd be coming too.

"This afternoon?"

"Around three. You know where we are, off Berkeley Square. By the way, what shoe size are you? Not that necessarily we'll be going down that far, knowing Damson, she's rather keen on close-ups, but it's best to play safe."

"I'm size four."

"What a tiny toes! This afternoon then. Don't forget your passport. We need that to arrange francs. Apart from that, you may take your choice. Either be paid a normal modelling fee or, if we use your name and do it as a personality piece as we've discussed, be paid nothing at all."

"I'll think about it, can I?"

"Of course, though if you're wise, you'll choose the latter. Such a lovely name to see in print 'Myopia'."

We sat in the garden discussing it, Rupert and me. He'd rung the doorbell as I'd put down the phone.

"Oh, how nice. Just who I was hoping to see."

"You don't mind me dropping in? A terrible cheek, I know, without phoning first. But I just happened to be passing in a taxi!"

We both knew that he'd taken the tube specially from Streatham on the off-chance that I'd be in, but it made no odds.

"I'm at such a loose end, Myopia. It's awful."

"Oh dear, let's go outside and sit down, you can tell me all about it."

He plopped into a blue and white striped deckchair. He was wearing white trousers and an open-necked white shirt, and around his neck he'd knotted the sleeves of his sweater, the colour of forget-me-nots. I smiled because he looked so perfect, like an illustration in a women's magazine. The handsome hero. Or one of those men in knitting pattern books.

"Smile, Rupert."

He tried. He opened his sculptured mouth, and pulled his lips back to show the stunning teeth. "You should be a model, you'd be very good at that."

He let his mouth relax, back into its about-to-cry look, and shook his head so that one blond lock fell over his eyes.

"I've tried. I've been with Boy's Agency for nearly two years, but they never get me anything. Now I'm getting too old, that's the trouble; when they took me on I still looked about seventeen."

"How old are you?"

"Twenty-six. Isn't it appalling? There seems to be nothing left now. Nothing to look forward to."

"What? At twenty-six? Don't be silly. Looking like you do?"

"That's all I've got though. I've never had anything else. I used to want to be an actor. I did a year at drama school, but in the end they told me it was a waste of their time and mine."

"But people can be late developers. Anyway, there are lots of jobs you could do. Where it wouldn't depend on your looks, Rupert."

"What? Like what?"

"Well, I always think if the worst came to the worst I'd be a lavatory attendant. They take anyone for that. You don't need qualifications. But I think you have to be over eighteen. Perhaps it's twenty-one. It could be very nice because you have a little room for making tea and there'd be a regular clientele and all you'd have to do is to train yourself to breathe through your mouth. So as not to be able to smell anything. I've trained myself already from changing babies' nappies. It's the first thing all mothers learn. You could say you were a civil servant, if people asked."

"Oh, you are funny, Myopia. It's a tonic just to be with you."

"You think I'm joking, but I'm not at all."

He stretched his legs, lay back and closed his eyes.

"This sun. Oh, it makes me die to be on a beach. Doesn't it you?"

I stared up through the branches of a tree. New spring leaves patterned the sky like a paper doily. "It would be nice." I imagined a smooth sea, crinkled at the edges like a lettuce leaf, sucking on fine bleached sand. Shining like a strip of sheet metal, disappearing into a distant sun-bright silver sky. And everywhere the smell of bronzing oils and melting ice-cream. Transistors crooning Latin love songs. Lots of bouncing going on, beach balls, babies, big-breasted women and boys with barely covered buttocks. "I like lively beaches best," I said, "with everyone sandwiched in like sardines."

"Oh, so do I."

"Do you? I somehow thought you'd prefer secluded spots. A private beach with a motor launch and a waiter in a white coat serving chilled champagne."

"I've done all that. But if you don't like who you're with it's no fun at all."

*　　　*　　　*

No. That's what I kept telling Jean but she wouldn't have it. "I don't want a repeat of Paris, Jean," I'd said.

"What do you mean? We had a super time!"

"Me saddled with the sugar daddies and you getting off with good-looking gigolos."

She sighed. "They were marvellous at making love."

"Of course they were. The tools of the trade."

"We ended up staying at the Georges Cinq."

"With me as bait. Me paying the price. That old man there was disgusting, what's more what he did was very dangerous. Sticking that strip lighting in. He could have killed me."

"It didn't sound very nice when you said."

"It's not how I'd thought of losing my virginity, not by neon."

"Mine was by moonlight. We left the window wide open. I could see the stars over his shoulder."

"Yes, and that's another thing. On my new red towel, why couldn't you have used your own?"

"What, my white one? I wouldn't have dared. Mummy would have guessed the worst If I'd brought it home all bloody."

"Well, now we're experienced women we must learn to pick and choose this holiday."

We were on the plane to Italy. I'd saved for the student trip by working the summer at the local Odeon. Usherette and ice-cream girl. Spot-lit at every interval. I'd sold 420 choc bars, 310 vanilla tubs, smuggled my parents in twice without paying and seen Walt Disney's *The Living Desert* eighteen times from start to finish. My neck was still aching from carrying the tray. While Jean had been fishing in Scotland with her father.

We sucked on the barley sugar we'd been given for take-off. "Was it nice in Scotland?" I thought of husky young lairds in shooting brakes, wearing hacking jackets and checked Viyella shirts. Strong like Heathcliff, striding over the heather in stone-coloured cavalry twills, and canary yellow socks.

"Not a sausage. Nothing in sight. I could have done with a couple of kilts and a strong wind I can tell you."

"What, no men at all?"

"Only Daddy's unutterably dreary friends. Chartered accountants and quantity surveyors. That sort of thing. With their wives. They used to send me to bed after dinner, can you imagine! I'd have died of boredom but I found this book. I've brought it. It's filthy. *The Life and Loves of Frank Harris.* Just our cup of tea."

We spent the rest of the journey sussing out the others and came to the same conclusion. No competition amongst the girls and nothing to write home about in the boys. Really nothing, but we let them carry our cases. Two Japanese students from Oxford were the most attentive. They both wore grey flannels, white stiff-collared shirts and serge blazers with badges on the breast pockets, which looked exactly the same as our Co-op Darts Team. My father had one.

"I didn't know they let Chinks into Oxford," I whispered to Jean. "Is it a new thing?"

"They're Japs, not Chinks. Look at what their cameras cost. Made of money."

Hers was short and fat with slicked back shiny hair which smelt of Lily of the Valley. Mine was short too, but made from pipe cleaners, his wrists were the width of my thumb. I wondered what he had in his trousers. Something the size of a cotton thread I supposed. "I wish they'd stop smiling. We haven't seen their eyes yet. Not once." But she would keep encouraging them, Jean.

"It's not as if our cases were even heavy." We were in our hotel room, unpacking.

"Honestly, you can't see further than your own nose."

She unzipped her skirt and put on a pair of dangerously short pink cotton shorts.

"Jean!" I said horrified. "You're not wearing those."

"Why not?"

"They're shorter than your knickers! I can see them at the back."

"Can you? I'll take my knickers off then. There, how's that?"

"All right. If you don't bend over." But I still had my doubts. "It's a good job your pubic hair isn't any longer. Otherwise wearing those you'd have to plait it up and sellotape it to your stomach or something."

"I could just shave it off."

"You have to be careful. You can get a nasty rash with a razor. I've tried it."

"What's it look like?"

"Very naked. Like a big baby with a nappy rash."

"Better with a bit of fur."

"The point is they could come in useful if we wanted to go somewhere ritzy. That's what I'm thinking of."

"Those shorts?"

"The Japs. Places where they won't serve girls on their own. Where we couldn't afford to go anyway. They're loaded those two."

"But I'd like someone to fall in love with this time."

"Yes, but not stuck on the beach with this lot all the time. You'd like to go in a speedboat, wouldn't you? Laze about on a yacht? Sit on the sun terrace of a grand hotel? Swim in their pool and get dressed up for a night club?"

"Well . . ."

"Well, all that means men with money. Leave it all to me. I understand how these things work."

"You do," I said. "It's easy to see your father's an accountant, I must say."

She came over and gave me a squeeze.

"Look, this is our holiday. Don't let's quarrel. We've got ten days. Long enough to do it all. Have a fling and fall in love. Both of us, I promise."

* * *

"What about going then? The two of us, Rupert? Next week?"

He lay in his deckchair, eyes shut, lashes as long as bootlaces. Like a beautiful corpse. "Are you dead?" I asked after a while. "Did you hear me?"

The tears slid out like tadpoles, separately formed yet still joined together. Leaving a shiny transparent path, they travelled his cheeks and melted into his mouth. I just sat forward and stared. I was fascinated to see if his nose would start running and spoil things. It wasn't till I looked at his hands, knotted together, nails digging in, that I knew he must be making a big effort to control himself. I went indoors and came back with a brandy.

"Nice big brandy," I said. "And a tea towel to mop up with. You can blow in it, I shan't mind. I haven't got a hanky."

That did it. He started to laugh and within seconds was sobbing, shaking all over and shuddering to catch his breath. It's best to let go when things get beyond you, the only way in the end to keep your balance. I lit a cigarette and wandered a few steps to see how my daffodils were doing. When the worst was over, I came back. He cleared his throat, a congested sound like the gear box of a car in need of a service.

"I feel so bad . . ."

"No, you don't. You feel much better now."

"In front of you . . ."

"Oh me! Oh, I'd far rather see a scar than a stiff upper lip. Go on, have a sip of brandy."

He blew his nose in the tea towel, one I'd bought with the children in Carnaby Street. It was printed with a map of London Underground. "At a rough guess, I'd say you've just blown your nose in Leicester Square Station."

He didn't look, just kept his finger and thumb squeezed on the spot.

"I'd say more like Baker Street, myself." He spread it out. "Too late to change your mind. Both wrong. Chancery Lane!"

"Well, what about it? Don't start looking sad again."

"What would it cost? I can't . . ."

"Cost? Who cares? I've got some money. We can go on that. No need to do it in high style. All we want is a bit of brown on our bodies, isn't it? Just what you need, it'll buck you up no end."

"But it isn't right, you paying."

"Why not? It's only luck that at this moment I have something in the bank and you haven't. Next year or even next month, it could be the other way around, couldn't it? And then I can come and lean on you. If you'll let me. I never worry too much about money—there's always some way out."

"I never used to either, but now I've begun to worry about everything. I've developed into a manic depressive."

"Has the doctor given you pills?"

"Yes, but I've run out. I should go back for more."

"Don't do that. See how you feel after our holiday."

"All right then. You've talked me into it. We can sit on a beach and sort out my future."

"That's it! And while we're at it, we can sort out mine too."

I persuaded Rupert, since he seemed so persuadable, to come with me to Chic House. He could see I was having second thoughts without me saying. That's what he said. I wasn't at all, in fact. I was quite looking forward to it, but it was still nice to have his moral support. I only had one big nagging worry. One that

Rupert might have found it hard to understand. The stretch marks on my stomach. They'd come with Harriet and had got even worse after Fanny. We used to compare, other mothers and me, in the post-natal clinic. Mine were always the worst. "Can't be helped," the sister had said briskly, "mere battle scars, with baby as bonus. Count yourself lucky they're not all over your breasts too." But I was obsessive about them then. Until Sam. "Christ almighty," he'd thundered. "What the hell are those? Lace curtains or a shoal of fish?" Then he'd seen my face. "C'mon, honey. We can get round it. Tomorrow you go buy a corset and wear it in bed." That relaxed me.

Not that they'd show in Joe's clothes, it was just that walking into *Chic*, that temple of perfection, I felt a fraud knowing they were there! The foyer was covered with big blow-ups of past copies. Centre spreads of beautiful girls in bikinis posing amongst bewildered peasants, nocturnal shots of flimsy nighties, floating through moonlit forests, a detailed study of fine-pored skin with a butterfly about to settle. The close-up of satin high-heeled shoes, arranged carefully amongst a pile of cripples' crutches.

"That's not in the best of taste is it?" I pointed.

Rupert glanced briefly. "Herman Bosch. He always does things like that. Goldfish bowls full of glass eyes to show off false eyelashes. Frilly bridal suspenders on skeletons. He's said he won't work for *Chic* again, though."

"Why not?"

"They refused to print his last lot of photos. The latest handbag by Dior. He'd shot it half-open but he'd filled it full of dentures!"

The commissionaire stared frostily as I started to laugh. Rupert pressed the lift button, it arrived immediately and we went up to the fourth floor. We were exactly on time.

The first thing that hit me was the smell. You could drown in it, like the perfume counter of an expensive store, like a room full of wealthy women, like a very high-class hairdresser's. Seducing you. A devastating bank of flowers faced us as we left the lift. I squeezed a petal as we passed to see if they were real. The carpet was as thick as double cream, peach. The walls were a sweet warm apricot.

Giant free-standing lamps cast the sort of amber glow you get when children put a lighted torch in their mouth and shine it through their cheek. Seated against the wall were six or seven ravishing models, their specimen books by their side, each a perfect example of their type. One in sawn-off jeans and faded tee-shirt, a carefully painted spattering of freckles on her sunburnt face. Another aloof and olive-skinned. Two talking together in pillbox hats and platform soles. And next to them a milky blonde with mile-long legs and waist-length hair. All of them waiting, cross-fingered, for work. How horrible to be hanging on the whim of the Moo Moffat-Paws of the world. A receptionist, with the best ironed blouse I'd ever seen, looked up and smiled. When she spoke it sounded as if she'd just eaten a plate of hot buttered mushrooms and enjoyed them very much.

"Can I help you?"

I scooped up all the charm I could summon from my blood-stream and smiled back. Rupert answered and we were directed on our way. "Here we are, darling." He knocked on the door. "The inner sanctum."

"Step inside," called a voice from within.

"Said the spider to the fly," Rupert whispered to me.

It was just like walking into a flock of sheep. There was so much mirror set at adjacent angles, with Moo standing in them all. She had on a particularly unfortunate curly woollen thing, a cross between cream and fleecy grey. From its high-collared neck, her mournful head emerged as if all set for the slaughter. The upper lip looked even longer than I remembered; when it began to quiver I half expected a bleat.

"My God," she moaned, "it's been an absolute bitch of a morning! Myopia, my dear, you look exquisite, do sit down. Rupert! Just the boy! I've had such trouble with Damson. Tell me, how well do you know her?"

I took the cigarette she offered, allowed her to light it and looked around the room. A portion of it was partitioned off into a large walk-in wardrobe; through the open door I could see piles of shoes, handbags, hats. On a shelf, a glamorous paraphernalia of bracelets, beaded necklaces, space-age sunglasses, bottles of perfume and a huge conglomeration of cosmetics. And, hanging amongst masses of others, my clothes from Garibaldi. It was like looking in a sweet-shop window when you've already decided what to choose. You can taste it before it even touches your tongue. I could feel on my skin the peach bloom of soft suede, silk slithering like cold jelly, the fine imprint of hand-made lace. I sat there, glowing greedily, sheer self-indulgence like the sumptuous houri of a Turkish potentate. Or for that matter some curious clothes fetishist. The thought had not occurred before.

"Very well. I got to know her when I lived with Joe."

So he had lived with Joe!

"Of course. And do you get on together?"

"Perfectly I'd say. Once you understand her there's no problem."

"This morning I was tempted to cancel the whole operation. I spoke to her on the telephone, agreed to pay the fortune she's demanding, received her assurance that the photographs would be within reason. I mean, I can't print all that animal stuff. She said she quite understood but she'd prefer not to have me on the session! I'd send an assistant but unless she knows them it's quite on the cards she'd bar them entry too. It's ludicrous. Someone must take care of the clothes. Be responsible for the accessories. Organise everything."

"What about Gilbert? Isn't he going to do Myopia's face?"

"That's another thing. She says his work is too hard. She's discovered a superb theatrical make-up man who's worked for years in the ballet and demands to use him. But it occurs to me, Rupert dear, that you might be the ideal person. Would you be free to go with Myopia tomorrow?"

"All expenses and a stylist's fee?"

"Naturally."

"I couldn't think of anything nicer."

"Oh, nor could I," I said.

For the first time since our arrival Moo smiled, a frightening affair involving yards and yards of pale pink satin gum. I never thought to describe anyone as plain but with her it was the only adjective to use, coupled with the terrifying intensity, it made my eyes water just watching her. She stabbed a finger in my direction.

"Well, Myopia, dear, shall we start? I can't tell you, my dears, now everything's settled I'm quite limp with relief."

We were there over two hours. Rupert was amazing.

"Invaluable," Moo kept crying. "Absolutely inspired."

Joe Garibaldi would have gone mad as white was spiced with ginger, dove grey with petrol blue, pale lemon put with brilliant pink. All done by adding, switching, subtracting tiny handbags, outsize earrings, strings of beads, a well-placed brooch, a different hat.

"Won't Joe mind?" I said.

"Mind what, darling?"

'Well, that his outfits won't be photographed strictly as he presented them himself?"

"Good heavens no. Fashion photographs, especially in colour, are never meant to look like life. Larger than life, yes. They should be fantasy. That's why we're asking Damson to do these. To create a mood."

"Oh dear," I said. "Am I the best person to use? I can look awfully ordinary."

"You, never, and certainly not with the make-up her man will do. If we know Damson that will be the exact opposite of ordinary."

"You'll keep an eye on that though, Rupert," Moo said anxiously.

"We'll shoot it lots of ways," he assured her.

"How about my hair? Should I wash it tonight or in the morning? It can go very frizzy if I leave it till the last minute."

They both laughed and looked at each other.

"There'll be a hairdresser," Rupert soothed. "And at least a dozen divine wigs in every colour, I shouldn't be surprised."

"I shan't know myself by the end."

"Myopia," Moo took my hand and set my flesh goose-pimpling. "It will be the new you. Damson will do her damnedest to see to that."

By the time I got home my period had started. Bloody blood! It hadn't been due for another two days. Brought on by excitement I shouldn't wonder.

Sam hadn't been able to believe it. He'd pulled me on to his knee and put a friendly hand between my thighs.

"Jumpin' Jesus! What the hell have you got in there? A loaf of bread or a leg of lamb?"

"That's my sanitary towel," I'd said with as much dignity as I could. And primly put his hand away. I'd only known him a few weeks then.

"But it's as big as a fuckin' bolster! You mean to tell me that every month you're walking round with that in your pants! Christ!"

"I like them large. I find it a comfort."

"But honey, those went out with the ark. Haven't you heard of internals?"

"I've tried Tampax, but I don't get on with them at all. It's like putting a white mouse in with his tail hanging out. A girl I knew mislaid one once. She forgot it was there, and went to bed with somebody and it got pushed up further and then went completely astray. She had to go to hospital in the end to have it surgically removed. They kept her there a week with complications."

"Didn't she try blowing her nose or was she too stupid?"

"Anyway," I went on, "since I've had the coil fitted it seems like overloading to use Tampax too. They give me backache, with the congestion."

"Aw, my baby! I love you and your little jam rags! You wear 'em all you want. Come on here to Daddy. I'm going to give my sugar an extra squeeze 'cos she's on the blob."

He took a special delight in my periods, Sam. More than any

man I'd met and certainly much more than me. It didn't put him off at all.

"Come quick," I'd shouted to my mother.

She'd run up the stairs two at a time.

"I'm bleeding," I said and started to cry. Ten I was. The first in my class.

"You're menstruating," my mother had said matter of factly. "Only two things to avoid. Head colds and hot baths. Remember that and you'll be all right. Now shush, you don't want your father to find out, do you?"

"This is something my mother always warned me against. She said on no account to do it."

Sam lay back in the bath drinking pink champagne. He wasn't listening. "Run some more hot, honey."

"We can't have any more, it'll slop all over the sides."

"Cuddle me. I'm getting cold. But don't for Christ's sake lose my cock."

I was sitting on it, facing him, knees squashed in each side of his thighs.

"It's a terrible squeeze, Sam, in here."

"Love it."

"It's not as if you're a normal size man, they should build special ones."

"C'mon, quit talking. I'm shrinking."

He let his glass roll into the water and placed two huge hands on my bottom lifting it slightly then pressing down hard. Although we were under water my inside skin squeaked dryly against his.

"It doesn't make for as smooth a run as natural juices," I said, then lay my head on his wet chest and just kept going.

I was freezing by the time we finished.

"Do you mind, Sam? I'm freezing."

"Aw, honey, have a heart."

"I have but it's gone cold."

"Just a little longer, that's all I need."

"It never is, though, Sam."

"Five minutes," he pleaded.

"Two then." I looked at the clock above his head. "But I'm timing it."

"You frigid little cunt—who the hell could come with you anyway?"

He pulled me roughly towards him, stuck his tongue in my mouth, and continued heaving with renewed energy. Cold water slurped from side to side.

"You sound like a whale in a washbasin," I laughed. "Two minutes up—I'm pulling the plug out." Then I sneezed.

He gave a roar of pleasure.

"Serve you right, you miserable girl. You should have listened to your mommy. I hope you've caught a fuckin' head cold."

We towelled each other dry.

"Do you love me?"

"Ever so much, Sam."

"What—an impotent, old, no-good screw like me?"

"I must be cracked."

"Here, let me put your little nappy in place."

"No, I'm trying a Tampax this evening. Just to get used to it for tomorrow."

"What is all this 'tomorrow' business?"

"I told you, Sam, I'm being photographed for a magazine."

"What magazine again?"

"Chic."

"Shit!"

"Why?"

"An unholy waste of time, honey."

"Oh dear, I've said I'll do it now."

"In hell's name, why?"

"Well, I suppose because they asked as much as anything."

He sighed. "You're a nice girl but it's time you grew up and learnt to say no to things you don't need."

I sneezed again. Twice. "I didn't need that bath."

In the morning I woke up flooding, just in time to stop it soaking through to the mattress. So much for internal security!

I bundled the sheets up, put them in the laundry basket, made the bed up with clean ones and went to put the kettle on. Then I got back in with a cup of tea and thought about what Sam had said.

"It's about time to think ahead, kid."

"Yes, where are we going tonight?"

"To the future."

"I'm not taking LSD."

"I'm too ancient a dog for all this crap."

"What crap's that?"

"This getting out at ungodly hours for the sake of your fuckin' brats. Like some college kid creeping off with the dawn. Jesus, at fifty where's the dignity?"

"Jesus never was fifty."

"Jesus was never dignified, for Christ's sake."

"Fifty! In fifteen years' time you'll be an old-age pensioner, Sam." I started to laugh.

"Yeah, and you'll be looking like my great grandmother. People will be saying 'How come such a fine handsome guy gets stuck with such a lousy old crap bag for a wife?'"

I stopped laughing.

In films the heroine always goes on. So does the young husband when he's told a little one's on the way. It doesn't sink in till six sentences later. Then it's "Darling" and "You mean" and a dawning comprehension in the eyes before the big melt.

But "wife", it hit me right away. Wham. In both ears.

"I heard that," I said.

"Then what did you say?" Rupert sat forward eagerly. We were on our way to Heathrow in the back of a car hired by *Chic*. It could have collected him first from Streatham but he hadn't wanted Moo to know that's where he was staying. So he'd come over to me in a taxi. When we left the girls were still asleep but I'd arranged for the same taxi to call back and take them to school

94

later. Rupert had followed me as I tiptoed in to kiss them goodbye. It was the first time he'd seen them.

"What did I say? I didn't say anything much."

"Except 'yes', I hope."

I looked out of the window. "No, not even 'yes'."

I could feel Rupert staring at me, sense his puzzled disbelief. Just how Sam had been. Thinking now of Sam's face a raw lump started aching in my throat. They have a wicked way of pleading, men. Even when they're not saying anything. It makes you do things you never dreamed you'd do and say reassuring, loving things which afterwards you're sorry you've said. Because you didn't mean them after all. This time I'd managed to keep my mouth shut. Imprisoned words which would have lit him up. Instead I'd enslaved him with unexpected doubts. And Charles would be the same. Why couldn't things just stay the way they were?

"Myopia! What are you thinking about now?" Rupert peered anxiously round.

I swallowed hard and cleared my throat. "I was just thinking what a lovely friend you are. How uncomplicated things are between us. Is it because there's no sex involved?"

"There could be sex."

"Could there?"

"There could be."

"Oh. Have you ever been to bed with girls?"

"One. One girl."

"What was it like?"

He raised his eyes and searched around. I prodded him with my handbag.

"What was it like? Rupert?"

"I'm looking for the word. Shush. I've got it. Ah! Obscene! Yes. It was obscene."

We both laughed.

"Ooh darling," he said shuddering. "I've got goose pimples remembering."

"There you are then, that's what I mean. Something like that wouldn't happen with us. The urge isn't there."

"It might be different with you. For a start, you're much more mummyish."

"Mummyish? Am I?"

"Not to look at, but you are inside. To look at you're quite the opposite. That's what's so attractive. The combination. I noticed you at that party long before we spoke."

"Oh, did you? With all those people there?"

"But Myopia, you're gorgeous. Lots of people must have told you that."

I lit a cigarette and thought back. Had they? "Oh look, Chiswick," I said suddenly. "I love going on this flyover. You can see right into people's back gardens. Rupert, look. This side."

"Ugh," he said and shut his eyes.

"Don't you like it?"

"Loathe it. Depressing. Reminds me of Streatham. Cleaning the car, mowing the lawn and minding everybody else's business. Suburbia, darling."

"Oh, I like looking at it. It's solid and safe. All the pieces fit, like a jigsaw."

"Looking isn't living."

"I didn't say living, did I?" Though on the other hand, I thought to myself, the mummyish side of me might find it very nice indeed. I smiled and stretched, then I yawned. "Will you wake me up when we get there? I'm going to have five minutes."

The clothes were packed in two large expandable suitcases. It worried me to see them whisked away after weigh-in. There were two young airline officials at the desk. One gazed steadily at me, the other at Rupert. Divide down the middle, just like with Jean. "Are you sure," I said to mine, "that we can't take those as hand luggage, under the seat or something? I'd feel safer keeping an eye on them."

They all laughed, Rupert too.

"Well," I said to him. "It will put the tin lid on things if they get lost. You won't laugh then."

He took my arm. "You're getting in a state. There's loads of time but let's go straight through. Have you got your passport? I'll buy you a drink."

"I'm not in a state. Why should I be in a state?" I shook my arm free.

We didn't speak till we reached the departure lounge, where he steered me to the bar.

"What, at half past eight in the morning?"

"Decadent. Deliciously decadent. What will you have?"

"Pernod for Paris, I think. I hope I don't puke up on the plane."

"I'll hold your paper bag if you do. You didn't say you were frightened of flying."

"I'm not," I said, drinking. "Not at all. If it crashes, it crashes. That's what I keep thinking."

"What, all the time you're in the air?"

"From the second I step on. I keep thinking of everything I should have done. Like making a will or saying what sort of funeral I'd like, all that sort of thing. Short flights are worse than long ones. On those you can at least sleep most of the way. Isn't it silly? I've never confessed it to anyone before."

"Poor Myopia. We can come back by train if you like."

"I'll be all right," I said. "Here, let me buy you another."

"Gladly, if you find it a help."

We boarded the plane in a cloudy yellow glow, completely reckless. I fastened my seat belt and watched the hostess mincing in the aisle, while another read out the life-saving instructions. I couldn't care less.

"Would people remember all that at the last minute?" Rupert turned to me.

"I wouldn't," I said, "I can never make head or tail of it. I can't now."

A head of frizzy grey waves in front of me swivelled round, put her finger to her lips and frowned. I nudged Rupert and started giggling.

"Fusspot! First time up I shouldn't wonder," he said loudly.

We were off the ground at last. I'd sung *You're the Tops* in my

97

head twice all through take-off. Word perfect, start to finish. Easy peasy!

"I wonder what plane we'll be catching back, Rupert?"

"When?"

"Well, today of course," I said, surprised.

"I wouldn't bank on that, darling."

"But I've promised . . ."

"Well you never know with Damson how long things will take. It will probably go into tomorrow. We've got enough money to stay the night. You can easily phone Sam."

"Oh dear, I didn't bring my toothbrush. I shall have to buy one. It wasn't Sam I was thinking of."

"The children then."

"Oh the children, yes. Tomorrow I've got to buy them things for their father's honeymoon. And something to wear at his wedding."

He raised his eyebrows.

"He's getting married on Monday. He asked me but I can't."

"Marry him?"

"No, go. I have to go to Brighton on Mondays."

"We'll be back by then. Can't he buy them himself?"

I thought about it. "Don't see why not. He can take Françoise with them and do it altogether. Oh, aren't you clever? That was my chief worry." I had Charles's number in my purse. "The other I can sort out easily—I suppose."

Unreliable, that's what he'd say. Irresponsible, that's what Paul would call me. Turning well-planned arrangements upside down at the last minute. Typical. I blew a raspberry which came out much louder than I'd intended. The man to the right of me looked up, astonished. I smiled at him alluringly so that he coloured up and quickly returned to the newspaper he'd been reading. Shy. A shy businessman. With two boys at prep school and a wife who played golf. I could have had a bit of fun with him, teasing till he wouldn't know where he was—but I couldn't be bothered. I snuggled down into my seat, pressed the button which shot it back to its lowest level and hit the head of the person behind, who'd been leaning forward.

"I say! Go easy!"

Rupert laughed. " 'Nother little snooze."

I shut my eyes. "Good night, Rupert. See you in Paris."

I dreamed I was flying. Running first, faster and faster, then leaping up, legs and arms doing the breast-stroke, like swimming. All along Oxford Street. High above Selfridge's and C&A, past John Lewis, right on to Oxford Circus, where I took a graceful curve, right into Regent Street. I glanced down when I got to Piccadilly. A crowd had gathered and was looking up. At me. I was naked from the navel down. I had a hat on, my Auntie Doreen's turquoise tulle and a home-made knitted jumper which didn't go at all. I pulled my knees up tightly over my stomach to try and hide my stretch marks and I tried to spread my toes to cover my crack, but they wouldn't go. They weren't long enough. Which only left my arms for flying. I was breathless and beginning to cry as I felt myself falling.

"Fasten your seat belt, Myopia. We're nearly there." Rupert shook me gently.

"My God," I groaned, "I dreamed I was flying."

He raised one eyebrow. "Hardly inventive." Very dryly.

"You weren't there though. I had no knickers on. With a lot of people watching!"

He raised the other. "Hardly the first time."

"Oh shut up, you," I said and started powdering my nose.

Our cases were the last to come out of the chute. We stood for ages watching everyone else's rotating around.

"About time," Rupert said. He'd looked as anxious as me for a minute there.

"They did it on purpose, I expect," I said. Airports make you like that, hostile.

We took a taxi from Orly. All the way in to Paris I kept saying, "Gosh, this has changed." In the end, Rupert was forced to ask, "All right, you've been before. When?"

"When I was eighteen," I answered promptly. "You can work

99

out for yourself how many years ago that was. I lost my virginity, as it happened, that time."

"Nice?"

"Nasty. Very nasty. More obscene, I shouldn't wonder, than you and that girl. Really bad."

"No fear of losing it this time."

"Will we have any adventures do you think?"

"Sexual ones?"

"It seems a waste to be in Paris and not have anything happen."

"Something always happens when Damson's around. You'll see."

"I keep trying not to think about Damson. I can imagine what she's like, very bossy and tough, built like Southend Pier. German or something. About the same age as Moo. Fiftyish."

"Moo's not fifty. She'd faint if she heard you."

"What is she then?"

"Forty-five."

"She doesn't look it."

"No, she doesn't. It's her illness. I remember her when she looked wonderful. About five years ago. People say she's dying now."

"Wonderful? Really? Dying? How dreadful."

"She was still with her husband then. He was divine."

"How can she be married if she's a lesbian then? That's what I want to know."

Rupert laughed. "She's got children. Two of them, grown-up. Why not?"

"Well, it doesn't seem right to me."

He laughed again. "You are funny, Myopia. You must go round with your eyes closed. People aren't half as cut and dried as you think. It's possible to be all sorts of things at the same time. Haven't you found that out yet?"

*   *   *

We lay on the bed, Jean and me, naked, covered in boys. There must have been seven of them, three on her, three on me, and

Sergio, that was his name I remember, he was odd man out. Scrabbling around for any bit of bare flesh he could find. My left breast, Jean's right buttock, now and again a mouth. Siesta time, the rest of the hotel asleep. What a holiday we were having. Better than Paris, much better, heaps. We'd ditched the Japs on the second day. I'd got Jean to agree to that.

"It's a great pity," she'd sighed. "We're saying adios to molto lire there."

"Oh, come off it. If that's what you're after we can do better on our own. I've never been so self-conscious as last night. A grand place like that, all dressed up and me dancing with a grasshopper. He opened his flies on the way back. It was pathetic. Like an eyelash dipped in gelatine. I haven't come all the way to Italy for that."

But what we'd got! Help! We'd never bargained for that. They'd arrived at our hotel on the fifth day, the boys. Students too. All Italian. Smashing age, twenty-oneish. Medical students, not much English, but that made no odds.

"They're used to working with bodies. It will be all right," Jean assured me. "They'll know their way around without dialogue."

We looked at them, they looked at us.

"That one there, green eyes, black hair, yellow shirt. Bagsy me," I said.

"Welcome. Looks like a hairdresser. I've seen mine."

"Which one?" I felt a bit miffed.

"The one next to him, very blond."

"Right. I'll have him then too."

That's how it came about. We had them all.

Tomorrow we'd be going home. I turned my head on the pillow to talk to Jean. We often did that, had a chat in the middle of things—they couldn't understand what we were saying. One of them, I can't possibly remember which it would have been, took my movement to mean I wanted my neck love-kissed. I already had a neat string of passion bruises all the way round, which meant I'd have to go home in a scarf.

"Dracula's at it again," I said.

"I see he is."

"Me in polo-necks for a month."

"We're going to miss all this when we get back."

Someone came inside me. "Mmm."

Our heads lay close together, so close that I could smell her breath.

"I can smell your breath," I laughed.

"Ooh. Is it bad?"

"It's beautiful. A soupçon of garlic overlaid with grape."

With difficulty she disengaged one arm, cupped my chin with her hand and put her nose against my mouth. "Open up."

I'll never forget that first kiss. I swear her tongue got as far as my tonsils. There was no getting away, her hand held me firmly in place but after a bit there was no need, anyway by then she was putting it to better use.

Neither of us noticed the boys leave, at least so we said after. I did see their faces though. All of them registered the same emotion. Horror, I would have put it at. They didn't come in to dinner that night and we didn't get a chance in the morning to say goodbye because the coach left before the hotel breakfast time. That was a shame, I should have liked to at least exchange addresses.

"We must have really upset them, Jean."

"Their egos," she tossed her head. "Their miniscule mannish pride. We made them feel superfluous that's all."

"I liked them though. I thought they were lovely."

"Well," she said triumphantly. "It all came true, didn't it then?"

"What?"

"What I said. My promise. I promised we'd both have a fling."

"And fall in love you said."

She looked at me for a long time, her eyes suddenly shiny and very bright, like someone hugging a secret. "Well," she said at last. "We have, haven't we?"

*   *   *

"Look, Rupert. Galeries Lafayette. I'd love to pop in there."

He looked at his watch. "No time for popping anywhere. This driver's taking us a funny way, I must say."

"Is he? Do you know Paris that well?"

"I lived here for two years."

"Oh Rupert. I keep forgetting you're the international set."

"Piss off."

"How coarse."

"Shh, I'm concentrating," He tapped the driver. "Monsieur!" And they went into a long discussion about the address.

I couldn't understand a word. My French by now must be non-existent, I thought. But Rupert was doing marvellously.

"What a wonderful accent you've got," I said when he stopped.

"Quite good in all modesty."

"Very good! Very good on the R's, all in the back of the throat. I couldn't ever get the hang of that bit. I'm hopeless at languages."

"They're easier to pick up if you live in the place."

"How many do you speak then?"

He counted on his fingers. "French, German, Italian, Spanish and a smattering of Arabic."

"Good Lord! You've lived in some places."

He looked all around. "We're here. I'll pay. My francs are handy."

"I can do it." I opened my bag. "Well, all right. It makes no odds. We're sharing everything." I watched him counting out the fare. "Isn't it funny, seeing you doing that makes me feel for the first time that we're abroad. It takes spending different money, it wouldn't be half as much fun if all countries had the same currency. This way it's more like playing Monopoly."

I got out of the taxi and stood holding one of the cases. Rupert picked up the other as the driver drove away. "What a miserable sod he was. Do you ever win?"

"With taxi drivers?"

"At Monopoly. I never do."

"Always, at the end. I come out owning everything. After crippling financial setbacks I effect a startling come-back, as they say in stockbroking circles."

"You'd go a bomb in the city. Come on, this is us."

He pushed at a peeling brown door, it opened on to a small courtyard around which sagged a high building with masses of mostly broken shutters—the ones which weren't tightly shut. There wasn't a soul or sound anywhere.

"Ooh, Rupert. It's rather sinister. I don't like it. Can we go back?"

He took a piece of paper out of his pocket and read aloud. "Cross courtyard. Take right-hand corner door, up stairs, top floor. Apartment 20."

"Top floor," I echoed. We looked at each other and burst out laughing. "Your face!"

"Yours!"

"There won't be a lift."

"I've got it. There will be a lift—but..."

"—Broken!"

We walked past the broken lift and started up the stairs. "They usually have little old ladies in that bottom room who come out to see what you want."

"Concierges," Rupert gasped. "Now stop talking for Christ's sake."

On the fourth landing I sat down for a rest. "This separates smokers and non-smokers. There was a time I would have run up these," I said and lit a cigarette. But Rupert soldiered on.

"These bloody cases," his voice drifted down.

I must be daft doing this, I thought, all this way to get doshed up for some photographer to live out her inner fantasies. Involving a tender plant like Rupert, getting him lugging a caseful of fancy clothes heavy enough to break the strongest stem.

"Mind you don't get a hernia," I shouted up.

"Hernia-hernia-hernia," the building shouted back. What if she wouldn't use me, didn't like my face, caught sight of my stretch marks? I'd have to go back to Moo Moffat-Paw and say, "I'm sorry but I simply wouldn't do." My powder compact had a mirror in it. I took it out to have a look.

It wasn't a face I would have made so much of a fuss about

myself. Everything was in the right place. Exquisitely so, perfectly proportioned—neat nose, narrow chin, wide cheekbones. A perfect oval—which is what true beauty is all about. I'm always reading that. They usually give diagrams and exact measurements so that you have to take a ruler to your face to find out what you are. Round, square, long or heart-shaped. Or oval like me. They never put hatchet in, though there are plenty of hatchet faces around. Or lantern jaws. Beauty writers won't allow their readers lantern jaws. Or jowls or piggy eyes or prissy mouths or stumpy necks, so I was all right because I certainly don't have any of those. In fact, looking at my face now I could see that if everyone believed what they read they would consider me to be devastating. As Rupert had said, "simply gorgeous". Jean used to grumble about it in the beginning. "I must be crackers going around with you. What chance will I stand—except with your leftovers?" But as it turned out we ended up equals.

"You've got the gift of the gab, you see, Jean. They soon get tired of staring at me. I would too if I was them." Though now that I was older there was somehow strangely more that you would stare at. There was artifice for a start. Clever highlighting which modelled the bones and made them even more dramatic. And luscious heavy eyelids which experience had taught the grown-up trick of drooping, just a little. The lips had lost that apprehensive tight-together touch, they'd turned into a loose and lovely kissy pair. I parted them into a different shape, blew cigarette smoke straight at the small mirror and watched my image slowly blur.

"What on earth are you up to now?" Rupert's flushed faraway face peered down over the banisters high above.

"Are you at the top?" I stubbed out my cigarette. "I'm just coming."

"I've rung the bell already," he shouted.

He'd gone by the time I got there. The open door faced me. I heard his voice, inside. He was laughing excitedly, chattering nineteen to the dozen like a child. From time to time he'd say her name, Damson this or Damson that. She couldn't get a word in edgeways. When she did I had no doubts at all. The accent had changed but there was no mistaking the voice. I knew at once who Damson was.

"Jean!"

"Mother of Jesus!"

"You've met before." Rupert looked amazed. He watched us hugging. "You know each other!"

"Intimately." Jean stood back to look at me and chuckled appreciatively. "But bye-bye and hello again I'd forgotten what I'd been missing."

I'd only just have recognised her. I totted up—twelve years. She spun round and waggled her bottom. "What do you see, love?"

"A change," I said uncertainly.

She gave a fruity laugh, full of freshly baked bread, plates of pasta, chocolate gateaux, whipped cream, laced coffee, sweet liqueurs.

"You've put on a bit, Jean."

She dimpled delightedly. "Five stone. Brings me up to thirteen. Lucky number. Do you like it?"

"You look amazing. I must say that."

Like a lampshade, with a high watt bulb burning inside. The sort of lampshade you'd see in an eastern brothel, all fringed and beaded and tasselled. As wide as it's high. Brightly coloured from top to bottom, that's what she was. Her hair was very long, about to the middle of her back, a dark rich cherry red, it hung like corrugated cardboard. Horizontally. She saw me looking and held a glowing strand in her hand.

"I try to make it look as creased as possible, as opposed to curled. I used to have it permed but it came out too frizzy. Now I get someone to iron it, the woman who does my laundry. She fits it in after the sheets. Folded in just the same way."

She held it to her eyes and squinted. "Mm, needs more crimson. This Paris air is shocking. Fades everything. Good colour though, isn't it? That's how they came to call me Damson."

"It's a far cry from Jean." Rupert pulled a face. "My sister's called Jean. I'm glad I didn't know you then."

"Well," I ventured. "She was quite different. You probably wouldn't have bothered."

"Oh, I don't know." Jean tossed her hair back, soft flesh shook gently all over her face and rippled down her neck. Fascinating. "He'd have liked my bum. It was smaller than a sparrow's fart. Tighter than a spy's tongue. You'd have liked that wouldn't you, Rupe?"

"Impossible to imagine, with all due respect, darling Damson. I adore you as you are now. How about Myopia? Has she changed?"

They both looked at me. Damson critically, I thought.

"No," I said for her. "I feel at a dreadful disadvantage. Static. I haven't changed one bit, have I, Jean? Go on, say it."

Her brown eyes, smaller now in so much extra skin, but still bright like a naughty bird, danced mischievously all over my body. Then returned to my face. She smiled with the same wide happy mouth she'd always had and the eyes took on a warm and different glow. "No."

That's all she said, "No", but in such a soft, insinuating, seductive way that I began to blush self-consciously and feel as shy as if I was with a stranger. Which made me mad and more defensive. "Better clothes, though, surely now?"

She put her head on one side, considering, but her expression didn't change. "A veneer of sophistication, but basics unaltered, I'd say." She ran a small plump hand over my breast into my waist and let it rest lightly on one lean hipbone. "Structurally superior, in fact. Have you had children?"

"Two."

"Improved you. Tightened you up. Does that to a lot of women."

She took her hand away and with the other touched my chin and swung it round so that my head was in profile against the light.

"Face leaner, eyes larger, mouth more relaxed, skin marvellous. Time has treated you well." She spoke briskly like a professional, which, of course, was what she was but I'd forgotten that. "I'm more interested in the mind for my photographs." She tapped my forehead. "And what has altered up there."

Rupert looked on silently as if now he was in awe of her. Which, most irritatingly, was a bit of how I felt myself. She spun round to him and laughed. "Believe it or not, Rupert, this beautiful beast, this femme fatale, was my best friend. We were students at this crappy college until my family left for the States, then we lost touch altogether. For one whole term I used to just stare at her. Everyone did. All the men were mad about her, staff included. And guess what she was going out with?"

"Don't be awful," I said.

"This blind bugger. This music student who couldn't see what he'd got hold of and in the end chucked her and turns out to be queer anyway. Went off with an organist."

"Sounds sweet," Rupert murmured.

"Anyway when we eventually got chummy I see that inside she's like a child. As daft as you make them. No idea of what she looks like, obsessed with ideas of social inferiority. Brought up by a family on the edge of being certifiably insane."

"Jean!"

"They were, love. Crackers! The whole lot of them. Your father was mentally defective, I swear it. He used to sit there. Rupert—"

I opened my handbag. "Where's the bog?"

"He used to sit there picking his nose and . . ."

"I said, is there a lavatory here?" I moved towards the door.

"Oh, don't go. Isn't it true? Tell Rupert." She turned to him. "They lived in this place, honestly, there was no bathroom and her mother used to . . ."

"Jean!"

"No, let me just say. Her mother, when they . . ."

I slapped her right cheek so hard it hurt my hand and then, with the back of it, I slapped her left so swiftly I didn't know I'd done it. Inside I felt cold and completely detached as if my limbs were working of their own accord. She thinks she's riled me, I thought, driven me to such anger that I have to strike out. But, in fact, it isn't so at all. She's a fat unhappy girl for reasons of her own and likes to play a childish spiteful game. And to please I've gone along with it. What she'd like now is for both of us to cry, become emotional and make it up. I felt the tears spring to my eyes and the next moment her arms were around me.

"Girls, girls," Rupert said anxiously.

Jean hugged me tightly and raised a tear-stained radiant face. Each cheek was scarlet from my blows. "That's what I wanted to find out," she choked between sobs, "what's happened in your mind. Had you learnt to be less passive, always out to please . . ."

I took a hanky from my bag. "What's happened to your glasses, don't you wear them any more?" And wiped her nose as kindly as I could.

"Gave up glasses, gave up girls, grew my hair and took to gourmandising all in the same year!" Jean skewered a steaming snail with a two-pronged silver fork and sucked between her teeth. Then she tore a piece of bread from her roll, soaked up garlic butter and swilled the whole lot down with red wine. Rupert and I sat in the crowded café watching her. Two dozen snails she'd polished off. Just like that!

"Oh yes," I said politely. "And which year was that?" Like an historical researcher making certain of his dates. She glanced at our two empty glasses but poured the remaining wine into her own. "Thank you, darling," Rupert said pointedly.

"Lowest form of wit." She took a swig and smacked her lips, then burped so loudly at a passing waiter that he spilt the entire contents of his tray. Two Pernods, three Perriers, and one small cognac. He swore and scowled in her direction. In answer, she held our empty bottle up. "Un autre, s'il vous plait." Then turned to us and laughed. "The only way to get attention in this place! Now, what were we saying? Oh, yes. Well, let me see when. One, two, three, must have been five years ago because Freddie's been dead two. It's terrible, you know, I still miss him. I wake up in the night and swear he's sitting on my bed. I still can't see steak mignon on a menu without thinking of Freddie. He was mad about good food. The more I ate the more he loved it. After a particularly fine meal we'd go home and he'd lick me all over. It was as much as I could do to stop him biting! He would have eaten me if I'd let him." Her voice shook. "Strangely enough, this place was one of his favourites. We used to come here all the time. He was great friends with the owner—" She broke off abruptly and stared across the room, then she started waving and stood up. "Oh, excuse me, I've just seen Babette. I must go and have a word."

She moved nimbly, no mean feat, between the closely packed tables. As she went, I felt my energy ebb away as if without her igniting presence my life supply was lowered. It was extraordinary.

"Phew." I let out a long and gasping breath, then turning to Rupert asked, "And who on earth was Freddie then?"

"Freddie?" he said simply. "Freddie was her dog."

I timed it. She was away from us for twenty minutes. The centre of attention, the other side of the room, laughing loudly, greeting new people, kissing everybody. I watched her. Rupert looked at me.

"You're thinking she's on something, aren't you?" he said.

"What do you mean?"

"You're wondering if she's on pills or something stronger. She's not you know—"

"No, I wasn't—"

"She's just on life."

"Yes," I said. "She always was."

What I was actually wondering was when we were going to get down to work. I looked at my watch. It was half past two. In just over two hours' time I'd be ringing Charles. "I'm sorry, Charles. We don't seem to have quite finished. It looks very much as if I won't be back till tomorrow. By the way, have you buried Deirdre yet?" I wasn't exactly understanding mistress material.

Rupert stood up. "She's beckoning. Come on, we'd better go over. Take a tip from me and forget about time. Damson starts work when she wants to. It could be when everyone else is half dead on their feet, so don't squander any stamina you've got. Not at this early stage."

I stood up too. "You mean grin and bear it?"

He shook his head and looked vaguely worried. I laughed and touched him reassuringly. "Ah, it's all right. I'm getting it now. 'Hang loose!' Is that better?"

He looked at me quickly but I smiled innocently back and by the time we'd reached Jean, or rather Damson as I'd now decided to call her, I was hanging looser than I'd ever done in my life. So loose in fact that when five o'clock came I did nothing about calling Charles and couldn't have cared less if Deirdre was six foot under or still receiving callers in her coffin.

Over the hours our group enlarged, sometimes to over twenty, even more, but through it all a solid core remained, with Damson at centre, holding court, and me at her side. The new consort. That's how it felt.

"I'm not calling you Jean any more," I said to her early on. "It's Damson from today." Her eyes flickered for a second. "And you might as well call me Myopia to stay in the mood of things."

"Mercy me," she'd blinked. "We've just murdered each other."

The girl called Babette sat on Damson's other side staring at us. A strange expression on her face, watchful. She hardly spoke at all. She had an extraordinarily long neck, like a Modigliani. Or, nearer the mark, a young giraffe because when she stood up, which she did quite often for no apparent reason, her arms and legs went on for ever too. She was dressed from neck to toe in yellow, slightly shiny so that she put me in mind of an old-fashioned fly catcher. Those thin long sticky strips that used to hang from people's ceilings. My mother always had one in our kitchen. Dotted with dead flies, like the flag of death waving above your dinner. Yellow.

"Babette is a model," Damson had introduced us. "She works for Dior."

Something clicked, I studied her complexion.

"What beautiful skin you have. Flawless."

"Christ, yes!" Damson shrieked. "But you should have seen it before! Craters of the moon. Covered! Acne Virulus. Pimples, spots, boils, scars—"

"Oh, I believe we have a friend in common—"

"Seven layers of the stuff they sheared off. She had the operation last summer. For a beauty article. I did the before and after snaps. Miraculous success. A perfect peel."

"Yes, she's living in London. Her name's Françoise."

Babette spoke for the first time. "Ah oui," her eyes lit up. "Françoise."

"She actually lives in my house."

She frowned suddenly. "Françoise? She live with you?" And glancing quickly at Damson, began a low-pitched, highly charged conversation. From time to time Damson snorted or turned her back deliberately. I sat watching now; they were obviously having a quarrel.

Rupert sat opposite. I leaned towards him. "I think those two are quarrelling." He didn't move his eyes. "It's Babette," he whispered. "She's impossibly jealous. I'd go easy if I were you."

Me? What had I done? There was a sudden commotion to my left. Babette stood up, glass in hand, while Damson remained seated, drenched in wine. It ran slowly down her dimpled face, glistened in the glorious hair. She looked up, laughed and licked her upper lip. Babette gave a strangled sob and pushing past the people next to her disappeared through a door labelled Dames. Everyone went on as if nothing had happened.

I picked up a napkin from the table and started mopping. "That's the second time today," I said crossly as if to a child. "Whatever has come over you? Do you like these emotional scenes? Is that how you go on all the time?"

She twinkled wickedly. "I thrive on disturbance. I like to scratch away the surface—"

"Like a rat—"

"What's underneath is so much more inviting—"

"An avaricious rat."

"A conjurer with a pack of cards."

"You'll drop them all one day."

"When I'm dead."

She always liked the last word. "You're still the same, Damson. A blockbuster."

She patted her hips and plaited ten small fat fingers over her swollen stomach. "What do you think of this belly?"

The thought struck me. "Are you pregnant?"

She laughed and laughed till the tears came to her eyes.

"It looks like it," I said nastily to make her stop.

That brought on another burst. "Oh dear, oh dear!" She gasped at the end and weakly wiped her eyes. I stared coldly with what I hoped was open dislike. "What's so funny?"

She gave one last happy giggle. "You are, my love." She leant forward and tickled me under the chin. "I can tell you've been wasting too much time with pompous asses." She wagged her finger. "You have to be careful, certain qualities can be very catching."

I took a deep breath, she was doing it again, deliberately provoking.

"You're a monster," I said, "let's leave it at that."

She looked just slightly put out. "But we haven't started yet—"

"I realise that," I cut across, "however, we're postponing further action for the moment."

"Why?" she persisted.

"Why?" I sat back and faced her squarely. She looked sumptuous, like over-ripe fruit, insistent, disturbing, self-confident, exciting. "Why? Because you're beginning to bore, that's why."

I caught a glimpse of Jean, just for one split second, standing pigeon-toed in tarty shoes with film star glasses on her nose and a mouth which trembled very slightly. Rupert leaned towards us.

"Going over old times, you two?"

Damson didn't answer. I lifted my glass and clinked the one in front of her.

"Preparing for new, more like." And started hanging loose again.

* * *

"How I'll miss you when I go." It had been like a bombshell. America.

"How I'll miss you, Jeannie, too."

The evening before she left we bought two bottles of strong cider and locked ourselves in her room. Her mother had looked in on her way out. "We won't be back till very late, darling. Make sure you're all packed." And to me, "Goodbye, my dear. I do hope you'll write to Jean. You've been such good friends. She'll be fortunate if she meets someone like you over there." Then almost absent-mindedly, "Such a beautiful girl."

Jean winked slyly behind her mother's back. "Good night, Mummy, have a nice party. I'll be asleep when you get back, I expect. Don't bother to look in."

I watched them briefly embrace. What niceties they knew. A car horn hooted impatiently outside, a rich imperious signal.

"Oh dear," the mother became prettily confused. "Daddy is anxious to be away. He's started fretting. Blow him a kiss, darling." She left the room as Jean ran to the window.

"Coo-ee, Daddy, kiss kiss." She spread her fingers wide and brought them to her lips, then threw these parcels of daughterly affection over the front lawns, down the drive, past the clipped privet, to her father in the waiting car.

We listened to them drive away.

"That's that." Jean began a slow grin and opened the first cider. "Now what about this?"

We drank a full glass each, slowly, non-stop, staring at each other over the rims. We were sitting on the floor and I wiped the bottom of my glass carefully before setting it down in case it should stain the carpet.

"Your mother and father are mad about you, aren't they?"

She looked surprised. "What a funny thing to say."

"No, but I mean they show it so much."

"In no more than a normal way. All parents are like that."

"Mine aren't."

"No, well, yours—" She broke off and looked embarrassed. "I

mean I think you'd find most normal middle-class families behave like mine. Boring, isn't it?"

"I think it's nice."

"What, sitting on Daddy's knee and arranging his hair in little curls—"

"I wouldn't dare do that to mine."

"I've always done it. It's his favourite thing."

"Yes, but don't you think it's funny? Now? At your age?"

"What do you mean? You think it might get him going? If it did he certainly wouldn't let on. He sticks too closely to the code."

She imitated her father's Scotch-on-the-rocks-just-a-spot-of-water voice. "Oh, my goodness, yes!"

I let the cider slip along my skin until it reached my wrists. I held them both up and watched my hands dangle loose. Then I dropped my head heavily on my chest and thought about sitting on my father's lap, running my fingers lightly through his hair, shifting slightly to redistribute my weight, feeling his shoulder press against my breast.

"Oh, no, I wouldn't dare do that to mine." I swear it's the last thing on earth that I'd dare to do.

Jean poured a second glass for us and we drank it as we had the first. I felt the pressure mounting in my bladder. "I'm bursting for a pee," Jean said, "but I'm not going."

I stared at her, my own need suddenly receding. "Why not?"

"Haven't you ever tried it? Holding out till the last minute. It makes you really randy. I discovered that years ago." She laughed and started rocking on her heels. "An exquisite pain. Ooh. I've even had a few accidents, leaving it too late."

"What do you mean?" I was secretly appalled, and unexpectedly excited.

"Pissed my pants. Wet my knickers. It makes you feel wonderfully naughty."

"Jean!"

"Try it now. Holding on. We both will."

I stood up, needing now urgently to go. "I'll have to keep on the move." I crossed my legs. "And cross fingers."

She stood up too, hopping from leg to leg. "I'll put a record on, we can dance. That will help."

The music was very loud, good for dancing but with a steady, insistent beat which only served to heighten my discomfort. We pranced about the room, going redder and redder. The record came to an end, I put on another. When I turned round, Jean was wriggling furiously behind, one hand between her legs. We both wore skirts, hers was all hoicked up at the front so that I could see where her fingers pressed against the gusset of her knickers. My eyes started watering; what she'd said was true. I did, despite the agony, feel unbearably aroused.

"I can't hold on much longer, Jean." I bit my lip and crossed my legs tightly.

"I know." She came towards me, scarlet-faced. "I'll hold yours and you can hold mine." She caught my hand and pulled it to where hers was.

"No."

"Harder than that. Press harder or I'll do it."

"Jean!"

I felt the warmth seeping through the thin material, felt at the same time her fingers on mine. We both, standing closely, our hands on each other, let our insides stream out together.

"All over the carpet," I remember thinking anxiously, but then I surrendered to the unbelievable joy of the moment, releasing tension like air from a child's balloon. Warmth, wetness, dribbling down our legs over all four feet into toes, until at last there was nothing left. Except the hammering of her heart against my own, her arm held loosely round my waist and her happy mouth kissing busily in mine.

"Well," I said, as soon as she'd let me, "that's the rudest thing I've ever done."

She laughed slyly. "There's ruder things than that to do. There must be, otherwise there'd be nothing to look forward to, would there? That's why people live as long as possible, to get it all in."

The pleasant warmth was beginning to fade, replaced by an uncomfortably soggy coldness. I looked down, our two separate pools were puddling into one. Anxiety and guilt flooded through the elation I still felt.

"Ooh," I said, "I feel awful now. It's just come over me. As if I could cry."

Right away she started bossing. "Down with your drawers. I'll wash them out with mine. I'll put them on the radiator. Be ready in no time! Here, hand me that hair drier, it will do for the carpet. Now you, you take your skirt off, dry yourself with this towel and when you've done that, get into bed and wait for me."

I stood there numbly. She clucked impatiently, stepping out of her dripping clothes and, giving me a small shove, she added softly, "Go on, dopey. Do as I say. Don't I always know best?"

A whole year, it had taken, to get going again. After she'd gone. Six or seven letters I wrote to her, but I never heard a word back. "Any news of Jean?" people were always asking. I'd shake my head. "Nice friend," my mother would say meaningfully. She'd never liked her much. But I felt as if one half of me had died. The lower half.

*   *   *

Half past seven. We hadn't stirred. Even Rupert looked concerned. I stood up. Damson put a cheerful hand on my arm.

"Where are you going?"

Back to London, you self-opinionated, fleshy lump! You mad, mindless, middle-aged . . . hippie!

"I'm going to use the telephone," I said.

She smiled with a sudden rush of enthusiastic energy. "Don't take too long. Here are some jetons, you'll need them for the phone box. I'm waiting to talk about work."

I fumed all the way to the phone, frowning at a handsome sullen face ahead which seemed to be approaching until I reached the wall mirror and saw it was my own. With the sulks? Why?

A thick-set, swarthy Frenchman was talking on the only telephone, shouting into the mouthpiece, shrugging his shoulders and stressing conversational points with his free fist. An empty packet of Gauloises lay at his feet. I thought of Paul. Posh voice, fast car. That had been enough for me then. And a way with him in bed that had put me in mind of Jean. Pushy, forceful. Both products of the middle classes. The man kicked savagely at the paper packet, gave a guttural grunt and then suddenly noticed me waiting behind him and turned to face me. He gave a dazzling grin, showing two gleaming gold teeth in the front. Quite nice, gold teeth. Funny things to think of having. I smiled back, rather wanly, and sagged wearily inside as I saw his eyes begin to wander. I turned my back deliberately, lit a cigarette and leaned against the open door, looking into the length of the café. We'd been there eight hours. Incredible. You couldn't do that in London. All over the world, just about; talking, drinking, eating for hours on end. But not in London. Not unless it's a club. Where people have to be passed before they can be members. Then it's pointless because you're always meeting everyone that you'd expect to meet. No element of surprise!

I jumped at the pinch and turned round quickly. The man had finished with the phone but kept his hand on my bottom. I brushed it away, remembered "Merci beaucoup" and began dialling London.

Françoise answered. I could hear the children in the background.

"First of all," I said, "is their father there? Oh Paul, hello," and I began to explain. It was only when I'd said good night to the girls, got Paul to agree to the new arrangements, that now I'd probably be back on Sunday night, and replaced the receiver that I remembered I'd forgotten to tell Françoise I'd just met her friend Babette. Closing my purse I caught sight of Charles's number on a piece of paper. He won't be there now but I can at least in all honesty say I tried. Two and a half hours late.

He answered immediately. I heard the ringing tone, it went twice. He sounded awful, no sign of anger, just strained and very sad. "I've been waiting. I knew you'd ring if you possibly could."

"It's the first chance I've had, Charles." I crossed two fingers to cancel out the lie, one polished nail was chipping I noticed.

"My darling, when am I to expect you?"

For one surprising second the pleading stirred up a fierce and cruel streak. Before I could stop I'd said it. "Have you buried Deirdre yet?"

The coarseness horrified me more than him. "What? Oh! Funeral tomorrow. Now which plane will you be on tonight? I'll meet it."

"Charles." I seemed like someone else, not me at all. "What are your plans exactly now?"

"My plans?" He sounded surprised. "Well, I thought I'd meet you, then chance dining in a little place I know. No fear of bumping into anyone . . ."

"No, I mean not now tonight, but from now on." Why in God's name was I asking that?

There was a silence at the other end. When he spoke he sounded very quiet, but confident. "Ah, well, that. That is something we have to discuss. The telephone is hardly the way in which I would have liked to . . ."

"To what, Charles?"

"To—well—ask . . ."

"What? Ask what?" Like a rat myself! Avaricious!

"Very well," he blustered irritably, coughed, cleared his throat —I knew he had one hand on his spectacles. "Ask a lady for her hand," then he said it again, but with better delivery. His public speaking was standing him in good stead.

"My hand?" I said into the phone. "Charles."

"Don't be deliberately obtuse," he said suddenly, shouting. "Darling, did you hear me?" His voice rose to its fullest pitch. "Goddammit, girl, I'm asking you to marry me. Wasn't that always the idea, once the obstacle was removed . . ."

"Your wife." I said it softly, gave him a lead.

"The damn woman's dead," he was still shouting. "And jolly good riddance too. A fool's trick that jump. And she knew it. Been warned time and time again! Died in triumph, actually laughing.

The expression on her face—challenging! The poor undertaker had the devil of a job to reset it into some semblance of dignity . . ."

I held the receiver away from my ear, his voice went on and on, Deirdre as powerful in death . . .

"Charles," I interrupted. "About my plane."

He was still excited. "Yes, darling?"

"I shan't be home till Sunday, I'm afraid."

When I turned round I found Damson talking to gold-teeth. She had her arm round his neck and they were laughing together, like very old friends.

"Come here," she said, "André wishes to be introduced."

He clicked his heels and bowed from the waist, then he held out one hand. It had a gold ring on the third finger. I pointed at it and said foolishly, "To go with your teeth."

He laughed and said in French-American-English, "Aw no, to go with the woman."

They both looked at me, Damson and him, expecting something witty back but I'd given up the ghost. I looked down at my hands, one of which Charles had just asked for. A fact which only now was beginning to sink in.

"Is your wife dead?" I asked.

André looked surprised and burst out laughing. Damson took my hand and led me gently back to our table. André followed. "I can see you're tired," she said. "André owns this place. He's the proprietor." As if that simple fact explained everything.

I lost the evening. It approached like an ocean, each hour a large and powerful wave which broke above my head and swept me further out to sea. Several times I was sick, but in between these bouts I floated, staring at the sky. At times it was completely black, at others full of blinding lights—and faces that I knew. Rupert's smiling encouragingly; Damson's. But an unfamiliar Damson, gazing up from down below, her mouth concealed by a crinkly dark moustache which I knew to be my pubic hair. A man I'd seen before, but only once, with a mouth of gold pressed close to mine. And another that I didn't know at all who came repeatedly with coloured crayons in his hand. Often I was tossed and turned and felt upon my limp skin the slithering touch of rich and varying sensations, some smooth like water, others soft as smoke . . .

Once, as a child, I'd had a long and dangerous illness. Death's door was where they said I'd been but I could only remember the hospital. And sleeping out of doors at night on a high veranda inches from the stars. Towards morning clouds would form, shepherded like sheep, into some sort of formation by a bigger, billowing shape that I took to be an organising angel. I knew it even then, I say it, since angels come neutered like cats from the vet, it hung each day throughout that bandaged summer directly above my bed. While the clouds drifted slowly about their business this angel didn't budge. Its wings were as wide as the hospital grounds, beautiful, and beckoning—but it had a grotesque and dreadful double chin. Like a well-filled shopping bag which hung from each ear and billowed about in the middle of its chest. A strange woman would come each day and sit silently by my bed. We'd stare without speaking at each other until eventually her eyes would fill with tears and I'd shut my own and hope that when I opened them again she'd be gone. One day when the angel was closer than it had ever been before I lifted my finger and pointed. "Do you see?" I whispered to this woman. "Up there, an angel with a double chin?" Two nurses took her away sobbing and another placed a cold thermometer in my mouth.

I was reminded of that angel now while white distorted shapes floated haphazardly before my eyes and for an instant formed into a shining pair of wings—without the shopping bag. I smiled and laughed. Chin up! It's learnt to stretch its neck! Then I opened my eyes.

"At last Sleeping Beauty awakes!" It was Rupert's voice.

"Welcome to the land of the living. How're you feeling?" Damson's.

I sat up. "Slightly sick. Seasick."

They came over and stood above me, smiling down. "You

won't be. Nothing left in you now. We saw to that before we put the clothes on. Couldn't have you soiling the spoils."

"Or spoiling the shots," Damson added.

A dull ache prickled slowly over my scalp, my mouth felt as dry as a dead moth. I ran a swollen tongue over my upper lip and, surprisingly, tasted a perfumed film of lipstick. Rupert laughed. Two gold teeth twinkled beside him. André of course. It was André. He handed me a cup with black coffee in it. "Drink up, honey." A nice voice.

"And then come and see how you like yourself," Damson said. My head prickled painfully again. I put up a hand and felt a mass of tiny tight coils kept in place by hundreds of small hair pins. An anxious voice with a heavy French accent said, "They are hurting you, no? The pins? I will remove them at once."

A boy stepped towards me, very much like Rupert, amazingly so. "Jean-Paul." Damson held my hand up. "This is Jean-Paul. He's been making you pretty! You must say thank you, Myopia."

I sat there stupidly, staring at them all. "Thank you, Jean-Paul." And drained my cup.

"Another?" I nodded.

"Oh, come on," Rupert put an arm around my shoulders. "She looks so amazing, let's show."

I'd been lying on a chaise longue, velvet, the colour of violets. "We should bring that with her. Honestly, darling, if you could have seen yourself! The colour—" He kissed his finger tips and closed his eyes. "Mm, mm, deevine."

I allowed myself to be guided to the mirror—was I drunk or drugged or what? "I'm hallucinating," I said and gave a ghastly grin. The technicoloured film star smiled gravely back. I watched the glossy lips move. "That's not me, is it? My God, my own mother wouldn't know me!"

"Oh her, she wouldn't—" I heard Damson's voice begin, but I'd stopped listening.

"Perfection," I sighed and allowed a soft and pleasurable gasp to escape under my long skirt.

"She's farted," Damson said. "Well, I'll be buggered. We've

all worked our balls off." She spun me round. "Ten outfits we've fitted you into—photographed them all with you snoring like a pig and your first reaction is to fart."

I stared at her wide-eyed, suddenly awake. "You've done all that?"

Rupert answered. "Don't you remember? It was your idea! Just before you conked out you told us about your dream, so Damson's done the first part already—'Beautiful Girl Dreaming'—"

Damson interrupted eagerly. "We run those pictures along the top of each page, shows the whole thing. Hair, shoes, outfits, the lot, and then printed large we show the dreams, close-ups of you in different situations. Like your dream—only with variations—"

"I can't remember anything. Was I very drunk?"

"It was the hash. You foolishly ate hash fudge. Hussein gave you it. He's always doing that. His idea of a joke. Really strong stuff. He'll kill someone one day. It doesn't mix with booze. You'll be okay, now, with a good few hours' more sleep. We've all been waiting to go to bed but we were waiting just to see you were all right."

"How awful. I am sorry. Whatever is the time?"

Rupert yawned and looked at his watch. "Six a.m.!" He and Jean-Paul glanced at each other. "Are you sure you're better, Myopia, because if so we'll be getting along."

"We? Who?" I said, stupid again.

He kissed me on the cheek. "I'm camping round at Jean-Paul's. Damson's only got room for you here. We'll report for work later in the morning. Goodnighty, darling! You were wonderful!"

"Wonderful," echoed André and hugged me. "I too shall see you, yes? Today," he whispered in my ear, "my sweet darling."

Before I'd known it, they'd gone. Damson saw them all out. When she came back I was still at the mirror. How much had I imagined? One thing I suddenly remembered, one physical fact that must have been obvious to all of them over the hours. The thought turned me scarlet. I heard her cross the room, then stand behind me, gazing in the glass at our two reflections. I didn't turn but said slowly and with considerable embarrassment, "What on earth did you do about my period and all those clothes?"

She flung a plump and friendly arm through mine, squeezed it and laughed. "I threw away your old towel and put a Tampax in!" Then she lifted my chin. "Was that in order, madam?"

I gave a mortified nod.

She laughed again. "Right then. Now do as I say and get to bed."

But I couldn't sleep. I lay on my side of her large bed and she lay on the other, nowhere did our bodies touch. A small amount of early morning light filtered through the wooden shutters, enough for me to dimly see her face. She'd fallen asleep almost at once. Without so much as a goodnight peck. But, was I pleased or piqued? I couldn't tell, myself. I flicked my lighter, lit a cigarette and holding up the flame looked with interest around the room.

Everything went on in it, a cooker and sink in one corner, the chaise longue I'd been lying on, a huge workbench table running down the centre and along one wall a battery of lighting equipment and cameras. There were photographs everywhere, covering the table, on the floor, pinned to the walls. Hundreds of her dog. Freddie, that was it. A Saluki, with a fine aristocratic face and graceful, greased lightning frame. Not what I would have chosen for a pet, but then I liked cuddly little animals, guinea pigs or pekineses, or fluffy things like day-old chicks and Persian cats. Or even bright pink squealing things like pigs. Not that you could keep a pig in Paris. Not in this apartment at any rate. The stairs for a start. The poor thing couldn't cope with those each time it went for a walk.

I studied Damson whilst she slept. She looked not unlike a pig, I thought, a pretty one with a little nose and deep-set eyes and curly laughing lips. But mostly it was her skin, so pink and soft and squelchy. I felt an irresistible urge to prod her, push a finger in and see how far it sank. To the knuckle or nearabouts, I would have said. On really fleshy bits—her thighs, her breasts, her bottom—right up to the wrist! I shut my eyes, and turned over. I'll tell her that in the morning, I thought. I'll tell her that—and try it out.

But in the morning she was nowhere to be seen. There was a note on her pillow—"Sleep on, see you soon." I got up when I read it, put the kettle on and looked around for a clean cup. Everything was fouled and filthy. Mrs. Bowen would have gone clean out of her mind, that or asked for her cards. Half a ham roll, dead, stuck out of the sugar bowl. Stale ground coffee stood in all the jugs, one with furry green verdigris growing on its surface. A broken egg lay on the floor, with a bloated fly inside. I found my cup from last night, recognising it by the lipstick stain, washed it out and drank my coffee black. There seemed to be no milk. My heart began pounding, pumping nineteen to the dozen. I spat the rest away, then started cleaning up. I knew what she'd say when she came in. "Proper little pit wife." Well? And so what? But by ten to ten, when I'd turned it into a presentable palace, there was still no sign of her. So I ran a bath and got in and while I was at it, I washed my hair. As I was rinsing it, a slow job done by filling a jug from both taps to get the right temperature, she came in. I stopped in mid-pour, and squinted through the dripping strands, on my knees, my bottom high in the air, nipples hard and pointing down.

"Good morning, my love," I heard her sing out. "Myopia?"

"Here," I shouted back. The bathroom door opened in a rush.

"Do you mind? I've got this turd up my ass! It's bigger than a battleship."

She sat down on the lavatory and grinned cheerfully. "Only hope it doesn't break the bowl. I've carried it over from the other side of Paris."

I heard the splash.

"Ah, that's better." She stared at the ceiling, concentrating. "To be followed by several smaller vessels." Then she wiped herself with paper, half a roll it looked like, pulled the chain and sniffed. "Not too bad! Now, how are you today?"

It had happened so quickly I hardly took it in. I noticed that she didn't wash her hands. "Can I make you something to eat? I've got fresh bread, milk, eggs . . ."

"I'm just washing my hair," I said quickly. "I'll do my own in a minute," and started on the taps again.

"Hey," she said slowly. "Look at me."

I lifted a wet and sudsy face.

"Don't move," she pointed imperiously. "Just stay like that, I'll get my camera," and darted away.

When she returned I was in the same position, bubbles sliding down my skin, streaming over each breast.

"Good girl." She put the lavatory lid down and stood up on it. "Now to me, your chin. That's it."

Soap ran into my eyes.

"Don't do that!" she shouted when I shut them.

"It's stinging though, the soap."

"Keep your mouth still! Now laugh! Not like that, really laugh. Teeth, teeth! Yes!"

She clicked through a whole roll of film then put another in and kneeled on the floor beside the bath. "Now sit on your feet, go on, just sink back on the heels. Straighter back. Titties out. Point them! Point, I said, not pout. Now fill that jug and pour cold water over your head."

"Cold? I'm not pouring cold." I turned the hot on. She turned it off impatiently, filled the jug to the brim with icy water and tipped the whole lot over me. I swear my heart stopped with the shock—my arms involuntarily lifted to shield my breasts.

She clicked unmercifully. "Get those arms down," she said so fiercely I did so right away.

Wet hair hung like a thick straight curtain all over my face. I pushed it to one side and glared at her. "You cow, you bloody cow."

"Beautiful," she cooed, "keep that look."

"Keep it yourself," I snarled and stood up, goose-pimpling all over. My teeth started chattering uncontrollably and I reached for a towel.

She didn't stop, quickly reloaded the camera and just went on snapping. In the end I took no notice, dried myself all over, wrapped the towel round me and with another started rubbing at my hair.

"That's enough. I think we've got it. Okay. There'll be some beauties in those, unless you're totally, irredeemably unphotogenic."

"I am," I said sourly.

She laughed. "We'll only know that later today. They're rushing through the stuff I shot last night. That's where I've been, to my printers. We'll have them by six. Isn't it exciting?" She tapped her camera. "But these, I'll develop myself. Now, I think."

Curiosity overcame me. "Yourself, where?"

She pointed to a door in the large living-room. "My dark room. I always do my own black and white. You can experiment so much in the printing. That's the best part."

"Why not do last night's then?"

The question bored her but she answered patiently. "That was colour. It's a different process. Has to go to a colour lab. What we'll get back this afternoon are transparencies. You experiment with those in a different way, like laying one or even two on top of the other, but all that will be done in the art department at *Chic*. I shall come over with them and have a say in the laying out. There's not an art director in the world that I'd trust with my work."

I stared at her, it was a different Damson today.

"Can I stay with you?"

"What? I was just thinking!"

"Can I stay with you—in London?"

"Yes! Yes, of course you can. I've got plenty of room."

She laughed. "I thought you would. I can imagine your house. It is a house, isn't it?"

"Yes." I felt almost defensive. "A nice house. In need of decoration though," I added.

"And does that worry you?" She looked at me very seriously.

I thought carefully. "Well,"—well, did it? "Well," I said again. "Well, if it did I would hardly have let it get like that, would I?" And right away felt better.

She nodded encouragingly.

"In actual fact, I don't know why I've stayed there. It's a family house meant for a husband and wife with children. Like living in the past."

"You've got children—"

"I haven't got a husband, though—"

Her eyes widened.

"I mean, I had one, but we're divorced," I said quickly.

She laughed easily. "Yes, I'm divorced too."

The shock had as much impact as that cold water. I don't know why. I stared at her in disbelief. She laughed again.

"We've got a lot of ground to go over," and taking the towel from my hand, started rubbing at my damp hair. "Don't worry, we'll do it. But there's plenty of time ahead." She stopped rubbing for a moment and said reflectively, "It will be strange to be in London again. Funny to see Moo." There seemed no answer. I remained silent. "Five years," she went on, "that's when I saw her last—that's how long it's been since I was there." Her hands towelled briskly over my head. I relaxed, soothed by the firm but gentle pressure. She had a fine, experienced touch. I wondered how often she'd shampooed Freddie.

"She's changed, so Rupert says. Looks completely different now. Isn't she meant to be dying?"

Her hands rubbed more fiercely, I imagined, for a moment.

"Dying? Yes, so I've heard. But we're all doing that, aren't we, dying?"

"Well," I said, "then she's doing it faster."

"My goodness," Damson said heartlessly, "she'd better watch out. She'll lose her licence for speeding."

"Her life anyway."

We both laughed.

"Spot on, old girl." She sounded like her mother. "You're dry now, I'd say."

"Thanks." I took the towel. "Shall I wash this out?"

"Don't be boring. I'd leave it on the floor. Let's go and have a bit of grub. The boys will be here before we know it."

I followed her, the towel tucked around me, my hair now haloed round my hair like a curling cloud of sooty smoke. She glanced back, her expression changing. Click, click.

"Oh, don't do any more!" I protested.

She took no notice. "Just finish the reel. I've got a good idea here. If it works out we can both make ourselves a lot of money."

I gave up, obeyed each curt command, tossing my head, when she said to, smouldering straight at the camera, staring stonily through my long fringe. It got so that I gradually began to enjoy it all. Like flirting with the lens, having a private love affair. But I didn't laugh once. That would have felt too false. She stopped at last.

"That was really great. You're getting the hang of it now. Much better than the last lot."

"It felt better." Adrenalin was high. I could have done it all over again for two pins.

"You could well become a real pro. You should practise expressions in front of a mirror and play around with your body. Make it fall into your own sort of angles, really get it working for you."

"I don't feel right laughing."

"Don't do it then. That's what I mean. Get your own special look going. Savage or sulky, whatever feels right."

"I'd like to look soft and friendly most of all, that's how I feel inside, but it's not somehow how my face falls. It's funny that, don't you think?"

She turned away. "Bollocks!" she said shortly. I had been about to enlarge, clumsily, granted, but still prepared to go on. Giving her the benefit of . . .

"What?"

"Bollocks!"

I stood still to let it sink in. "Right," I said eventually. "Bollocks back."

"That's better," she said. "Now lay the table."

She cooked like an artist, the sort of arty artists they show in films, flinging colour at the canvas and stepping back appreciatively. Slap dash. On it went. Egg shells thrown to the floor and four winds. Butter browning to burning point. Cheese flaked furiously everywhere. I watched my recent houseproud efforts reduced once more to havoc.

"Omelette," she said and banged it on the table. I took a mouthful dubiously.

"Delicious," I said as it melted away.

She smacked her lips juicily, grease glistened on her chin. "You should taste my soufflé—sublime, though I say it myself. Not that I cook that much any more. Usually eat out. At André's or other places. Creates too much chaos here." She waved a fork. "As you can see."

I looked around. "What would your mother say?"

"My mother? Who's she? I'm a grown-up now, I've got no mother." She leant forward. "And nor should you. At our age we've learnt to cut family connections, surely. That dependence, and not daring to do—"

"But you were very close to yours," I protested. "You all liked each other."

"They liked me." She gave a short laugh. "They probably still do—if they're alive—"

"You mean you haven't kept in touch at all?"

"Listen, I got married at twenty. Six months later I was a mother myself and divorced to boot."

"I didn't know you had a child."

"I haven't any more."

"Oh dear, did it die? I am sorry." I touched her hand timidly and pulled a tender, sympathetic face.

She laughed cheerfully. What courage she had. "It might have died for all I know. No, I gave it away."

I froze. "Gave your child away?"

"Yes." She laughed again. "Your face, it's a sight. Yes, I didn't like it, so I gave it away. What's wrong with that?"

"It's honest," I said stiffly. "But I couldn't do it." I bent my head to light a cigarette and saw Harriet and Fanny in the flame. Each side of Paul. "Going up" in Harrods' lift. Turning left to Children's Clothes, with Françoise trailing moodily behind. Paul fighting it out, oh so subtly, with some assistant as to who should show the snootiest front. Harriet cleverly sensing it, exulting in her father's victory. Fanny missing me. And me, instead of being where I should, with them, me smoking in a Paris studio, listening to Damson telling me how she'd calmly given away her child.

"No, well," she was saying, "I expect you see your children as your life."

"Not all of it," I said, on guard.

"Them and a selection of lovers," she said shrewdly. "Is that right?"

"On the nail!" What else was there to say? I suddenly felt completely pointless. My life laid there amongst the dirty dishes. Appropriate placing. Like yesterday's left-overs. To my horror, my eyes went wet. I swallowed hard. "It's not enough, is it?" I said dejectedly.

She stood up, smiling like a satisfied sphinx. "Oh, I wouldn't say that, not by any means. After all, I expect you spread a lot of love around and that's good stuff, isn't it? Now," she said briskly, "don't for Christ's sake start indulging in self-pity, there's a good girl. I've got to get started." She moved across the room and left me sitting all at sea. "When the boys come, bang on this door. I'm in the dark room, okay?" I nodded miserably. She laughed wickedly. "Cheer up! It does everyone good to get it in perspective."

She banged the door behind her. I got up suddenly, strode across and, standing close to, I shouted through, "So sayeth the bloody prophet!" But all I heard was her answering laugh from the other side.

They'd been at it. I could tell the minute they came in. Rupert and Jean-Paul. But now things were going badly. It's ugly when it ends like that. Enchanted evenings, laced in heady anticipation—undressing, a bit embarrassed, cleaning teeth, closing the lavatory door, aiming urine carefully so the sound won't carry. Lights out, let's make love. But then the rhythm's wrong, or the smell close-to, or something in the skin. My ideal is smooth skin like my own which people think in men is nancyish. Not me though. I like it fine-grained, rather soft, no hair, with a body temperature similar to mine. Like—I tried hard thinking just who like. Well, like no one that I knew. Not now at any rate. Charles had a hairy body, hairy from top to toe, like coconut matting on his chest. When he sweated, wet strands clung together, went shiny, looked not unlike a river rat. Felt slimy to the touch. Sam? Sam never sweated which for such a large and heavy man was something I found very strange. Well, never sweated much that is. And yet was hot. Hot and dry like the desert, with skin as coarse as sand. You could have cut it up in squares and sold it at a hardware shop. Sixpence a sheet, no trouble. Physical facts, not serious, but if encountered just by chance and added on to other things, enough to put you off. Like buttocks pocked with pimples and roughly peeling nails. And chins that need a shave. And breath turned bad by dawn.

Looking at poor Jean-Paul and Rupert now, each so conscious of the other but communication temporarily abandoned, I wondered idly what had been the cause. They greeted me separately, both with a kiss. Jean-Paul gave two, being French. One on each cheek, but I'd turned away before the second came so that it landed in my ear. We both laughed.

"Where's Damson?" Rupert said abruptly as if now he was at odds with me too.

"In there." I pointed. "In the dark room. She said to bang on the door when you arrived." I looked around trying to locate my own clothes. "I'd better get something on I suppose. Oh don't worry, I can dress in the bathroom. That is when I see my stuff. Do you know where it is, Rupert?"

He shrugged irritably and shook his head. Jean-Paul put up a soothing hand.

"No, Myopia, for me to do your make-up you are perfect as you are. This first shot I think you are wearing only the hat and skirt so that I shall also be applying foundation on your upper half."

I stared at him and then at Rupert. "What?"

What. I could hear them all saying it. Back in London, buying *Chic* from Smith's counters. Charles frowning, "What the devil!" Sam smiling, "What the hell!" Paul perplexed, "What on earth?"

And the children giggling, "What are you meant to be doing, Mummy? What—"

"What?" I said again.

"Oh, just a little painting on the bosoms. Such as one would apply to the cheeks—"

"Cheeks?" I sat down on them quickly.

Jean-Paul touched his face delicately. "I polish and shine your oh-so-pretty breasts and on those charming nipples apply a little rouge."

When had he seen them then? Last night? "Well," I said uncertainly.

Jean-Paul twinkled flirtatiously. "It will be a labour of love for me, Myopia."

Rupert snorted and began banging. "Damson!"

There was a short silence the other side of the door then it opened slowly and Damson came out.

"Contacts," she said trimphantly and waved two long strips of shiny paper along which were printed small grey photographs, about the size of postage stamps. "Mind, they're still wet, but it gives you an idea of yourself." To me, "Here, look at them through this," and she put a square heavy slab of magnifying glass in my hand. I don't know what I was expecting but it wasn't what I saw.

We'd come across the place unexpectedly. One Saturday in a narrow street somewhere behind Tottenham Court Road. 'The Doll Museum.' "Shall we go in?" I'd said to the girls. "Oh yes," answered Harriet right away. But Fanny had hung back. I took her gently by the hand, a tiny bell tinkled as we stepped inside and an old woman with a crumpled face like a Christmas cracker took our money and directed us upstairs. It was a narrow dark building on three floors, formerly a house, late eighteenth-century or thereabouts. There were dolls everywhere—over the walls, all the way lining the stairs, each with neat detailed labels giving dates and origin. Harriet was ecstatic. I looked with interest at them on the slow voyage up. Fanny said nothing but held on tightly. But by the time we'd reached the top her uneasiness had communicated itself not just to me but Harriet too. "Oh look," my voice sounded unnaturally loud. "Oh look," I continued in a whisper. "This one's made of wax." We all three of us studied it in silence, a hundred eyes stared back in that one small room alone. Unblinking, blind in delicately modelled perfect frozen features. Faces which had in the past given untold pleasures to their child owners and yet known none themselves.

That's how I looked, like one of those. Damson watched closely for my reaction. "What do you think then, soppy?"

I shivered, the suddenness of the question and the sight of the cold pale face had set off a strange creeping sensation over my skin. That and the barely suppressed excitement in her voice. I cleared my throat, but kept on looking, moving the enlarging glass slowly up and down the strip of images. These were the last of the lot she'd taken. About ten towards the end of it, even to my inexperienced eye, seemed far superior to the rest. But by then I could remember I'd fallen more into the swing of things. She made a sudden movement of impatience as I continued to say nothing.

"Here, let the boys have a look. Go on, Rupert, you go first."

I stood up, suddenly self-conscious. "Anyone seen my cigarettes?"

No one answered. I hadn't expected that they would. The packet lay on the table, close at hand. I saw with surprise that my fingers shook slightly as I lit it. I wished they'd hurry up looking so that I could have another go. That was the bare bones of the matter.

Jean-Paul spoke first. He looked at me and said very slowly, "Last night I make a big mistake. I make Myopia like a beauty queen. I make applications of colour that are crude and far too obvious. Damson, I wish to make a fresh start today!" He stood up.

"Oh sit down," she said. "Everything's perfect, don't you see? Those, if they turn out as I expect—those will be just right for ordinary, well not ordinary, but conventionally beautiful. How-every-woman-longs-to-look, sort of stuff and that means that the dream ones can be much stranger, more like—nightmares." She tapped the strip in her hand. "This face denuded, raw, has much more impact, I agree, but let's make it even paler, emptier, more alienated . . ."

"I do that," Jean-Paul said eagerly. "I use greys and amethyst so that she look like a ghost. Like someone dead who walks in the sleep."

"Now you see," Damson looked reflectively at me. "I'm not so certain how I should do it. That first idea seems a little crass. What do you think, Myopia?"

"Who, me? About what?" I'd lost track.

She tutted and raised her eyes to the ceiling. "Wake up!"

"Well," I said defiantly, "nobody has told me yet what the first idea was, have they?"

Rupert softened. His bad mood was beginning to fade. "That's right. We hadn't properly explained." To the others, "Well, Damson had decided to do you as you were in your dream. That is flying over not London of course, but different parts of Paris. And not even flying necessarily but appearing in crowded places but always with some particle of clothing missing. So that for instance in this first shot that Jean-Paul mentioned you'd be nude from the waist up. The rest of you beautifully dressed of course—hat, gloves, skirt, shoes, but with your breasts bare, or in another—"

"Ah, you see," I saw him floundering. "That's where you run out of erogenous zones. There wouldn't be enough for six pages—"

Damson cut in. "Don't be silly. It's not a question of that at all. I'd shoot profile, front, back, from above, below. It's not the content that's important but what the camera does with it."

"Thanks," I said, but cheerful.

Everyone laughed. "Well," Damson put up her hand, "since then we've seen these, so what do we think? It introduces a new element, wouldn't you say?"

"I would," I said, "me."

*　　　*　　　*

"Go and say goodbye to your granny," my aunties clucked. Maiden aunties, all of them, which meant they weren't allowed to wear finger rings or go without their pinafores. Or put curlers in their hair. Or stuff on the pale, slab-pastry faces. In case there was a chance their maidenhood or something should be snatched away from them when they weren't looking. "Go on," they pushed me towards the parlour door. "Go and say goodbye to Granny."

I'd shrunk back. "No."

Coarse, capable hands caught me by the shoulder. I struggled, but it was not an equal fight. The door was opened, shut, the key clicked in the lock and I was inside alone.

Alone with Granny who lay in a long wooden box, its top leaning against the small piano. The blinds were drawn and it was very black, as black as the armband they'd sewn on my cardigan. I'd been the centre of attention in school, all week, because of the armband. Asked to join in all sorts of games in the playground. Accorded with a new respect. Next week they'd said they'd take it off. Two candles burnt by Granny's head, on each end of the mantelpiece. I went right up to the box to get a better look. She was wearing her new nightie, the one she'd sent me to get from the shop, the day she'd been taken bad. It hadn't been paid for yet, I knew that, since she'd asked me to get it on tick. I'd taken a bit of time choosing, made old Miss Tidy show me all there was. By the time I'd got back she was dead. But I'd got her a nice nightie. I picked it up to see if they'd left her knickers on. But there was nothing there except a matted, mossy grey triangle which looked to me as if it could have done with a comb. Her hands, knobbly things, normally with cuts and countless chilblains, were folded smoothly like a pair of gloves. And her face was very smooth too, as if someone had taken a scalding iron to it. It looked like Sunday best. Her eyes were shut, not tightly like they used to be when she was crying, but easily, just right. The lids sat on the eyes like a shell covers an egg. I poked at one with my finger but jumped back at the cold. It was colder than the toad my teacher had at school. And very white. Very sickly white. Like the maggots and lice you find under a stone. Sort of "see through" white.

*   *   *

Jean-Paul stood back proudly to survey his one and a half hours' steady work on my face. I stood up slowly and looked at it too.

"I won't sit you before the mirror as I do it—"

"Oh please," I'd begged, "I'd love to see how you start and go on."

"No," firmly, "you must wait till is all complete."

"My God," I gasped, "I look just like my granny."

His face went strained and disappointed.

"Oh no," I said quickly. "Not meaning rudely. Really! But the colour. It's the colour of a corpse—"

He gave a brilliant smile and a little bow, almost a curtsey. "Then I have achieved exactly the effect I was after."

Damson was in the dark room, printing blow-ups from her morning's contacts. Rupert was with her, helping. Jean-Paul hugged me, carefully keeping well away from my head.

"I call them now, yes?"

I nodded and laughed. "I won't turn round till they're in the room. Wait a minute. Take that white sheet off the bed. That's it. Drape it round my shoulders. I'll stand by the window. Looking out."

We giggled like schoolchildren. He suddenly stopped, frowning. "Not too much, the laughing. You might crack your maquillage."

I nodded solemnly and stared at him with cold and distant eyes. He seemed mesmerised momentarily, then gave a little shake like a puppy faced with something deeply disturbing. "You are, Myopia, far too lifelike," he said in a funny voice.

I continued to stare and murmured softly, "Life*less*." Then, at his silly expression I winked one eye, remembering to keep my face as straight as possible.

They came in excitedly. "Look at this blow-up. Look, it's sensational," but I didn't turn round, not immediately anyway. I wanted to savour the moment.

"Let's have a look, then," Damson said.

I swung round in my sheet, quietly, like a film in slow motion and held my arms out straight on either side. Since I'd chosen to look, eyes wide, at a distant point above their heads I'd done myself out of the satisfying sight of their faces in first impact. By the time I focused on them fully they must have had time to collect their senses and gather up their dropped jaws.

"Jesus wept!" Rupert whispered. Jean-Paul looked delighted. He turned to Damson enquiringly.

She swallowed, then croaked, "Fucking fantastic, boy."

I started to glide towards them. Each involuntarily took a step back. "Now look here, get off all that," Damson said, but I was beginning to really enjoy myself. "Bloody death's head," she said again. I went over to her and softly laid my fingers on her cheek. She jerked away. "Feel her hands, they're freezing." She sounded really angry.

I stopped. "Does it give you the willies?" I said in a normal voice, and looked at them with a friendlier face. Rupert took a deep breath.

"It's pretty strong stuff. Do you feel all right inside? You look— I don't know—drained." He stared closely into my eyes. "There's no blood in there at all, no blood vessels or veins or anything."

"Eye drops that I have put in." Jean-Paul spoke. The first dealings of the day with Rupert, I noted. "That makes the whites of the eyes very clear so the pupil and iris become more dramatic." He shrugged. "An old trick, of course, but this, this is a new Italian make. Is excellent, no?"

I looked in the mirror and paused. "I'm doing more of this looking in the mirror since I've been in Paris than I have for the whole of the last half of my life."

Jean-Paul looked surprised. "But of course. You are doing a professional job. How else can you become able to know your face?"

"You're muddling it up with vanity, Myopia," Damson agreed. "Quite a different thing."

I looked at their three faces glowing with life and good health and then back at my own. My grey eyes, always grey, grey as cigarette ash, grew lighter as I looked. I found by concentrating, lasting as long as I could without blinking, that I was able even to control the colour. That by turning my head whilst keeping my eyes on the same spot they reflected and echoed the waxy subtleties in my skin. "Perhaps it does help to practise." But it was as if I were talking to myself. "Wouldn't it be strange if you, knowing what you looked like, glanced in passing at a mirror and saw yourself like this. The same but as if you were dead."

I stopped. Damson listened carefully.

"Well, of course," I continued, "and also the other way round. As if a ghost or someone looking dead like me now were to see in a mirror herself but alive."

"Yes," Damson dragged the word out slowly. "Yes, the mirror image . . ."

I took from her hand the large print that she'd come running in with. Apparently now forgotten. Black and white, just of my face.

"This is beautiful." Rupert and Jean-Paul clustered round. "Isn't it?"

"What do you think of yourself then now, Myopia?" Rupert said teasingly.

I considered seriously. "Well, I think there's a lot there that you can do things with." He laughed. "No, I mean it's got me thinking myself . . ."

Damson snapped her fingers. "It bloody has. Could be great that idea of hers. I could do it, you know, the mirror thing."

We stared at her, she'd gone bright red with excitement.

"I've thought of something else," I started.

"I mean," she interrupted, "the semi-nude dream thing. You see tit and bum everywhere now, nothing new . . ."

"Anyway," Rupert added, "you never know, Moo might not think it 'quaite naice' enough for *Chic* and just run the normal sleeping ones we've done. She's always an unknown quantity. Lots of snaps get chucked out last minute if she doesn't quite 'see' them . . ."

"I've thought of something else," I tried again.

Damson gripped my hand so tightly I flinched. "You've thought of enough, my beaut."

"No, listen. What about if it's the dead image in the mirror doing that in black and white . . ."

She opened her eyes wide.

"Well," I said uncertainly and held up the big print.

"It just seems to look so much stronger without colour and . . ."

"And," she nodded, "we'll have the rest of the photograph, the real you in colour, which means the clothes . . . Yippee, God almighty, it's going to be tricky. But let's get going. We'll start with a head shot first. If that comes off a treat I can see it ending up on the cover."

We all us of beamed, carried by her enthusiasm.

"What excitement," Rupert cried.

I laughed out loud till I caught sight of Jean-Paul. He shook his head mournfully. I put a quick finger to my face.

"No!"

"But yes," he replied sadly. "You have cracked your beautiful maquillage. Now I, I must set about repairing it."

At six o'clock Damson sent Rupert to collect the previous night's colour transparencies. He was back with them by half past. Damson took them carefully out of their small plastic boxes and switched on a square light box in the corner. She placed them on top of it so that they looked like brilliant gems on a jeweller's cloth.

"Now," she took a deep breath, "the moment of truth."

They had me arranged beautifully, conscious or not, head resting on one limp arm, hand hanging gracefully weighed down with jewelled rings. Each frame contained a clearly consistent colour theme with only the violet chaise longue to link them. In every one the hair was arranged differently and looking closely I could see that in all not only had the face been repainted but so had even the finger nails to match whatever I was wearing. Like a bird of paradise, a peacock, the pure stuff of dreams.

Rupert sighed. "Jesus, I've got a job on now." I looked at him. "I'll have to go all through that lot and list every bloody thing— lipstick, Thunder Pink by Elizabeth Arden, Rose Soufflé nail lacquer by Helena Rubinstein, eye shadow, Azure Haze by . . ."

"Oh," I said, "did you use all those different makes, Jean-Paul?" They all laughed. He shrugged. "But of course not. I use everything that I have collected over the years. It's mostly theatrical but I have done many jobs like this for magazines. I know that always they must label untruthfully."

"To do with advertising, love," Damson said cheerfully. "Whichever beauty house has bought most space, that is placed most ads that month, they get the most editorial mention. Only practical, eh?"

"Well," I said, "I've been caught by that then. Liked the look of a lipstick somewhere in a beauty article, read what it was, bought it and found it's not the same at all."

"That's it. You shouldn't believe all you read then, should you, soppy?"

"Stop calling me soppy, Damson."

"Dopy, then, is that better? Now, let's choose the best of these and get on with it."

"Oh," I said, "can you still use those? With no mirror in?"

"Let me worry about that. Tricks of the trade. As it happens everything's perfect—better than we could have bargained for. In these your eyes are shut, so we're giving a good show to eye shadow that'll please old Moo. She likes keeping in with the cosmetic queens. And then as the ghost or as death your eyes are open. Makes it stronger you see. You're now not looking into the mirror, merely sleeping in front of it, and lurking death is looking at you. Whew." She looked triumphantly at all of us. "What do you think of that?"

"Should she be wearing the same outfits exactly though, Damson?" Rupert pondered. "I mean we've given enough coverage to Joe's clothes in these colour ones and I'm worried that in the black and white mirror ones they won't register so well because I put everything together in terms of colour and not tonally."

"Well," Damson puckered her eyes. I looked carefully amongst the glowing squares. Redcurrant reds, piercing pinks, plum, blood, purple, dusk blue, sweet strong leaf green, lemon, canary, and melon yellow, brown, brown sugar brown, bitter chocolate, dark rich treacle. Something missing.

"There's something missing," I frowned. "White! Rupert, what about, what's it called, 'Snow Siren'? Did we bring that? I'm sure we did."

"We did, yes. But then I decided not to use it after all. It didn't seem to fit in with these."

"But it would in the mirror."

"In black and white."

"Perfect! Get it!"

Damson sat down. "Christ! What a team. Well, kids, we're inching forward. Let's have a look at this 'Snow Siren' then."

Rupert brought it from the wardrobe. It had travelled well. Crêpe de chine, not a crease in sight. He held it in front of me. I moved to the mirror and drew the batwing sleeves to their full width. The silky pyjamas rippled around my bare feet. Jean-Paul placed the crystal skull cap loosely on my head. White from top to toe. Immaculate. Pure. An angel. A moonlit creature. Someone from the other side.

Damson stepped back and placed her fingers to her eyes, making a small square of them through which she looked, as if through the eye of a camera.

"Sensational," breathed Jean-Paul. "Ça c'est sensational."

Damson glowed happily and nodded. "It'll do," she said grudgingly but her eyes held that special look again.

"There you are, darling, didn't I say you should have this?" Rupert said smugly. "Now just look how useful it is after all."

I looked at myself and saw two wax candles flickering on a shabby mantelpiece casting shadows along smooth and waxy flesh. Picking out impoverished rayon lace, more suitable for a bottom drawer than a going away dress on the dead. Old Miss Tidy's best.

"Yes," I said slowly. "It has come in useful. Nearly as nice as my granny's nightie."

Jean-Paul painted my nails white, they looked like pearls by the time he'd finished. And over my hands he smoothed the same foundation that he'd used on my face. But he was disturbed by my hair.

"This," he said, lifting it and looking at Damson. "This I think is too dark."

She agreed. "Do what you think."

He tried pinning it flat and pushing it into the skull cap. "You agree?" he said to me. "We should have no hair."

I nodded. I knew perfectly what he meant. It was no good, strands kept falling out, there was just too much of it.

"Well," I said in the end. "Cut it off then. Go on, all of it, I shan't mind."

They looked at me approvingly.

"Really short," I went on, encouraged. "And what about while you're at it plucking my eyebrows? They're surely too dark aren't they?"

Damson nodded. "Be better with none at all."

"Yes," I said recklessly. "I can always draw them on till they grow again."

"What the devil have you done to yourself?"

"I've cut all my hair off and shaved my eyebrows, Charles. Do you mind? It looks a little bald I know, but it will soon grow back."

"Am I to understand that alopecia is now all the rage?"

"Something like that, yes."

"Perhaps," I said a little fearfully to Jean-Paul, "you could at least leave me my fringe."

We worked until past midnight. Damson drank steadily all the way through. Red wine.

"I could do with some of that," I said at one point.

Jean-Paul frowned. "Oh no, it will spoil your white lips."

"She can have it through a straw." Rupert fitted one carefully in but removed it too quickly while I was still drinking. I felt a thin trickle run from the corner of my mouth and heard Jean-Paul curse.

"No, wait! It looks good, like a vampire," Damson shouted from behind her camera. "Let me do some before you clean it up."

I'd got the no-blinking off to a T by then. In fact I'd slowly turned into this other self completely. I made my mind an empty room and allowed its walls to ripple with imagined horrors. Harmless particles of dust drifted together, turning into nests of insects' eggs which, feeding on each other's warmth, metamorphosed behind my eyes. Until the surface of the room became a heaving shuddering mass of minute beating wings and threadlike sawing legs. Entering this space, at first confidently, drawn to my full height, erect, I was stricken by the inability to breathe. My flesh hung pouched and withered like an old balloon, with nothing left inside. My bones shrank and grew soft, took on the consistency of the toothless gums in the aged and infirm. My tongue quivered, forked inside my mouth, darting helplessly towards the throbbing life surrounding it. And they, the insects, gradually grew in size and with it, altered in their shape, exuded monstrous rotting fumes. Began to fly. But being now so swollen and inexplicably without their wings they drifted down on unseen winds and settled on the slimy floor and me. Into my still moist eyes they came, so that when, with gigantic effort, calling on my last reserve of strength, I closed my lids I found with mounting panic that I had unwittingly trapped them there inside. And that now they were doing exactly what they wished to do. Devouring me internally. But still I stayed alive, though not in any physical sense at all since my body had long been sucked apart by those who surrounded it.

"Right, that's it then! Done!" Damson's voice reached me out of another world. The one to do with morning tea and putting on of radios. And blowing noses and buttering toast. All the ordinary actions that let you know there is no other world at all beside this one where these things exist. And that if you think there is you certainly are a very foolish person indeed. And serve yourself right for going off like that alone.

"You must stop this screaming in your sleep. Your poor father and I couldn't get a wink last night. Do it once more and we'll get the doctor to you. I won't warn you again. Now hurry your food down and be a little more sensible. You look awful. People will be wondering what I'm feeding you on."

Damson snapped her fingers. "You in a trance or what? Come on! I'm dying to eat. We'll have a big blow-out at André's, eh? He'll be open still."

I blinked for what seemed like the first time all day. "I went all funny then. It was awful. Was I all right? Did I do it well?"

"Superb! You want to be careful though, Myopia, not to get too fanciful. It runs in families they say."

"Don't be silly. Jean-Paul, can we take this face off now? I feel it's eating me away somehow."

He laughed. "Well, it isn't wise to keep it on too long. The pores can't breathe, you know. It has in it a certain substance, like lead white, that if I had put it all over the body in two hours you would indeed be dead."

"Good God," I said, alarmed. "Now is a nice time to tell me."

"Could have made good pictures though," Damson said cheerfully. "Now, Myopia, what's it to be when we get there?"

Rupert's tired voice said plaintively, "Champagne surely is called for. I don't know about anybody else but I'm completely buggered."

Damson laughed. "Uncross your legs, Rupe, and tonight you might get lucky."

I glanced at Jean-Paul but he was bent over his tin of cleansing cream, lifting out a scoopful on his fingers like delicious cold ice-cream. I wondered what would happen tonight. Rupert went to the bathroom.

"You oughtn't to have said that, Damson," I said to her reproachfully, quietly, so that Jean-Paul shouldn't hear. "You go trampling in until before you know it you could kill something beautiful."

She pulled a face and said mockingly, "Oh dearie me. I must mind my Ps and Qs, must I, madam?"

It came right out of the blue. "Why didn't you ever write back to me?"

"What?" She looked taken aback.

"You heard! I wrote and wrote and never had a word from you. I was terribly unhappy, you pig."

She glanced over at Jean-Paul. "I wasn't entirely unmoved myself." Rupert came back into the room looking sulky and withdrawn. "We'll go into it later." Hurriedly, "Now get a move on, Jean-Paul. Tell you what, Rupert and I will go on ahead and warn of our arrival. What about that?"

I nodded, I felt like a spot of peace and quiet. As if it would take time before my feet could realise they were actually touching ground. Jean-Paul took my skull cap off and carefully helped me step out of 'Snow Siren'. I put a towel around my body as I had that morning before it had all begun and closed my eyes whilst his firm fingers lathered the comforting cream all over my face. It smelt like Harriet and Fanny had when they were very small. Sane and sweet. Dimpled and damp and everydayish. Tomorrow I'd be back and Paris would be in the past. Except, of course, before then there'd be tonight to get through.

I'd had my fill of fine clothes for a bit. "I can't be bothered to dress up now, Jean-Paul. This is all right, isn't it? I'm not in the mood to be looked at any more." I stood in black trousers and polo-neck sweater, cropped head like a boy, thin long fringe almost in my eyes.

"The urchin, but why not?" he said.

We smiled at each other. "The end of a long day." I felt aglow all over, deeply satisfied, like after a strenuous ocean swim or when you've done the week's wash and you're piling it clean and pressed into the airing cupboard.

"You're a very, very clever boy, Jean-Paul." I put my arms around him. "And I love you dearly."

I was thinking of food as I said it, with all four of us sitting down and tucking in. And André in charge and taking care. And I was hoping in a generous flooding tender way that things would work out nicely for Rupert and the boy in my arms. I dropped them lightly to my sides.

"Time to go," I said brightly.

But he didn't move, just stayed glued to my front all the way down, his cheek hard against mine. I felt him trembling slightly, and turn a searching mouth towards my own.

146

"That's torn it," I thought. I made my body go as hard and sexless as I could, stiffening the spine and trying to squash back my breasts to be as small as they'd go by taking little shallow gasps of air. I don't know why I bothered, it had never worked before. And it certainly wasn't now. You could try anything when a man's in full flow. You could cross your eyes, put snot on him, cut orange peel teeth and place them on your own, begin to sing in high soprano, but nothing of it puts him off. Not with that sticky, stuffy goal in sight. I tried a kind, long-suffering sigh and a dose of solid British good sense.

"Look here," I said. "Jean-Paul. This just isn't good enough you know. Now pull yourself together, there are people waiting after all."

Quick as lightning he frogmarched me to the bed, yanked my trousers to my knees, threw me on to it and pulled his own pants down. A sweet pork sword, a tender chipolata. Much earlier on that day my troublesome period had disappeared. They do that some months, put in a quick and painful appearance then leave a spotless sanitary towel as a visiting card. "Just as well," I thought. "Not today, tomato sauce, merci beaucoup, maître d'hôtel. We don't take it with all our meals you know."

Twelve thrusts and a sharp sly twist at the end, to make the cake perfect. Then out of the oppressive heat of the oven and back into the open air. Into the cold to shrink the thing into a reasonable shape again. He did his trousers up with difficulty and, shrugging, looked down at me and laughed.

"It is not ready yet for sleep, my friend." He reached down for my hand and placed it on the bulge. "You excite too much, Myopia! Now I once again prepare you for your next appearance."

I lay there pulsing like a stranded fish, my knickers round my knees, one breast still lower than the other, when eager hands had snatched it from its brassière cup. I looked beyond his head and saw the door, then froze. It was open. Just half an inch, no light on the landing but enough in the room to catch and hold a strip of colour. The width of a fly catcher. Shiny yellow. Jean-Paul saw my expression change and swiftly looked around. Not swift

147

enough. In that infinitesimal instant it had gone. I stood up, pulled myself together, literally in all ways, and walked across the room. The door swung back easily and I stepped outside. There was no one there, but there had been, the perfume lingered on. Musky, cloying, unmistakable. "Babette!" I called. "Babette!"

Jean-Paul joined me. "You imagine, Myopia. There is no one here."

"Well, smell," I said. "What's that?"

He laughed easily. "That is Damson's perfume. I know it is a special one which only she must wear. It has a musk base."

"It's the same as Babette's," I said, "because I smelt it on her yesterday."

"Ah well," he said, "Babette. Yes, maybe she has stolen some at one time to remind of her beloved Damson. Or maybe Damson foolishly has dangled it before her eyes to take yet more delight in her distress. But come, we must go. There is nothing for you to worry about."

So that was to be that. We walked along to André's, passed similar but smaller cafés, all still full. Passed dress shops labelled 'Chypre' and 'Chère'. Crossed cobbled streets and traffic lights with Jean-Paul's hand held companionably around my waist with not so much as a glance from anyone. "He's fifteen years my junior, doesn't that seem funny to you?" I wanted to shout. But, of course, in Paris what was that? And in any case I was deceiving myself if that was what I claimed to be disturbing me. I thought of Rupert crying in my garden, how stranded he'd looked this morning coming in with Jean-Paul. And how pleased and hopeful he'd been last night. I saw Babette's shut and watchful face, and the long yellow line of her dress at the door. And then I thought of Damson. "Well, anyway. So what. She didn't write back."

As we came to André's door I broke away from Jean-Paul's hand and entered separately, alone. They were sitting on the far side, Rupert, Damson, Babette I saw, and André. He rose to greet me, as I approached, his gold teeth glinting in the lowered lights. The others stared as I held out my hand. He bent to kiss it but kept his dark brown eyes on my face. "Myopia," he murmured.

"André," I answered softly, and thought as I said it, "Oh well, in for a penny, in for a pound."

Midnight. A corner table in a French café, criss-crossed with fierce undercurrents of emotion. Cutlery in hand. "You could cut it with a knife," I thought. "This atmosphere, scoop it up with a spoon and swallow it, except for fear of indigestion." Damson was tucking in to second helpings, so she'd be getting it anyway. Indigestion. Unless the gods and her innards were looking the other way. Enchaud de Porc à la Perigourdine, that's what she was on, which translated comes out to be Loin of Pork stuffed with Truffles. I knew that because André told me. "You run a very good restaurant." That's all I could think of to say back, but it pleased him. In fact everything I did seemed to please him, even when at one point my food went down the wrong way, bubbling up in the back of my throat. "Ugh, ugh," I coughed. "Ugh." Everyone laughed but then I felt André's hand rubbing my back, putting things to rights. Underneath my jumper! "Ugh." Final cough, last little splutter. "That's better," I said. "All gone. Thank you." But he kept his hand where it was and I sort of had to let him really. It would have seemed too churlish to do otherwise at that point in the evening.

We did a lot of talking about what we'd done. Damson reckoned they were the best photos she'd taken. Except for a one very secret session she'd had with Freddie. That's how she put it— "one very secret session"—and I bent over my plate blushing a bit at the terrible thoughts of what she could have been getting up to.

Whenever I looked up one or other of them was watching me, as if somehow I was to be the deciding factor for the events of the night. The other tables were emptying until by half past one we were the only ones left. André told one of the waiters to lock up, then he sent him and the rest of them home. A bottle of cognac was passed around between us and came quite naturally to rest in front of Damson. I wondered briefly who was paying. Rupert and I had plenty of francs—we hadn't spent anything yet, only on the taxi from the airport. He was sitting next to me.

"Rupert," I whispered, "we should pay for this dinner surely."

But his face when he turned it to me was so dreadfully miserable that I said quickly, "What I mean is that *I* should, don't you think?"

He nodded dejectedly. Jean-Paul was talking excitedly to Damson and had paid no attention to Rupert for the whole of the meal. "Perhaps I should think of keeping my money for a hotel tonight."

I was appalled. Oh dear. Dearie me. I took his limp hand.

"Is it all over then?" And cast a glance towards Jean-Paul to show what I was talking about. Well, I thought, I've surely got some influence in that direction now! "Would you like me to have a word with him, Rupert? I can't bear seeing you like this again."

That set him off. He stood up quickly, scraping his chair, and went off to Messieurs.

I looked at André. He shrugged and laughed, though I don't think he'd heard what we'd been saying. I leaned forward a long way towards Jean-Paul so that André's hand fell out of my jumper on to my bottom, right under it, fingers spread.

"Jean-Paul." I said it with great urgency, to get it over with before Rupert returned. "Jean-Paul, is Rupert staying with you tonight?"

His smile faded. "Rupert?"

"Yes. You haven't quarrelled or anything really, have you? Not really seriously, I mean?"

He lifted his shoulders, shrugged just like André, but he didn't laugh. "I do not know what I have done to Rupert but he doesn't speak to me all day so naturally I do not speak to him. That is all."

"Well." I could see Rupert coming back towards us. "Please try, Jean-Paul, he's very unhappy. It would be a shame to lose a nice friendship, wouldn't it?" I looked hard into his eyes and lowered my voice right down so the others couldn't possibly hear. "After all, I could have turned nasty and said no, couldn't I?" He looked astonished but I kept on staring until at last a slow smile broke out. We both winked at precisely the same moment. Rupert sat down, looking sulky. It crossed my mind that he must bring these situations on himself. You can't expect to always bring things off by being babyish. "A spoilt boy," my mother would have said.

"Would you like a cigar, you two?" They looked at each other and nodded back at me. André went to fetch some. "And me," Damson shouted.

"You say yes to anything going in your mouth don't you?" I said.

Babette glowered at her end. She really put me off, that girl. I wished she'd get up and go. Damson was taking no notice of her at all. But I seemed to have pulled something off for Rupert with Jean-Paul. They lit their cigars together and from there on remained engrossed in each other. I don't care what anyone says, that lighting-up lark is a sure winner for breaking the ice. With cigars more than anything because they take so much longer to get going. And when all at once Rupert said, "André, could we have the bill? I'm paying for this meal," I knew everything must be all right again.

André wouldn't hear of it, of course. He waved his hands and shook his head. "It is my pleasure, please allow me that. Tonight no one pays, okay?" But he kept his eyes on mine while he said it. Except me, I thought. I'll be paying indirectly. Not that I minded, not at all. I thought he was nice, very nice, and that was always enough. Anyway, I'd never had a man with gold teeth before. I thought of the schoolgirl joke.

"Tell me, André," I said, "your two front teeth, are they like stars?"

He looked startled. "Stars?"

"Yes. Do they come out at night or are they cemented in?"

He threw his head back and roared.

"I'm only asking. It's not that funny."

But he went on laughing, shaking helplessly. "You like them?" he spluttered. "Yes?"

"Oh yes, I think they're beautiful."

"Ah," he stood up, "one moment then."

I took the opportunity to change seats. Sitting in the lavatory, I tried to sort things out quietly. If I was Prime Minister or occupied the throne, that's where I'd rule the country from. The privy. Privy Councillor. Was that what it meant? Anyway, nothing like a confined space for clearing the head, clarifying the situation, concentrating on the central issue. It wasn't quite so easy in this one, too much effort had to be wasted in seeing that my trousers didn't get splashed. A tiled hole in the floor with ridged foot-rests either side. I'd have a word with André afterwards to see if he hadn't considered interior modernisation. This undignified squatting would hardly suit a Head of State.

Damson was the fly in the ointment. I knew now that I didn't want to get tied up with her again. Not in the way it had once been. Too much something or other had flown under the bridge. Working with her was great, but barging into my life and taking over, knowing everything that was going on, making my decisions for me—that was a different matter. I'd stay with André tonight, that should make things clear to her, spell it out so to speak. And tomorrow before leaving for London I'd say it wasn't convenient for her to stay with me there. Babette should be pleased, poor creature.

When I got out, there she was. At the mirror, making up. She watched me while I washed my hands. "Hello," I smiled. She didn't answer. Well, I thought, she's half mad. She really is. That's what Damson's done to her. Well, she'd done it to me too in a sort of way. The year she left. Lost, that's what I'd been. Shot through with self-doubt, irrational fear and a dreadful fierce possessiveness. Or is that just what love does to you anyway? Hadn't I been the same with Paul? Unequal love then. When one is giving more and getting less than the other. A better balance is what's needed, so that though on one side of the scales it's all sugar and on the other a steel weight, things can still work out even if the proportion's right. You can't say that to people though, like the onlooker you can only see the game. I took the bull by the horns. I love that expression—as if anybody in their right senses would! What, with big wide nostrils snorting at you like a steam kettle? And bulging eyes as red and ripe as wild strawberries? You'd have to be pretty wild yourself. But I did it.

"Babette," I started. She'd finished her face and was now filing her nails. I'd noticed her nails before, they'd reminded me of Moo's, the same shape, long and narrow coming to a fine point at the tip. Lethal weapons. I took a step back.

"Babette." She didn't look up. "You have no reason to worry about me. Not at all. Not about Damson and me, I mean." That was putting it baldly, but I was thinking about her understanding of English first and foremost.

She held the nail file as you would a dart towards the board, except if she let fly now it would have landed in my throat. When she spoke it came out a cross between a hiss and a curse, with her upper lip curled back like an attacking animal. "Françoise, she is your girl!"

I laughed but I felt a prickly uneasiness, a desire to escape. Why hadn't I left well alone? Whatever I said I could tell she couldn't be convinced. From the restaurant I could hear Damson's rich and fruity laugh, echoing the lighter sound of Rupert's. And André's strong and reassuring voice, binding the whole thing together. I wanted to be with them, back there in the warm. But Babette moved quickly. More swiftly than I would have believed possible, she slipped behind me, locked the door and stood with her back against it. Something jolted painfully against my ribs, if she'd been closer I would have said her nail file except that this was happening from the inside and hammering hard now, right up in my eardrums. It's always amazed me how terribly tiring fear is. Real fear.

Harriet had run across the road once, when very small. I'd turned round and there she was with people shouting and speeding cars screaming to a halt. A stranger picked her up in his arms on the other side. "Where's the mother?" they were saying but I couldn't move; from sheer exhaustion I couldn't take a single step—only sink down and sit where I was right there on the cold pavement.

I could have done with a nice chair now or tear gas or a cold water hose. Anything to get her out of the way. But somewhere the voice of reason came to my rescue. She looked insane, that was for sure, on the point of eruption, losing her cool, blowing her top, consumed, crackers!

"What a very pretty girl you are, Babette," I said. Her eyes flickered for a split second. "Françoise is always telling my children that, and how you model for Dior. She is my au pair. Next week you will be able to see her, she's coming home here for a holiday. Tomorrow when I'm back in London I shall tell her that we met."

Her hands dropped to her side, the nail file fell to the floor. I took a smooth step towards the door, but it wasn't over yet. I could tell by her tense face. She spoke slowly in a dangerously tight, over-controlled voice. "I should like to kill you. You are a hateful person. Like an artichoke, you give a little of yourself to everyone. I have seen—"

"Oh yes, Babette, I saw you seeing at the door—"

She stopped suddenly. Then threw back her head like a pony, puckered her mouth together and spat in my face. I felt it sliding over my skin, lifted one arm and wiped it away with my sleeve. Then I reached behind her and unlocked the door. As I walked back to the table I could hear her crying hysterically. "Your girl friend is upset, Damson. If you're at all kind you'll go and see to her," I said as I sat down.

Good in bed, I'd had lots of those without a doubt. Good at it. And I'm all for technical knowledge, knowing your job and using your instruments well, but you can still feel at the end of it a certain flat. Hard to put your finger on quite why. Perhaps when all's said and done it still comes down to conversation and not taking it too seriously. Or else taking it very seriously indeed. Like André.

"A bloke who knows what he's doing, believe you me, can get goose pimples growing on your eyeballs!" Who said that? Not Shakespeare. Mavis. Mavis and Lottie at old Pilsky's café under the pier. But would they swallow it at the optician's? "It would appear that quite suddenly I need spectacles. I've been to Paris and now have curious protuberances all over my corneas!"

Spot on it was, right from the start. "A small gift," he said.

"For you. It's what I went to fetch before your little scene with pauvre Babette."

"Oh yes. How sweet. What is it?"

He handed me a small white plastic box. "With my love, Myopia. So you will never forget me. You must wear it around your neck."

"Oh, André. Jewellery. You shouldn't."

His eyes twinkled wickedly. "Open it."

Inside lay two gold teeth attached to a fine mouth-shaped wire with metal loops at each end. I looked at them in astonishment. Then at him. He smiled. "Oh no, those you have there are my spare set. You were quite right, you see. Yes, my teeth are indeed like the stars. Except that I don't necessarily remove them at night as you will see." Then he kissed me, holding my head in his hands, gently as if it were a small bird and not part of my body at all. In the middle I burst out laughing, thinking about the false teeth and how they'd look hanging round my neck. Instead of being put out he joined in too and must have known what I was thinking because when we stopped he said, "You will, of course, remove the wires first." I liked that.

His apartment was above the restaurant. I sniffed when we went in to see if the smell of cooking floated up. He watched me. "No, you see. You smell nothing."

I nodded, he was quite right. It was a huge place on two floors, with art books everywhere and paintings all over the walls. "What a lot of paintings."

He shrugged. "That is my enthusiasm. I have collected since I was fifteen. It is where all my money goes. Like a disease of the blood."

"Your greatest enthusiasm?"

"That and beautiful women, of course."

"Of course," I said, but right away I felt cold. He knew. He pulled my head softly round again so I would look him in the eyes.

"Myopia," he said, "you are a child if you think at my age there could not have been others. And you? You are a virgin?"

I opened my eyes wide. "Me? No, of course not. Goodness, I've got two children."

"Ah," he said gravely, "ah, then you have done it twice."

"Oh, André, that's a very old one."

He nodded. "Like me it has been around."

"Well, I've been around too but if you're a woman you're not supposed to say that, are you? Though I've never understood quite why. People don't say of a man that he's promiscuous do they, and there's no such thing as male nymphomania, is there? They call it a Don Juan complex, which comes out to sound like a compliment more than a curse of the blood."

I stopped. "Am I going on too much?" Sam would have said so. "Jesus Christ, when I wish to indulge in a diatribe on the sexual psychology of the sexes I'll go to a fucking bookshop and buy one. Now shut up, woman, and start sucking."

"I'll get undressed now if you like, André."

But he took my hand and shrugged, smiling. "My Myopia. There is no hurry, we have until morning."

I looked at my watch. "Well, it's that now, after all—"

He covered the face of it with his fingers. 'Ssh, ssh, there are many hours left. But first we must prepare."

I must admit my heart sank at that a bit. My idea had been to get into bed, have a quick cuddle and a bit of a poke then drop off to sleep together. Not a big procedure such as he seemed to have in mind.

"Well," I said, "it's been a long day and I've got a bit of a headache." Which, as I said it, sounded a shade too housewifely for even my liking. All it needed was "Have you set the alarm, darling? I plan to start the spring cleaning bright and early." "I'm sorry," I laughed out loud. "Now I do sound like a professional virgin."

But he didn't answer. Instead he went out of the room and came back carrying a small glass with some treacly liquid in it. Just about a teaspoonful. "Drink this, darling."

"What is it?"

"Just drink it."

"Not till I know what it is. It could be anything."

He sighed. "You think I plan to drug you? And what use would you be then?"

"What use? What a horrible way to put it. I don't have to stay here, you know. I've got money. I can go to a hotel." My voice rose steadily. I listened to it in a detached sort of way with some amusement. It was years since I'd pulled that stroke, it always put them in a tizzy. Fish pie floating through the port hole! Fare thee well. Plop!

André stood calmly staring down at me, totally unaffected. He held the glass up. "This is part of our preparation. The other part is in the bedroom. Now drink it."

"Why?"

"It's a simple but immediately effective laxative."

"A laxative?"

"To relax you, cure your headache and prepare the way for our lovemaking. A necessary step as you will understand later."

I drank it in one gulp. "Now you come to mention it I am a little constipated. My bowels are never quite what they might be after a journey." What love talk! Quelle sweet murmurings! We smiled at each other.

"Good girl! Now I run you a warm bath."

I sat where I was, waiting for the desired results. "Constipation in varying degrees of severity is generally brought about by incorrect habits of living, chiefly dietetic. We therefore suggest a dietary of foods with a 'high residue', such as green vegetables, fresh and dried fruits, wholemeal products and nuts. Olive oil and nut oil will also be found beneficial. Correction of the diet will generally prevent constipation in time. *Herbalene* should be taken until adjustment of the diet has been satisfactorily effected." I knew that off by heart. It comes on the back of the *Herbalene* box, a pleasant packaging, bright yellow with a blue band across the top. *Herbalene* made by William E. Lusty. (None genuine without this signature.) A greyish powder smelling of aniseed balls with a large warning printed amongst the directions, *Do Not Masticate*. Just that, *Do Not Masticate*.

The desired results came sooner than expected. Speedy Gonzales. We used to dance to that song. Thank God the lavatory was separate from the bathroom. Divided off with the bidet next to it. I felt as if a snow-storm was raging in my stomach. Like an enema. André knocked at the door. A less sensitive man would have barged right in. I saw the handle turn. "Don't come in, I haven't finished yet." But he stepped inside, smiling, with a cup of coffee in his hand.

"Well," I said weakly, "there's not much privacy around here, is there?"

He lifted my head and tilted the cup towards my lips. "To give you a little strength."

"It'll go straight through," I warned.

"So much the better. It is only with a clear passage that perfect pleasure is achieved. Later you will express your gratitude."

"Later maybe," I groaned. "But at the moment I'm a little busy expressing something else."

I'd never liked it much before, in fact it was stronger than that, most of the time I'd downright refuse. I'd heard of it first, oh ages ago, of course. From this girl I worked with. We were talking together about sex. "Well, I'm a virgin still," she'd said. I looked at her doubtfully. Twenty-four if a day, with the phone ringing non-stop on her desk from men trying to make dates. "I'm saving it till I get married. I've promised my father."

"Oh yes," I said. "Each to his own. It seems to work anyway. Chastity. You've got them buzzing like flies. Good luck to you."

"Around my bum."

"Beg pardon?"

"Around my bum. That's where they're buzzing."

"Oh dear." I choked on my chocolate biscuit.

"Well, my father never mentioned anything about behind. A public schoolboy suggested it first to me and I've been at it ever since. It's nice, you should try it."

"No thank you very much. I don't take to the idea at all."

A few months later she got married, in white. And her father died the next day. A happy man. It had always surprised me how many men seemed keen on it that way. Of course they don't have to look at your face which saves a lot of embarrassment. How could they look at it, when it's dumped like an empty bucket upside down in the middle of a pillow? The most they get is a sideways view of your snout as you're coming up for air. Which is hardly romantic. Apart from that it hurts. Hurts like hell. Or so I'd found before. Men's things, if they were meant for there, should have a definite thread on them like corkscrews so that they could fit the puckers better—go in clockwise or anti, depending on your ridges. The normal way of doing things round the front it's not necessary. There are no ridges, only folds, like curtain folds, so it's simply a matter of parting them to let a bit of light in. That's what I'd always thought, anyway.

After my bath, André led me to the bed, a four-poster. "This is nice," I said, "I've never slept in a four-poster."

"It's been in my family for years."

"However did you get it up the stairs?"

"Oh," he laughed. "We had to dismantle it and then put all the pieces together again."

"Really?" I stretched myself out. "Well, I expect it was worth the effort."

"Not that way, Myopia."

"What?"

"Turn over please."

Oh God, I thought, here we go again. "I'm not very keen on it that way, André. Do you mind?"

"Say nothing." His voice was stern. I sighed and turned over on to my stomach. It was a high bed, surprisingly hard, a good working surface, I supposed. My head, I saw when I turned it to the side, was about level with his upper thighs.

"Goodness me," I gasped. "You're massive. I can never take all that up there." And I stretched out to touch it.

He smacked my hand lightly away. "Now get up on all fours and see what you can find under the pillow."

159

I did as I was told and brought out a shiny plastic penis. Slightly smaller than his own but still a pretty good handful.

"Is this part of your art collection?" I giggled stupidly.

He took it from me and pressed a switch. It started right away, trembling gently like a well-set jelly. Then he pressed again, at which it shook so violently it nearly jumped out of his fingers.

"See?" he said, "battery operated."

I nodded. "Keeps the place neater. No flexes to fall over."

But I felt as apprehensive as when I went once to have a wart removed. "It won't hurt," the doctor had said. "And afterwards all you'll have is a clean open hole." "What, always? Open I mean? What do you suggest I use then, Doctor? A safety pin possibly?"

"That won't overstretch it, that thing, André? I don't want to be walking round with a big hole in the back." I could end up incontinent, I thought, with a useless set of anal muscles. "And exactly what have you been up to, young lady?" they'd ask at the hospital. "I must have sat on something."

"Do we have to?" I said. "Honestly, André, I'd far rather—"

He took no notice. "Now first we anoint the temple."

I felt his fingers, firm, insistent, nice like a nurse's, massaging, probing, oiling with a warm, slippery jelly.

"That's nice," I said, surprised. "Have you heated it, that stuff? How considerate." Perhaps this time it would be different. He'd made a good start.

"Relax," he murmured. "Relax, Myopia."

I knew what he meant, despite what he was doing or possibly just because he was, I'd tightened everything. Even my mouth and fists knotted up like balls of string. Clamped together like a stamp on an envelope.

"Look at yourself," he urged. "Straight ahead, look."

There was a canopy of heavy brocade above the bed and all around it curtains of the same material. Drawn back now with tasselled ropes. The head of the bed was against the wall and in that space hung a large mirror with an intricately carved wooden frame. It had been tilted slightly so that it didn't lie flat but instead reflected completely the entire surface I was lying on.

I'd seen that already but hadn't liked to look. Now I lifted my head and gazed at us both. André smiled, his gold teeth shone rich and coppery in the lowered warmth of the shadowed lights. Like the Turkish Delight commercial. Full of eastern promise. If I'd had a box in front of me it would have been jelly, both ends. Then he started with his piece of plastic, the quivering tip at first, set on low speed. It wasn't unpleasant, if you concentrated on something else. I thought about the girls' last school reports. "Harriet is a child with a mind of her own." Whose else would she have anyway—the next door neighbour's? "Fanny must learn to conquer her left-handedness." I looked in the mirror, André was left-handed. He obviously hadn't learnt to conquer it but he was doing all right. Perhaps by the time Fanny was his age and still left-handed she'd be using it to wield a plastic weapon too. André smiled at me, he seemed a long way away. I brought my elbows up and rested my head on my hands.

"Are you enjoying it?" I said pleasantly.

"Are you?" he answered.

I let myself go to think about it. All I could feel was a dull drilling like at the dentist's when you know he's on a nerve but because of the gum injection you can't feel a thing. By the end it becomes sort of soothing, you miss it when he stops.

I nodded. "How much have you managed to get in?"

"About half."

"No! I wouldn't have guessed that. Well, go on then."

I said it cheerfully. I felt encouraged though. Not as yet carried away with any great desire.

"Hey look," I said into the mirror. "At least I've stopped gritting my teeth."

The excitement started slowly. On tiptoes, tapping softly like a blind man's stick, sneaking stealthily through to the front of me. A small washing wave at first which took me by surprise and set me all a-tingle. I lay quite still, conscious of a loud thudding heart, a rushing of saliva in my mouth and an urgent need to touch. I shut my eyes and began to spin. André knew, he must have sensed the difference.

"Now you are ready for me, Myopia."

"Yes," I murmured. Anything. A cold cucumber! A stick of Brighton rock! Anything so long as he wouldn't leave me empty. The plastic throbbing had stopped, there wasn't a sound now except the muffled ticking of a clock and my own heavy breathing. He rolled me slowly on to my side, brought my knees up and gently opened them. Then he slid himself inside me. I couldn't have said where first. Front or back, they'd become indivisible. When he was in one place the other ached for attention which right away his hand supplied. I curled around him, foetus-like, kissing him on to climax whilst wanting it to carry through till dawn. And so it did. Three times in all we did it, which wasn't breaking any record. Not in quantity that is. And each of the times he deposited in a different place. The last I swallowed, sitting up to gargle with it first. He pulled me back till, smiling in each other's arms, surrounded by the early morning sound of Paris streets, we fell asleep together.

I just about remembered the way back to Damson's place, although by day it looked quite different. "I shall come with you," André had said. "I shall come with you and then I will drive you to the airport."

"No, don't do that! Please. I'd much prefer to say goodbye to you here, without anyone else around."

He didn't argue. "You'll come to Paris again." It wasn't a question and as such needed no answer. I held his teeth in my hand.

"Next time you see them they'll be round my neck."

I bought a packet of Gauloises and walked along the street, smoking. Boulevard St. Germain. How excited we'd been, Jean and me, when we'd seen that first. Would my life have been different if I'd met André on that trip? I rounded the corner of Les Deux Magots and then on impulse retraced my steps, sat down at a pavement table and ordered a Pernod. I smiled up at the sky. Sunday. Sunday in Spring. And me full to the brim with light and bursting life, enough just about to get up and do a tap dance over the tables. Treat everyone to whatever they wanted. Take the whole of Paris on my knees and hug them half to death. If this was a film I'd be singing by now, I thought, and the string section would be twanging fit to bust a gut. Fred Astaire or Gene Kelly would be popping up out of nowhere to whirl me into the middle of the road, dancing like mad, stopping the traffic. Everyone throwing open their windows and tossing flowers down, all joining in the chorus. "I love Paris in the Springtime. I love Paris in the Fall. Chorus: I love Paris, why, oh why do I love Paris—because my—because my—"

"Myopia!" It came at just the right time. I couldn't for the life of me have finished. What was that damned last line?

I smiled up. "Hello, Rupert."

"What on earth are you doing?"

"I'm singing, but I just got stuck. What's the end of *I Love Paris*? 'Why, oh why do I love Paris because my'—? What comes then? 'Because my'?"

He sat down. "What are you drinking?"

"A Pernod. What comes then? I'm going mad." I sang it softly in case he couldn't remember the tune.

"All right." He joined in. People started looking from the next table. Looking and smiling. Perhaps they knew. "I've got it," Rupert said. "Because my love is there. Right?"

I looked at him. "That's not right. It doesn't rhyme."

"I know it doesn't, but that's how it ends."

"Are you sure? I'm not at all myself. I shall look it up when I get home. I've got Maurice Chevalier singing it somewhere if I can find the record."

We looked at each other and burst out laughing.

"Now," I said, "shall we start again? You come walking towards me. Go on, get up and come towards the table. I'll be sitting here sipping my drink and I promise I won't be singing this time."

"You're mad this morning, I can tell. Pots for rags. Crackers." But he got up, reapproached and we did indeed start all over again.

"Myopia!"

I smiled up. "Hello, Rupert."

"What on earth are you doing?"

"I'm sitting here sipping a Pernod, soaking up the sunshine and simply oozing goodwill and happiness. How's that?"

"We were worried. I've already been round to Damson. We rang André and he told us you'd left. I was afraid you'd got lost."

"I just felt like a daydream, that's all. Have I put you out? Where is Jean-Paul? Did things go well last night?"

He sat back and ordered a Pernod. "Will you have another?"

"Better not."

He ordered another anyway. "We'll drink it up half each. Now, where were we? Last night! Oh, Damson wasn't too pleased. You should have heard her. It was awful—"

I sat forward anxiously. "Not too pleased with me? You mean for staying—"

He looked surprised. "With you? For staying with André? I should think she was delighted."

"Delighted?" Something slight ached inside me, like seeing a one-time love linking arms with somebody new.

"In the circumstances it was the best thing that could have happened. With Babette. She became uncontrollable. Damson had to call her doctor. At one point she was trying to jump out of the window."

"On that top floor?"

"If you'd been there she would have dragged you with her."

"I don't doubt."

"Anyway, the doctor called an ambulance and they've taken her away."

"Poor thing," I said. Taken her away! Yes, my mother was always saying that. They've taken her away. In the end they came and took her away too. She pegged it before they'd even got to the traffic lights so they might just as well have left her where she was. "Were you there, then, you and Jean-Paul?"

"We had to be. Damson couldn't have managed on her own. Where did you disappear to?"

"I'm sorry. André said to slip upstairs while Damson was in the lavatory with Babette, and I thought it was best for her not to set eyes on me again. I felt I was the one who'd started it all off."

"You might have said good night."

"I didn't want to make a big thing of it, that's all. Anyway, was it? A good night, apart from all the trouble? Afterwards?"

His face slowly split in two like a sliced melon. It was lovely to watch. A Cheshire cat who'd been at the cream. Pleased with himself. Like an obedient angel who's been given the night off and then abused it by extremely bad behaviour. My own smile spread in sympathy. "So it's all been worth it, this trip to Paris?"

He sighed. "What?"

I sighed too. "I feel much the same myself."

He sat back, tilting his chair, folding his hands across his stomach as if after a deeply satisfying meal. "But I'm in love, Myopia."

An apprehensive breeze blew over me. "Oh lord! Are you? With Jean-Paul? Is he?"

"He is. I am. We both are. Isn't it wonderful?"

"Yes," I said lamely.

He brought his chair forward quickly and opened his eyes wide. "Oh, we owe it all to you. Really we do. Yes, Jean-Paul told me about," he bent his fingers in a dismissive gesture towards me, "you know, you and him. That's what decided him. He'd never tried it with a really beautiful woman ever. And he said if it couldn't even work with someone like you, then—then he'd be better off following his natural inclinations."

"So," I started to laugh. "So—" and couldn't go on. "Oh dear, oh dear," I gasped, then at last I caught my breath. "So," I gurgled, "having me has put him off girls for good." I took his hand. "Oh, Rupert, I am glad for you."

He looked bewildered. "Well, it was meant as a compliment, Myopia. He thinks you're the tops."

"I know. And I'm extremely proud to have been of service. Where is he anyway, Jean-Paul?"

His eyes grew luminous and faraway. His voice came low and sweet. "I left him in bed. He was exhausted."

Mm. That's where I'd left André. We both sat staring into space until I shifted uncomfortably in my chair. "These seats are very hard, aren't they? How about going?"

We walked back arm in arm, looking in shop windows on the way. What could be more out and out pleasant than this? I matched his footsteps with my own. "Oh Rupert," I said, "you're not looking. You trod on a crack then, the trick is to miss them, otherwise—"

"Otherwise it's bad luck, I know."

"Well, don't tempt fate, not when things are going so well." I stopped in my tracks. "Do you know what I was thinking yesterday?"

"What?"

"I was thinking that if these photos are as successful as we think, Moo Moffat-Paw will be offering you a job."

"Oh Myopia, didn't I say? Jean-Paul has asked me to do a job with him—next week—for French *Mode*."

"No!"

"Yes. They're doing a feature on British fashion and have already asked him if he knows someone good in London to get the clothes together. Well, I know everybody who's designing anything worth while. I can do it standing on my head. Hey," he stopped and stared at me excitedly. "So could you, Myopia, couldn't you? Why not?"

"What? Stand on my head? Don't be daft."

"Model. Model the clothes. I've only just thought of that. Let's ring him, Jean-Paul. Let's ring him now and see what he thinks."

"Can't we do it from Damson's? She's there waiting for us, isn't she?"

"No. She's not. She's working. Developing the 'Snow Siren' ones to see how they look. Anyway we daren't ring from there. I'm sure *Mode* haven't asked her to do the photographs. You'll probably be working with someone quite different. Whoever it is, you'll find it a dream after Damson."

"It wasn't that bad," I protested. "I'd far rather work with her than someone dead from the neck upwards."

166

He squeezed my arm. "Don't worry, I'm exactly the same. That's the thing about Damson—the loyalty her friends feel for her. But what you have to remember is," he paused, "that it isn't in any way reciprocated. She's a very much of the moment girl. Here today and gone tomorrow. You know what I mean?"

"Yes. Yes, I do."

I waited outside the phone box and watched Rupert talking. He kept turning round, winking and nodding through the glass. I had to laugh. I hadn't seen him so happy. I crossed my fingers and said a silent prayer that everything could stay like that for him and Jean-Paul. At least there seemed a likelihood that he'd be waving farewell to Streatham Hill. He must have seen my hands because he lifted his own crossed fingers too. Crossed fingers, crossed purposes, I thought. I couldn't have cared less about the job next week if it came off or not for me. I'd done my stint of modelling but it did occur that it might be nice to have a shot at earning my own money again. This could be as good a way as any. Independent. Independent of Paul. Free of the need to marry. Free to make love or not to whoever I wanted. To live in a place of my own choosing. To bring up my children however I thought. That wasn't bad. "By golly not," I said out loud. A small child with plaited hair, sucking an outsize lollipop, stopped to look at me.

"By golly not," I said to her. "Qu'est-ce que vous dites, ma petite?"

"Oui, madame," she nodded gravely and went steadily on her way.

Rupert joined me excitedly. "It's in the bag, Myopia."

"No!"

"It is honestly. A friend of his—Serge something or other—is the photographer and he'd already spoken to him this morning. Jean-Paul said he'd found a super new face, you, and Serge said if she lives in London why not use her."

"Oh Rupert."

"So they're ringing us tomorrow and will probably come over on Thursday. What do you think of that?"

"Thursday. That's all right if you can get all the things together."

"You can come with me, to all the places, so we can choose things on the spot."

"This week. Hey," I said slowly, "wasn't this the week we were going to go away? Sit on a beach and work out our futures?"

He slid an arm through mine and slipped easily into step. "Well," he said creamily, "there's no need for that now is there? Our futures have already been decided."

Damson had decided not to come to London. She looked worn and very irritable when we arrived. "I've been waiting," she said accusingly. "Where on earth have you been?" Then she turned away. "The hospital rang. I've got to go there. Babette keeps asking for me. They say she's refusing to eat or drink."

"Oh dear, poor thing."

She snorted. "Poor thing! Bloody nuisance! It's like having a dog around, a fucking bitch on heat! At least with a dog you can kick it or at best have it put down."

"Damson!"

"What? They should let people like that die. Put her out of her misery. Get her off my back anyway."

"What you suggest seems a little drastic, after all you must have given her some encouragement in the first place."

She turned to me viciously. "Oh shut up and go to hell."

Rupert and I packed in silence. Damson went into her dark room, banging the door noisily behind her. I clung for all I was worth to my memories of the night, to the sweetness of André, and all we'd done together. But it was no good, everything kept evaporating. I went to the window and looked down, hoping to catch again the lightheartedness of those earlier hours, but all I could see was the cold deserted courtyard below and the gloomy walls surrounding it. What a view! Sunlight struck the opposite wall like a shabby overcoat—threadbare, thin and weak. A pale reflection of the sun that shone even at this moment on Boulevard St. Germain. I shivered, my mood spiralling down, a hard miserable knot tightening in my chest. I hate rows, any heavy unpleasantness hanging in the air. I like things to be—well, to be—comfortable. Comfortable like warm water or clean sheets or smooth green lawns. Comfortable like high teas, soft centres, postcards in the post. Everyone friends and getting on a treat.

Rupert caught my eye and made a face. I made one back. He snapped the cases shut.

"Have we finished?" I whispered. He nodded. I tiptoed to the dark room door and knocked. There was no reply. I cleared my throat, and knocked again. "Damson?"

It came fast and furious. "Fuck off you!" Like a smack in the face. Even Rupert looked shocked. My knees went all trembly, for two pins I could have burst out crying. Ridiculous. Rupert came and put his arm round me.

"She's impossible when she's in this mood," he whispered. "Have you got all your things together? Yes? Right? Take them and wait for me downstairs. I'll get all the photographs and film from her, that's my responsibility, not yours. Leave everything to me. Now go on."

He gave me a small shove. What? Without even saying goodbye? Surely not! With so much still unsaid? "But, Rupert," I whispered back. "I must—"

He opened the landing door. "Get going."

I picked up my case uncertainly and took one slow step. "Should I leave a note or something?"

He lifted a finger and pointed without answering. Then he knocked at her door. Even from the top of the stairs, right outside the apartment, I could still hear her cursing. Then all was quiet. He'd calmed her where I couldn't.

I lugged the heavy case down, step by step. It seemed worse going down than it had coming up. I stopped and sat down in exactly the same spot to smoke a cigarette. Well, at least this trip had laid a ghost at last. Whose ghost? Jean's. Damson had done that without any help from me. Just by being over-greedy—for everything. My cigarette had gone out. I felt in my pocket for another light and my fingers touched a fine metal wire. André's teeth. I took them out to look at them. Then very carefully put them in my open mouth over my own upper set. A door banged high above me and the dragging sounds of a heavy case drifted down. I heard Rupert whistling though how he found the breath I don't know. As he came closer I adjusted my upper lip until only the two gold teeth hung down, then when he reached me I spun round smiling brilliantly. "Hello, Rupert," I said, "well, what do you think? Do they suit?"

Our taxi driver understood English. He was a handsome wolfish creature in the manner of Yves Montand with a lot of the rogue about him. Insolent and very sexy. I looked at him as we got in, without a word. But as soon as Rupert in his immaculate French had finished speaking and sat back I said, "Isn't he gorgeous? A rotter through and through, you can tell." Rupert frowned and put a finger to his lips. "Ssh." I stared out of the window. It hadn't occurred to me that he could conceivably have understood.

We travelled at great speed, shooting over traffic lights just as they turned red, overtaking, cutting corners, as if for all the world we had a special plane to catch. Paris was empty and depressing, no one in sight now we'd left the centre. All was withdrawn and shuttered. Shops bolted and barred.

"That's the worst thing about Sundays, the shops being shut, isn't it?" I said to Rupert.

"Well, at least there's nowhere to spend our money. It's practically still intact, you know."

"Will we have to give it back then?"

He laughed. "No. André gave me lots of bills after you'd gone to bed. We'll put those in as our expenses."

"How sweet of him."

"Well, I had to ask."

"You are clever. I would never have thought of that. I wish there was somewhere open though. I want to buy presents for the girls. I'll have to get something at the airport. I'd thought of a bottle of Chanel No. 5 each and cigarette lighters in different colours."

"What, at their age, cigarette lighters? Myopia!"

"Well, they make a nice flame. Children like that, a little bit of magic."

The taxi slowed down to normal speed and the driver swung round, braking to a halt. In very good English he said, "You want to spend your money?" I stared at him, blood rushing to my face. His smile went up at one end. Sardonic, that's what you'd call it. Rupert answered. "Well, yes, we do. We would like to buy a few small presents if you know of a place."

He shrugged. "But of course. The flea market."

"Oh," I recovered enough to speak. "Is that open on Sundays?"

"Sunday? That is when everyone goes there. It is their big day. I can take you, wait and then continue to the airport."

I turned to Rupert. "That sounds nice. I've never been to the flea market. What about it?"

"Well," Rupert looked doubtful. "We have a plane to catch at some point remember."

"Yes, but we're not booked on to any one particular, are we? And this will only make us an hour later at the most. Come on, let's go."

"All right. You've talked me into it. But you mustn't go mad there. Just in and out."

"I promise."

The driver twisted back and we shot off again, badly scraping a parked Citroën on the side of the road. We'd be lucky to arrive intact either at the airport or up in heaven at this rate. "How was Damson at the end?" I felt more confident keeping my eyes off other cars. Was he drunk, the driver?

Rupert sat with a bulky cardboard envelope on his lap. He patted it. "Well, I managed to get everything. All the films and colour transparencies are in here. Oh, by the way, I've got some contacts you can look at—'Snow Siren'—they're superb. Do you want to see them?"

I shook my head. "No, I don't think I do. Not now. We'll look at them on the plane. Would you like me to put that in my bag? It'll fit in."

"Okay, okay. If it will go. But for Christ's sake don't lose them. Above everything they're the most precious."

I fitted them into my red leather bag, more a briefcase than a bag. "They'll be safe in here. I won't let it out of my sight. It's got all my money and passport in anyway. Was she all right then when you left? I'm sure I should have said goodbye."

"She wasn't really, no. She was fairly scurrilous about you, I must say."

"Me?"

Rupert looked the other way. I could guess what she'd told him. "She must have minded about André after all."

"Well," I said slowly, "we used to be very close at one time—"

"So I gathered from what she said."

"But you wouldn't have guessed otherwise would you?"

"Not in a million years that someone as sane as you would get mixed up with Damson."

"Well, it's done with now. We'll put it down to the inexperience of youth. I knew it wouldn't be the same the minute I set eyes on her. Too much of her had changed, not just her shape and name—"

"She thinks you hurt her deliberately, to get your own back."

"Hurt her? Does she?" I laughed. "No, I don't think so and then on the other hand perhaps I did. In which case, yes, so I got my own back." I yawned. "Now I'm boring myself." I yawned again, and set Rupert at it. "Whew," I said when we'd got our breaths back, "it's easy to see we didn't get our full quota of sleep. I could nod off now for two pins, couldn't you?"

The taxi slowed down. "Don't do that," Rupert said. "We're obviously here."

It was never clear whose decision it was to leave the cases in the car but it was clear to both of us that they were far too heavy to cart around. "I wait here on this corner," the driver had said. A chilly streak of caution curled sluggishly round my head. I should have taken note. After all, I'd made enough fuss at the airport. I did say, "Will they be safe?" to Rupert but not until we were walking away. That's true. "Well, we're not going to be that long, are we? And I told him on no account to leave them. Not for a second, especially not round here."

"It's a mixed bunch all right," I agreed on that, but even as I said it I could still see a pair of treacherous teasing eyes and that sardonic slanting smile. I turned round quickly but the taxi driver sat where we'd left him, staring after us. He raised a mocking hand in acknowledgement. "I wouldn't trust him with money—"

"Myopia!"

"Well, I wouldn't."

He took my arm impatiently. "Well, we haven't done have we? Look, let's get a move on. We haven't got all day."

We could have done with all day, I said that after the first five minutes. All day and carte blanche at the Bank of England. The market was marvellous—a cross between Portobello Road and Petticoat Lane, Petticoat Lane as it used to be before they boxed it all in. You can kill an atmosphere stone dead when you cover it with a roof. Here it was all open air with narrow lanes and passages created by the positioning of stalls. You could buy just about anything—suits of armour, silver spoons, spectacles from the 1920s, feather boas, brimmed felt hats, Chinese clogs, candied ants, plastic boats and bottled ships. "My girls would go mad," I said. "Now what shall I get them?"

Rupert picked up a pale pink heart-shaped box filled with tiny lace-trimmed handkerchiefs each embroidered with a day of the week. "These are adorable."

"What? Hankies? How appalling. Rupert, you could be a little more constructive than that. Children don't have hankies any more, not since Kleenex came in. These days they just blow and throw."

"All the more reason to buy them these. They probably haven't ever seen a real handkerchief in your house, have they?"

"No, now I come to think of it, but who's going to wash and iron them? Not me!"

Rupert held up two boxes, one pink, one blue.

"They will. They'll do it themselves. They'll love it, like playing

Mummy. Here you are, my treat. Bet you they're a great success."

After that I allowed myself to be guided by him.

"Lots of little things, that's the trick with children."

"How do you know?"

"Because it's how I felt myself. And still do," he added.

Half an hour, that's all we allowed ourselves. Half an hour is what we'd said to the driver anyway.

"These unspent francs are burning a hole in the bottom of my bag," I said. "I never like it until I've spent the lot."

"You can change them to English when you get back and give them to the children for pocket money. Now, where's this cab?"

My red bag bulged with bits and pieces, the precious envelope still safely in the bottom. I struggled with the zip, head bent. "This bloody thing won't do up now."

"Myopia!" Something in Rupert's voice made me turn. Panic. "What?"

"He's not here. The driver. Nor the taxi. They've gone."

They had too. Nothing on the corner except a boy on a bicycle and an old woman selling hot chestnuts. "This is the corner, isn't it?"

Rupert was frantic. "For God's sake, of course it is."

"Well," I said calmly. "Are we early? He might have been moved on. No parking. He's probably cruising round the block." A bench lay under the nearby tree. "We'll sit down and wait."

"How can you be so cool?"

"Would you like some chestnuts?" I said. "Or will they give you wind?"

He sighed, sweat sparkled on his upper lip. I could see his hands were shaking.

"Rupert, keep calm. They're only clothes. He'll turn up in a minute. He's probably popped off for a cup of coffee."

But he was near to tears. "Only clothes! Over a thousand pounds' worth and that's without all the accessories. Moo Moffat-Paw will go mad, not to mention Joe Garibaldi."

"Why?" I said. "Why should they? Everything's insured, isn't it? That's assuming the worst and this chap doesn't turn up."

He stared at me. "What on earth are you saying?"

I drew him to the bench and sat him down. "What I'm saying is, my little love, that your reaction is all out of proportion. If the stuff has been stolen it's not the tragedy you seem to think it is."

He put his head in his hands. I gave up for the moment.

"I'm keeping my eyes peeled. He'll come back, I'm sure of it."

I glanced at my watch—11.30. Ten minutes later—11.40. And still no sign. I concentrated on tiny figures in the far distance. By the time that person reaches the third lamp-post from this corner our car will have come. Nothing. Right, by the time that blue Volkswagen gets to that empty hoarding it will have been overtaken by our man. No good! If I stare at my watch face for five minutes non-stop, he'll be hooting at the kerb. Like hell. Poor Rupert couldn't raise his head. Once or twice I felt his shoulders shuddering against mine. Oh Jesus Christ, come off the cross and find that cab. Please God, go round the corner and tell him to get a bloody move on.

We sat there for a whole hour. At last I shook his shoulder. His muffled voice oozed hopefully out of his chest. "What news?"

"None," I said briskly. "I think we'll have to accept, my darling, that the bastard's buggered off. Now!" I added brightly, "it's really not so bad. We've both got our passports and enough money to get to the airport. You're carrying the tickets and the photos are still all safe and sound. Let's have a look at you—it could be a lot worse. Come on. It's just a spot of bad luck. Let's forget it and go back to London."

"I'm not going, Myopia."

"Don't be silly."

"I can't move. I'm staying here."

I shook him gently. His head fell like a broken flower on to my neck. People walking past were glancing back curiously.

"Everyone is staring—"

"I don't care."

"Rupert." Alarm was setting in. "What's happening? Are you having a nervous breakdown or what?" We hadn't got enough money for luxuries like that, couldn't he wait and have it on the National Health?

He began moaning softly, talking to himself. "My first job! I'm finished. My very first job. Outrageous irresponsibility. Finished."

I sat there, cradling him helplessly. After all, they were my clothes. But they'd served their purpose now. That's how I looked at it. We had a record of them. Years later I'd be able to fish out that one copy of *Chic* and say "That's me. Do you like what I'm wearing?" Which would in itself be infinitely more satisfying than turning heads in restaurants or making small theatrical entrances into taxis on the street. Taxis on the street. Taxis on the street!

"Rupert, where did we pick up that cab?"

"What?" he mumbled.

"Where exactly? I know it was outside Damson's, but you found it didn't you? Was it on a rank?"

He shook his head dazedly. "No."

"But there was a rank there, just further up the street. I remember there was—"

"Yes." Rupert lifted his head a little. "But this one drove straight past it to pick us up instead of waiting his turn. Didn't you notice, that's why all the parked taxis started honking?"

I thought quickly. "They must know him. At least someone must know him."

I stood up. "Look after this bag—no, on second thoughts, just sit there, Rupert, don't move! Do not move, are you listening? I'm going to phone André. If anyone can help, he can."

One of the waiters answered. "Monsieur André? Un moment." I could hear the clatter of the restaurant, they must be right in the thick of things now. Twenty to one. He took ages to come. What on earth was he doing?

"Oui. C'est moi, André."

Relief flooded through me, right through, from top to bottom as though someone was filling my body with hot sustaining soup through a neatly drilled hole in my head. Tilt the jug a little more, there's still a small space in my toes!

"Oh André," I said feebly.

"Myopia!" His voice leaped over the line with such strength and joy, such deep pleasure and genuine delight that for a swift dancing second I was transported right back. Back to his high, hard bed, back to my own first, blinding, breathlessness, to slyly stirring inert skin and new fresh slow awakenings. We exchanged some numbed, shy sentences of love, and then I told him of our trouble. He was silent for a moment. No sharp words at our stupidity, no charge of carelessness, not a single scolding reproach. What a friend I'd found. I could hear him thinking.

"Well," I said, "we don't have the number of the taxi but I can tell you what the driver looks like. Sly eyes" (I could have said sexy but this was hardly the moment for such insensitivity); "a sort of foxy smile, sardonic. Tall, I would have said, though we didn't see him actually standing up—"

André interrupted. "Myopia—"

I ignored it.

"Actually, André, who he looked like more than anyone else was Yves Montand."

"Yves Montand?" I heard a sharp intake of breath. "Ah, I have it."

"Oh!" I said. "Do you know him?"

He spoke quickly, with great authority. "Myopia, where are you now? What precisely has he taken? Describe the cases exactly. And when, how long ago was this? An hour? You have done well to telephone me. You have money to take you to the airport? You are certain you must depart today?" He said that very tenderly. "Yes? Ah well! So I shall meet you at the airport—you travel BA? Very well, I shall meet you at the BA desk at, it is now quarter to one, at two o'clock. Until then, ma chérie—"

Quickly, before he hung up, I shouted desperately, "But André, what about our cases?"

I heard his throaty chuckle, could imagine a fiery flash of gold. "They will be with me." And then the line went dead.

The next hour was the worst. Rupert was inconsolable. At the airport I ordered him an omelette. "You have to eat," I said. "It

177

will help settle your stomach." He shredded a whole bread roll, waiting, and then when his omelette came he claimed he couldn't eat it. I tried scolding. "Now look what you've done, covered the whole place with crumbs. Come on, eat up, you can't offend the cook as well as the waitress."

I tried to jolly him up. "Why don't you ring Jean-Paul? He'll think it's a joke. Anyway, André seemed to know right away who I was talking about. That driver was probably not a driver at all, just a con man. I thought his English was too good to be true. Anyone can get taken in by con men."

His anguished face looked up from his fork. "Ring Jean-Paul?" he said, horrified. "He'd never work with me again. You only have to be unreliable once in this business and the word goes around right away."

I sighed. "This business, this business. It's just the same as any other. People allow for strokes of bad luck, surely to God."

"But it was all my fault." That's all he'd say. Again and again. In the end I gave up.

There were seats available on the three o'clock flight. I took Rupert's ticket from his nerveless fingers and booked for both of us. "What if André can't get the cases by two?" he said.

"Then he'll come here anyway and at three o'clock we'll fly off after thanking him for trying. That's all."

But by five to two the tension was beginning to tell on me too. I'd long since stopped talking. "Any luggage?" they'd asked at the BA desk. "That's just on its way," I'd answered. "Be here in no time at all." God forgive me if I tell a lie. Bastard.

At dead on two I turned to Rupert. "Sit up, love, and at least look a little less hopeless."

"Why?" He slumped even lower.

"Well, I don't know, but it shows such lack of faith if André comes in now and sees us both—" I hadn't time to finish. André was striding towards us, grinning wide, teeth flashing, arms flailing all over the place. He wore a fine pale camelhair overcoat like an affluent gangster. It shocked me to see how distinguished he looked. He lifted his arms as if inviting me into his embrace—empty arms.

Rupert said it first. "Where are the cases?" But I'd gone past caring. I wanted to touch something solid. I ran towards him and threw my arms round his neck. Over his shoulder in the second before shutting my eyes I spotted the porter staggering towards us, a heavy case in either hand. Of course André would get them! Whoever doubted? Who on earth?

Rupert cried. Really cried. Tears of pure relief. Straight into his champagne. André and I kissed, pretending not to see. And then we all toasted each other. Again.

André wouldn't explain. "Do tell," we begged. "What happened? How did you find them?" But he'd only shrug and pour us yet another glass. I drank, adoring him. Power is a pretty potent aphrodisiac. I didn't want to go when they called our flight. He squeezed my hand very tightly. "Now at the last minute I confess to you. I arranged everything. The cab to pick you up. The driver to take you to the flea market. His disappearance with both the cases—all in order that you would call me and I should have the chance to see you once again."

I held him very close then looked him in the eyes. They twinkled back at me. "And impress me with your cleverness," I said.

"Of course."

"But how did you know I'd call you?"

He gave me a last long hug and whispered softly in one ear. "Because, Myopia, my Myopia, I am your first French lover. Real lover. And as such your lasting friend. When you are in trouble you will always call me, of that I hope I can be sure."

"Yes, yes. Oh my God, I must tell them when I'm coming back. Here's my number; tell them I've caught the three o'clock plane."

Oh dear, how can you wave a man farewell with mascara running right down into your mouth? I turned to try but saw that sensibly he'd gone. Rupert put his arm round me, fully recovered, he was now a pillar of strength.

"He's a marvel that man," I blubbed. "A bloody marvel, that André. Do you know, so far he hasn't put a finger wrong."

Rupert wore a grave and soothing expression, like a clerk from the Citizens' Advice Bureau. "No," he nodded. I had an hysterical urge to laugh. "Not one finger wrong," and then I gave another sob.

London looked lovely, bathed in the dusty glow of late afternoon. The river looped like a satin ribbon round Maidenhead, patches of green dotted here and there like discarded billiard tables. We slanted over it then steadied up for touch-down. "Are you glad to be back?" Rupert shouted. The plane shuddered to a grinding halt. I rolled my eyes slowly. "Whew, I'm glad that's over anyway. Now, what did you say? Am I glad to be back? Well, since you come to mention it, no. No, I don't think I am at all. There are too many complications awaiting me back here."

"Are there?"

"Yes, complications of the heart. You know the sort of thing."

"I can only think of Jean-Paul and how to last till Thursday myself."

I sighed. "Well, when there's only one on the scene it's all much simpler."

We hadn't talked much since Paris, most of the time we'd spent in a companionable silence, both preoccupied with our own thoughts. Mine leapfrogged from Sam to Charles then on to Paul getting married tomorrow. But underneath lay the hard solid core of André. I could have asked André what to do about the others, he wouldn't have minded I was sure. And I could have told him about my weekly trip to Brighton. Yes, I could have told him all about that, every detail, which was something I couldn't have started to explain to anyone else in the whole world. Paul had never known, not the ins and outs of it, and we'd been married after all. We'd been married a whole year when it first started. But then it's common knowledge that women have more secrets from husbands than they ever do from lovers, or even from the hairdresser if it comes to that.

Rupert unfastened his seat belt. "Who exactly are the others, Myopia? You still haven't told me. Sam, I know. But who is it you go to see in Brighton?"

"In Brighton?" I laughed. "Oh, he's not the problem."

"Well, who is he?"

"He's—" I hesitated. "He's just a sad and lonely little old-age pensioner."

"Myopia, you're breaking my heart." He said it mockingly. I didn't answer. Yes, I thought, it breaks my heart too sometimes. "Well, who else is there? The man you were meant to come to Paris with in the first place."

I turned. "Isn't it a good job I didn't? What! I would never have met André if I had."

"Who is he then and why couldn't he come at the last minute?"

"His wife died," I said briefly. "Yes, a form of insane suicide really. She threw herself out of the saddle. At least that's what Charles claims."

"Died riding? Earl's daughter! I read about it. Lady Deirdre! Yes, I read that in the papers."

"You would have done, just before we left."

"Charles Glossop's wife. Is it him then?"

"Yes."

"Oh Myopia."

"He proposed on the phone to Paris. That's the trouble. It's been going on for ages, before Sam even, but I never thought it would come to this."

"But, darling, he could end up Prime Minister, that would make you First Lady."

"Would it? After the Queen? Yes, I suppose it would. Unless marrying a divorcée would wreck his chances. Though knowing Charles he will have sought advice on that already."

"I could be coming along to Number Ten for tea."

We laughed. "Only if I accept, Rupert."

He sighed dreamily. "Decisions, decisions. What a choice! A brilliant politician on the one hand and a bloody millionaire on the other. Oh for the chance!"

I stood up, brushed myself down and smoothed my fringe. "They're only men, Rupert. And neither of them much good in bed, come to that." I smiled. "Not like André. Or even for that matter like Paul."

"You're not still sleeping with him?" Shocked!

I picked up my bag casually. "I did the other night. It was very nice."

He looked bewildered. "Why on earth do you bother with all these different men, Myopia? Doesn't it ever occur to you to say no?"

"No? Yes, of course it occurs but I can't do it."

I stepped into the gangway and turned back smiling. "I love them all, you see."

The air hostess greeted us as we were going. "Goodbye. I hope you enjoyed your flight." Affable, that was the word. The only thing to be was affable back. "Tremendously," I assured her. A clutch of aircraft mechanics in white overalls stood waiting at the bottom of the steps, looking up all the ladies' legs. My trousers must have been a bit of a let-down. Shame.

Rupert and I walked down a long plastic corridor, then waited in the queue to show our passports. "What are your plans now—straight off to Streatham Hill? Would you like to come and have tea in my house first? The girls will be there, we can give them their presents."

He looked grateful. "Yes," he said, "it's a bit of an anticlimax coming back to nothing."

Fifteen minutes later I would have given my eye teeth for it—to come back to nothing. They were all there! It was unbelievable, but they were. All there, waiting for me. Paul and the girls at the front. Sam somewhere to the left, and at the back, standing on his own, Charles. I saw them as a big crowd of people before us pushed through the swing doors. So far, none had caught sight of me. I gave an agonised wail. "Rupert, oh God," and, case in hand, I turned and in panic ran back. He followed me. "Myopia! What is it? What's the trouble? Tell me—"

I sat down on a seat against the wall. Unable to speak. Frozen. What could I do? Just stay there? Take up residence, permanent residence. Yes. "Three meals a day, please, brought on a tray. Just leave it on the floor, that will be perfectly all right." Go out? And ignore all, sweep past as if I didn't know any of them? But not the girls. What about the girls? Jesus wept!

"Jesus wept," I groaned.

"What?"

I pointed with a shaking hand. "They're all out there. The whole slam bang shoot of them."

"Who?"

"What I've said. Charles, Sam, Paul with the girls."

"Together? Do they know each other then?"

"Don't be daft." I spoke viciously. "All separate."

His face tightened.

"Oh, I'm sorry, Rupert. But what can I do?" I gave an animal wail. "Go and sit in the Ladies' all night? You could come and fetch me when it's all clear."

He sat down beside me. "How on earth did they know? That you'd be on this plane?"

"God only can tell. But what difference does it make? They're all there now."

Rupert began to laugh.

"Don't be awful. Come on, do something—"

He went on laughing. "What's there to do? You'll just have to walk out there. Greet them all like a great lady acknowledging your public. This could be your solution, darling. At least it will separate the lambs from the sheep."

"What do you mean?"

"Well, grown men don't give up in the face of rivals. It spurs them on. Let them fight it all out together. Like dogs over a bone."

"Thank you."

"All you do is stand back and watch. But you need to dress the part. With all due respect, Myopia, at the moment you look a positive mess."

"I feel worse inside—mincemeat, 5p a pound."

"Go and put 'Snow Siren' on. We know that won't be creased. Quick, into the Ladies'. It will be the first time you've worn it in public. They'll be so flabbergasted by how you look, it'll take their minds off each other. Go on, quick."

I arrived like an international film star. Rupert as my personal valet, weighed down with all our luggage, stood at my side. People started pointing, and staring, somewhere a flashbulb snapped and I smiled, posing for an instant on the threshold. The girls were the first to break the spell. They ran towards me. "Mummy, Mummy!"

"My darlings," I gushed and bent down to kiss them both. Harriet rubbed her mouth with the back of her hand. "You've put all lipstick over me!" Fanny giggled and pointed at my legs. "Why are you wearing your pyjamas?"

Paul stepped forward stiffly. Something had happened. I could see it in his face. The wedding was off! I offered my cheek for a kiss in a theatrical manner, then pretended for the first time to see Sam. And Charles.

"Sam!" I shrieked as if he was a long-lost chum that I hadn't set eyes on since school. "Charles!" I gave it a low vibrancy, an intimate thrusting ring. The voice you reserve for the family doctor. How good of you to come.

I held tightly to the girls, one on each side, like small protective poodles. My chaperones. All three men stood their ground, staring at me, stunned in their separate ways. A curling, leaping flame of pure mischief unfolded inside me. I turned, not attempting to introduce them to each other. "Oh, I don't believe you gentlemen know Rupert, do you? Well," I looked at him, my eyes full of laughter, "this is Rupert, my colleague. We've been working all weekend in Paris and now we're so exhausted we thought a nice quiet tea somewhere. Any suggestions?"

Afterwards, Rupert rang to say it had been absolutely unbearable. I didn't see why, in a wicked way I'd quite enjoyed myself. "You should have stayed to see it through, Rupert, instead of rushing off like that. They all took to their heels, there was no tea! I had to come home on my own. I'm here now doing nothing at all."

"Alone? Are you feeling awful? I'll come over if you like."

"Awful? Why should I feel awful? I love it. I'm luxuriating in bed, looking at television. I've got a face mask on which, wait a minute, what does it say, which 'contains a highly efficient counter-active agent—discourages unsightly blemishes, tightens pores and banishes blackheads'. There, it's doing all that at this very moment. I'll hold the phone closer, perhaps you can hear it."

"But, Myopia, where are the girls?"

"Gone! They've gone to Greece with their father. The wedding's off. He's jilted her. Isn't it cruel? Serve him right if she sues for breach of promise. That's what I said. He claims he couldn't go through with it because of me. I'd fanned the flame of his original passion by letting him make love to me the other evening. I wouldn't have done it if I'd known. I'm trying to cut down on suitors, not accumulate more. He asked me to go to Greece with them right there and then, on her ticket. Cheeky thing. 'No,' I said. 'I'm a working girl now, I can't go gadding about the world when the spirit moves me. I have commitments for this week which can't possibly be broken.' That was right, wasn't it, Rupert? He can't expect to just creep back into my life like that, can he?" I lit a cigarette. "He must learn to stand in line like the rest of them."

"What about the rest of them? How did they react, Sam and Charles?"

"Sam stormed off as you would expect. Said the last thing he had in mind was a teddy bears' picnic with my dithering brats, and that if after seeing his way through a bottle of brandy he was still capable of doing so, he would call me. He hasn't yet, so perhaps he's not."

"And Charles?"

"Charles carried it off with great dignity, upholding the honour of the British nation. He said he'd moved for too many years in diplomatic circles not to recognise an insoluble solution when he saw one and would I do him the honour of dining with him on the morrow. Then he tactfully withdrew. So I gave the girls their handkerchiefs each, which were a huge success by the way, waited to see them on their plane and then came home! Françoise isn't here, Paul said she could go to Paris a day early. We must have crossed flights, isn't that funny? She will be there by now. I wonder if she'll bother to go and see Babette."

"Babette. All that seems worlds away, doesn't it?"

"Doesn't it! I still can't believe I'm back. I've been walking round all the rooms, opening cupboards and peering in the back of drawers just to see that everything's the same. And I've counted all the knives and forks and broken an egg in the sink to check if it was real. Insanity! Anyway, how is Streatham Hill?"

"Still the whirling cosmopolitan centre of South London. My mother's not here, she's gone to stay with her sister in Eastbourne. So later on I thought I'd take a cruise round the Common. Sundays can be very lively. You get a lot of vicars about."

"Rupert! You're not considering being unfaithful to poor Jean-Paul?"

"Only physically. That can do no harm."

"Well, watch you don't catch anything, that's all. Except of course with clergymen the one thing you can be sure of, I suppose, is that they're thoroughly clean."

"Cleansed. Cleansed with holy water."

"In that way. Baptists would be the best bet. You ought to enquire first before you embark on these casual encounters as to their denomination." I gave a sudden yawn. "Oh dear, I'm sorry. I've started yawning. My bedtime."

"Well, Myopia, you're off to Brighton tomorrow. Will you be taking the old fellow a rattle or is he not quite in his second childhood yet?"

"Don't be cruel. I shall be taking him a pot of Marmite. He's very fond of that. Perhaps you should take some into Moo Moffat-Paw. Say it's the very latest thing in Paris."

He laughed. "Cross fingers that she likes the snaps."

I woke up much later than usual—no children rushing in, that was the reason. I'd probably have gone on even longer but for the telephone. It was Sam.

"Are you fucking still asleep? I've been ringing hours, you slob."

"Oh have you? I was in the bath. I couldn't hear. How is your head?"

"What head? I have no head. I have a cage full of ferrets

wearing hobnailed boots but I have no head. I'm holding the phone at arm's length. Can you hear me?"

"Perfectly."

"Then stop fucking shouting! Now explain to me exactly what that scene was about yesterday. You never told me you wanted to be a movie star. Is that what you're after? A little part, my precious. Because if so I tell you now you turned in a lousy performance—"

I started to laugh. "Oh Sam, how sad. I thought I was rather professional. I shall have to approach another producer."

"Like hell, shit face! I happen to own all options on whatever you decide. Let's get that straight for a start."

I saw through the window that my daffodils were dying off, the first fierce yellow browning at the edges like burnt butter. What a surprisingly capable cook Damson had turned out to be. This summer I'd fill the window boxes with scarlet geraniums and buy a canary each for the girls, pale lemon, the colour of cowslips.

"Canaries can't talk, can they, Sam?"

"Cheap! Cheap!"

"Yes, that's what I thought. They just go cheep."

He roared down the phone. "What the hell are you talking about? I said cheap. A cheap trick to change the subject—"

"Oh, what were we saying. I've forgotten. Anyway, I can't stay talking all day. I've got to get off to Brighton. It's Monday, remember."

His voice altered. Became almost pleading. "Honey. What are you trying to do? Play hard to get? Have me run round in circles? Chasing your tail?"

"Certainly not, Sam." I said it kindly. "But I've been thinking about what you mentioned, about getting married, and it's made me very panicky to tell you the truth. I've got two children, whether you like it or not, and to judge by the way in which you refer to them I take it—"

"Jesus Christ! What the hell have your brats to do with this?"

"Don't interrupt. It's crossed my mind that you wouldn't make the most suitable of stepfathers—"

"Stepfathers! Holy ghost! Couldn't they go off to an institu-

187

tion—school or something? You mean I'd actually have to see them?"

He sounded so appalled, I laughed. "That's it, you would. So couldn't we leave things as they are? Surely that's the best, till they grow up at least?"

"But honey, I can't get enough of you this way. I want more, you rat bag. More and all to myself."

"Well, Sam." I looked at my watch. "You'll just have to make do with what you've got for the time being anyway. Now, I must go."

His voice changed again. "Say, honey. Can you get away this weekend? Take a trip to wherever you like. Charter a little plane and fly off? Sit in the sun? Sail? What do you say?"

"Well, you see, now you're making sense. As it happens, I can. The girls are away and I'd love to. We can do lots of things like that together. Isn't that more fun than just being married?"

I'd just shut the front door when the phone rang again. I hovered on the step, half knowing who it would be. Charles. I took a deep breath and went back in to answer. May as well get both of them settled in the same morning. Surprisingly, he was even easier than Sam.

"My dear, I understand exactly your apprehensions about matrimony. It is a serious decision, not to be embarked upon lightly. We both of us have already made foolish errors of selection. Mistakes which neither would wish to repeat. However, as I regard the current situation, the likelihood of remarriage at this immediate point is rather remote. I have spoken, in the greatest confidence you understand, with a certain colleague and he is of the opinion that to remarry within certainly two years would from my point of view be political suicide. Added to this the delicate fact that you yourself are a divorcée, albeit the innocent party—"

"Yes, you should think of that, Charles. It could lose you half the votes of your churchgoing constituents for a start."

He droned on and on. In his dear, dead, boring voice. He'd have got my vote for certain if only to shut him up. I interrupted. "I'm afraid I have to go now. I have a train to catch, Charles."

He sounded taken aback. "Nine o'clock tonight."

"What? Oh sorry! Where?" Was he talking about our dinner?

"On BBC2. Look in. I think you'll find it interesting. We're discussing World Economy and the Individual. I deeply regret the postponement of our dinner together. However, could lunch on Tuesday be a possibility?"

"Yes," I said quickly. "What, just the usual arrangement? Here you mean? Oh, I'd love that, Charles."

"A bottle of Dom Perignon, wouldn't you say? We can toast each other on our unofficial engagement, my darling. Two years is a long time to wait I know, added to which we will have to continue meeting in our usual clandestine manner. However—"

"I think it's perfect, Charles," I said, "perfect." And added coyly, "After all, it always has been in the past."

I whistled all the way to the station. Found a parking place with no trouble at all, changed my clothes in the Ladies' lavatory and deposited what I'd taken off in the locker. I loved that part of it. No one at home had seen my Brighton clothes. Dull green beret, skirt and blouse like a school uniform. Solid stockings, flat shoes. Sensible raincoat for possible showers. Even a change of handbag. "A mystery woman was seen boarding the 12.25 for Brighton!" I bought a paper and saw with horror that my nails were still white. Pale shiny pearls from Paris. Oh dear, he wouldn't like that. I'd have to get some varnish remover and cotton wool from the chemist's shop. I glanced at the clock, ten minutes, still time.

I got into the nearest carriage and started scrubbing at my nails. By the time we'd left Victoria they were back to nature and bare again. Peardrops, that's what the remover smelt of. Nice. All finished, I stood up and moved along the corridor to the buffet car. Now what should I have today? A cup of tea? Or something stronger? Going to Paris had put me on drinking, that was for sure. I'd have to watch myself. My Auntie Doris was a big one for the booze. They were always saying that in our house. My mother was anyway. "Bottles and boys! Boys and bottles! She can't get enough of them, Doris." Perhaps I was taking after her.

"Gin and tonic please," I said. On the other hand, he'd be able to smell that. "No, wait. What's got no smell?"

There was a new man behind the bar. I knew all the usual ones. "Oh," I said, "you're new, aren't you?"

He winked, cocky, young, about eighteen. When he answered it was with a marked Irish accent. Fresh from the Emerald Isle. "First day, lady."

I didn't like that. Lady. It held too well the distance of years and counter.

"You're very young for the job, aren't you?"

His eyebrows shot up in mock surprise. "Young? Young, you say? And me twenty-five."

"You never are. Not twenty-five. I know that. More like eighteen, I'd have said."

He was built like a brick house, whatever his age. With wide wrists and a strong straight neck like a Corinthian column. His hair was the colour of caramel toffee, tight and curly to his head, but his eyebrows were black, black to match his curly lashes. And his eyes were a marvellous blue. Really marvellous, spectacular, smiley. "When Irish eyes are smiling". Those sort of ones. Paddy. A puckish Paddy. It would be pleasant travelling with him each Monday.

He laughed to see me looking at him for so long. Well, he must be used to that by now. And it wasn't as if he hadn't taken his fill of me too. Had your pennyworth?

"You haven't answered," I said. "What's got no smell?"

"Ah. Ah now." He did everything with a great animal flourish. Gusto. Glad to be alive. How I felt too as a matter of fact. "Rum. Rum and coke. No trace at all. You might have been at your mother's breast. No one could tell the difference."

I was sorry when we arrived. I was really. I'd not enjoyed a train trip, not like that since—ever. We'd made a date. Oh yes. Seven o'clock at Hammersmith Palais. He wanted to show me his dancing paces, that and his extraordinary drinking abilities. I was looking forward to it. Why not?

I walked from the station humming. Breaking at one point

190

into a neat paso doble. Six days non-stop of sun and Brighton bustling with the heady excitement of a good season ahead. I took a deep breath. Ozone.

When I got close I stopped at the corner shop for Marmite. "Large one please. And a packet of Osbornes while you're at it. Oh, and a nice malt loaf, and a tin of peaches with a small condensed milk." Onnie connie. He couldn't get enough of that, straight from the tin sucking on a teaspoon.

"A regular feast," the woman said. "How is the old fellow anyway?"

"Fine. I'm just in to see him now."

"I caught sight of him last week. He seems to be breaking."

I pocketed the change and turned to go. "Seventy-two next month and not getting any younger."

But still keen on it. The old devil. We could be had up for what we did, surely we could. Comforting the aged, that's what I'd get my counsel to plead. "For years, m'lord, this young woman has given freely of herself body and soul. Unstintingly complied to the strange requests of this venal old man. The raw truth, the bare bones, the actual fact that in this relationship he happens to be . . ."

I'd reached the door. He was at the window waiting. In a hurry again. I laughed, easily. What the hell? Where's the harm? Charity begins at home, my mother was always saying that. He opened the door and grabbed me in. Same as ever. Nothing changed in seven days. Teeth on the mantelpiece, trousers down. A terrible old trout, tortoise neck, knees like turnips. The oldest by far of all my men, but with a greater need than the whole lot put together. I looked at him, warmth, love, pity and a fierce protectiveness flooding through me.

"Hello, Dad," I said cheerfully, "have you had a good week?"